POSTCARD HISTORY SERIES

Peoria

A POSTCARD HISTORY

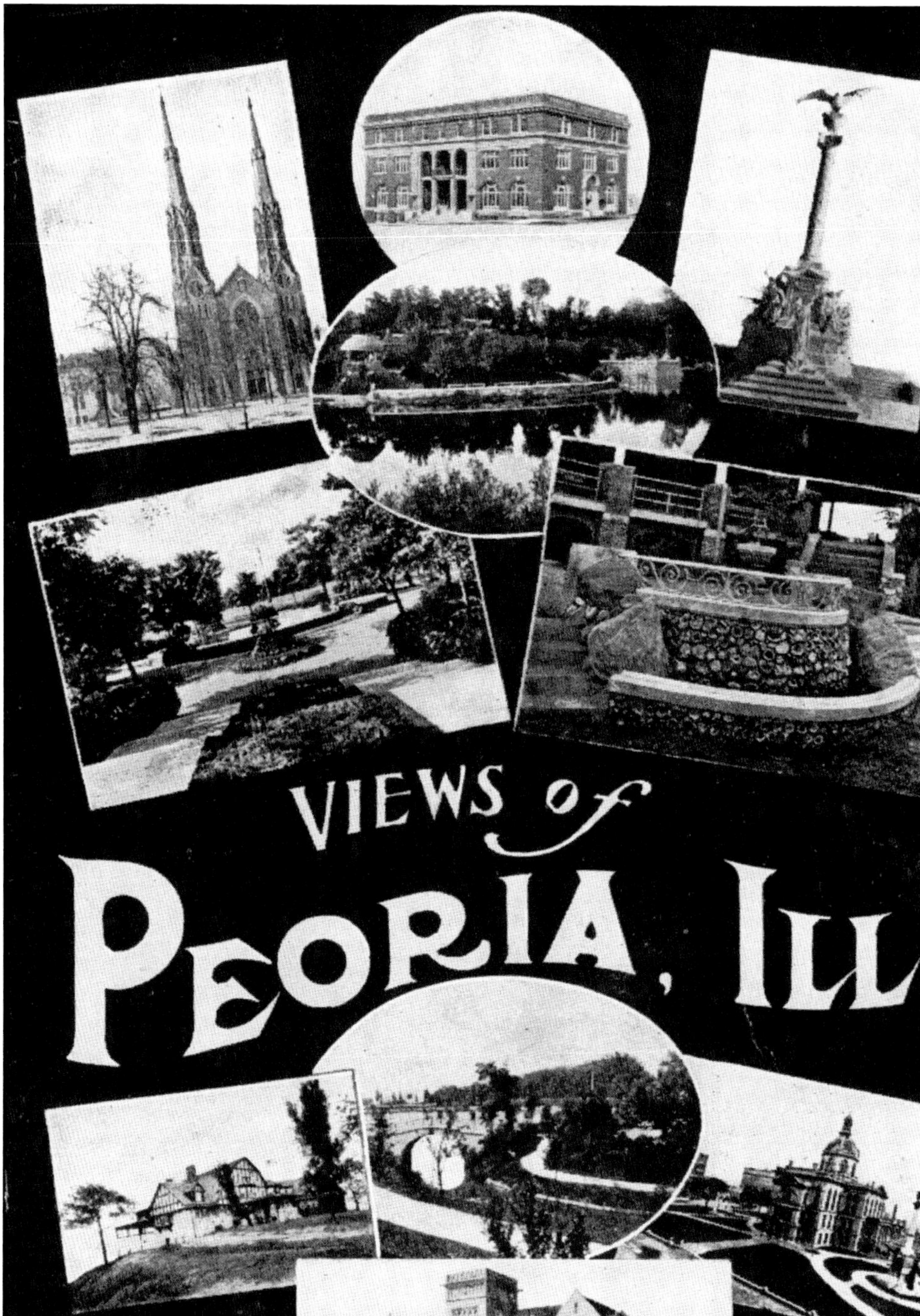

Peorians boast of two important facts regarding their town—the first is the beauty of its name, and the second is the beauty of its location. "Peoria," a word of Native-American origin meaning "the land of fat beast," is derived from the tribe Pe-o'rias, one of the five tribes (the Kaskaskias, Peorias, Cahokias, Tamaroas, and Mitchigamies) that comprised the "Illini" confederacy ("Illini" means "perfect manly man"). To this the missionaries add the French "ois," giving us the harmonious name Peoria, Illinois.

POSTCARD HISTORY SERIES

Peoria

A POSTCARD HISTORY

Charles A. and LaDonna Bobbit

ARCADIA PUBLISHING

ISBN 978-0-7385-5469-3

Published by Arcadia Publishing
Charleston, South Carolina

Printed in the United States of America

Library of Congress Catalog Card Number: 2007924358

For all general information contact Arcadia Publishing at:
Telephone 843-853-2070
Fax 843-853-0044
E-mail sales@arcadiapublishing.com
For customer service and orders:
Toll-Free 1-888-313-2665

Visit us on the Internet at www.arcadiapublishing.com

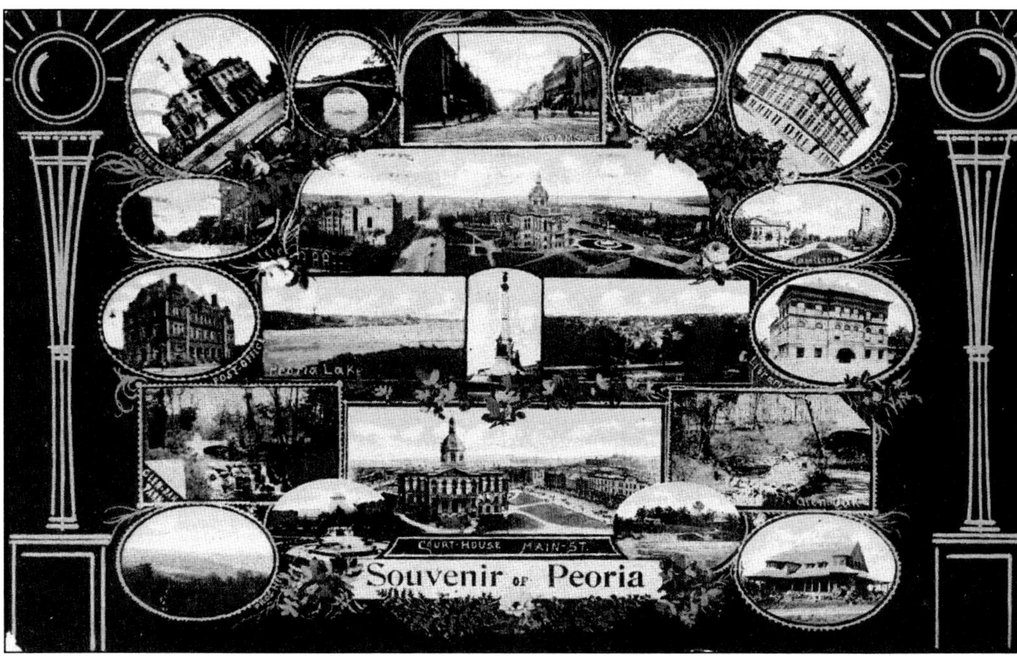

On April 1818, Illinois was admitted to the Union, and in the spring of the following year, a party of seven venturesome pioneers found their way to the east banks of the Illinois River. They then ferried across and landed at what they believed to be the burned Fort Clarke. Assembled here they found the walls of two small log cabins, which stood on what is now Water Street and almost directly in front of Thomas and Clarke, and they set to work to finish up the dwellings. These cabins were the first American dwelling places on the site of what is now the city of Peoria.

Contents

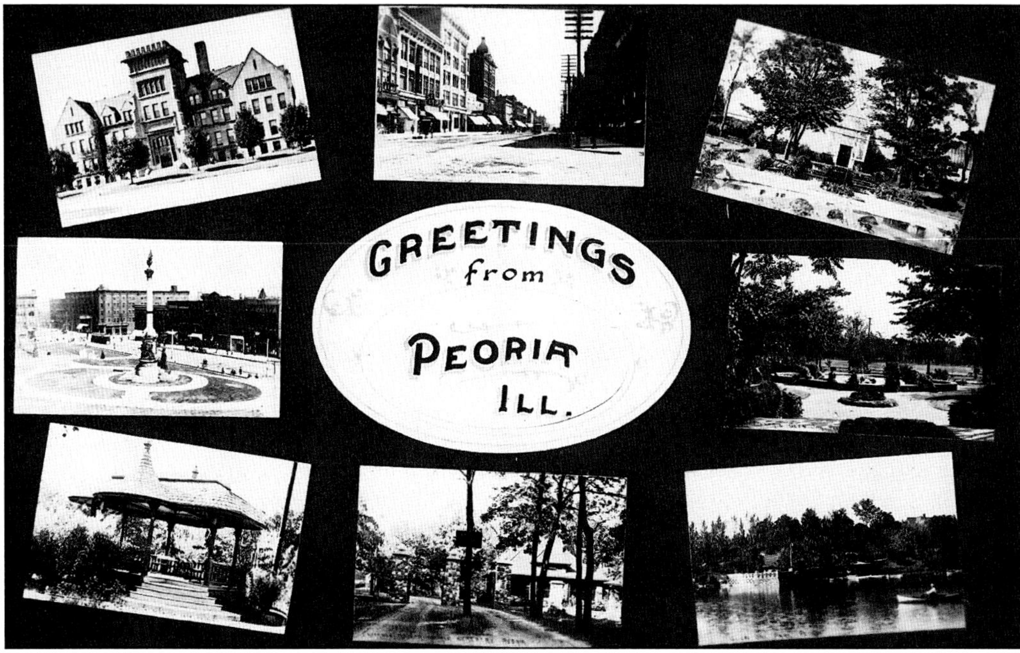

This card, mailed in 1912, best exemplifies Peoria. Many of the highlights, such as Bradley University, a downtown street, the Civil War monument, and scenes in Glen Oak Park and Springdale Cemetery, have changed very little. However, several of the scenes in Bradley Park no longer exist. Each of these views would eventually be photographed independently as postcards.

ACKNOWLEDGMENTS

The authors would like to thank those who made this book possible. Without the guidance and encouragement of these people, this book would have remained merely a hope.

Thanks go to Jon Austin, executive director of the Illinois State Historical Society, for introducing the authors to Allison Carpenter and Patrick Catel of Arcadia Publishing. We are also grateful for Arcadia's confidence in allowing two postcard collectors the opportunity to bring to Peoria another postcard history.

We would also like to thank the Peoria Public Library staff, and most especially R. Howard Courtney, Betty Hoberson, Suzanne Buchanan, and Sue Kaufman. That facility provided vital data from former newspaper clippings.

Special thanks go to Richard and Karen Deller, whose knowledge of Peoria and postcard publishing was invaluable.

Published histories of Peoria by Bill Adams and Jerry Klein, as well as *Peoria: Impressions of 150 Years*, were all vital references.

In addition, thanks go to the many church staff, ministers, and volunteers who were so gracious with their time on the phone.

Thanks go as well to Mark Gobeyn, associate professor at Bradley University, for editing and moral support throughout this project.

Finally, the authors would like to personally thank Mr. Ernie Grassel of Mountain Home, Arkansas, for sharing his personal recollections in addition to allowing for the use of the famed Grassel Collection.

INTRODUCTION

Peoria: A Postcard History, is more than just a souvenir—it is also an illustration of what Peoria once was, and a glimpse into how it became what it is today.

As non-native history buffs, we discovered that one of the easiest ways to quickly learn the history of our newly adopted home was through collecting its postcards. From this beginning, we assembled a collection of nearly 1,500 different cards. Clearly, the challenge of selecting merely two hundred cards for this book was our most difficult task. The research was difficult at times as well, since many businesses associated with these cards came and went, and many times their histories were never recorded.

Postcards of Peoria have been used to a very limited extent in past publications of this city. However, the more recent printed work reflects their new-found value. Rare or unusual postcards of Peoria have soared in value in the last 20 years. Prior to that time, cards were bought and sold for less than 50¢. Collectors could find Peoria cards in many places. The principal places were the antique malls specializing in collectibles. However, flea markets and estate sales are both excellent sources for rare postcards. Today, a collector may expect to pay upward of $25 for a special card.

We believe that recent publications by several authors well-versed in Peoria's past have adequately covered the story of the town's history. Our goal here is to share with our readers a part of the photographic history of Peoria seldom viewed prior to this publication.

When asked if we are finished collecting, the answer is always a firm "no." We are always anxious to see new views of a familiar building, or a painted-in automobile or wagon, or new and unique views which include people of different historic decades. The postcards have been mailed to many places, but thanks to the efforts of postcard collectors throughout the United States, many have found their way back to their Peoria home.

About Postcards

As deltiologists, or postcard collectors, we are frequently asked about postcards. How long have picture postcards been produced? If a card is not postmarked, is there any way of estimating its age? Where can I find old postcards? What is the easiest way to determine the value of a card? And the list of questions goes on.

The term *postcard* describes privately printed cards that usually have a picture or message on one side, while cards printed by the government are called *postal cards*. Postcards have been around for about a hundred years and most can be classified according to their date of publication. The list to follow describes the types of cards that were produced during each era.

Pioneer Cards (1893–1898). These cards are quite rare; many of them are labeled as "Souvenir Postcards."

Private Mailing Cards (1898–1901). These cards have the term "Private Mailing Card" printed on the address side, usually along with the statement, "Authorized by Act of Congress of May 19, 1898."

Undivided Backs (1901–1907). Cards printed during this period are called *undivideds* because postal regulations did not allow a message on the address side. This was also true in the case of pioneer and private mailing cards.

Divided Backs (1907–World War I). On March 1, 1907, the United States Postal Service approved the divided back, which allowed for a message on the left side and the address on the right. Many of the undivided and divided back cards were published in England and Germany.

White Borders (World War I–1930s). After World War I, most of the cards sold in the United states were printed in this country. Since many of them had a white border, this term is used to describe cards published during this period. Some of the cards in this book fall into this category, but a few of them from this period lack the border.

Linens (1930s–1940s). These cards have a rough finish and were made using paper with a high rag content.

Chromes (1940s–present). These cards are printed mainly in color and most look like a photograph made from a colored slide. The two most common sizes are the standard 3.5 by 5.5 inches and the continentals, which are about 4 by 6 inches.

As with any classification system, there are exceptions. For example, real photo cards are printed on photographic paper with the word *postcard* and a stamp box printed on the back. These are currently one of the most collectible categories.

Flea markets, yard sales, antique shows, and friends with attics are all sources of postcards. Or you may want to attend one of the dozens of postcard shows held around the country each year. How much will you have to pay for postcards? The answer depends on the kind of cards you wish to collect, their age, and their popularity with other collectors.

One

The River

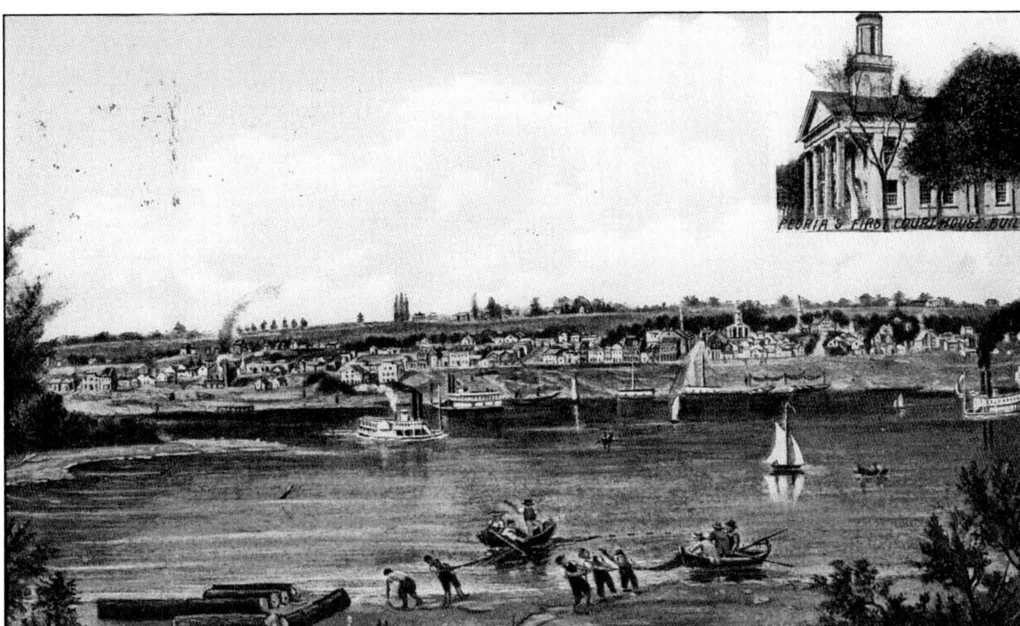

Our Peoria postcard journey begins appropriately with this 1909 mailed card of an 1846 Henry Lewis painting. It is believed to be one of the earliest descriptions of Peoria. This detailed card presents a Peoria without bridges and very little development on the bluffs. Isaac Underhill, a Peoria Real Estate Developer, paid $100 to commission the painting. In the upper right hand corner is an insurrect picture of Peoria's second courthouse, built in 1835.

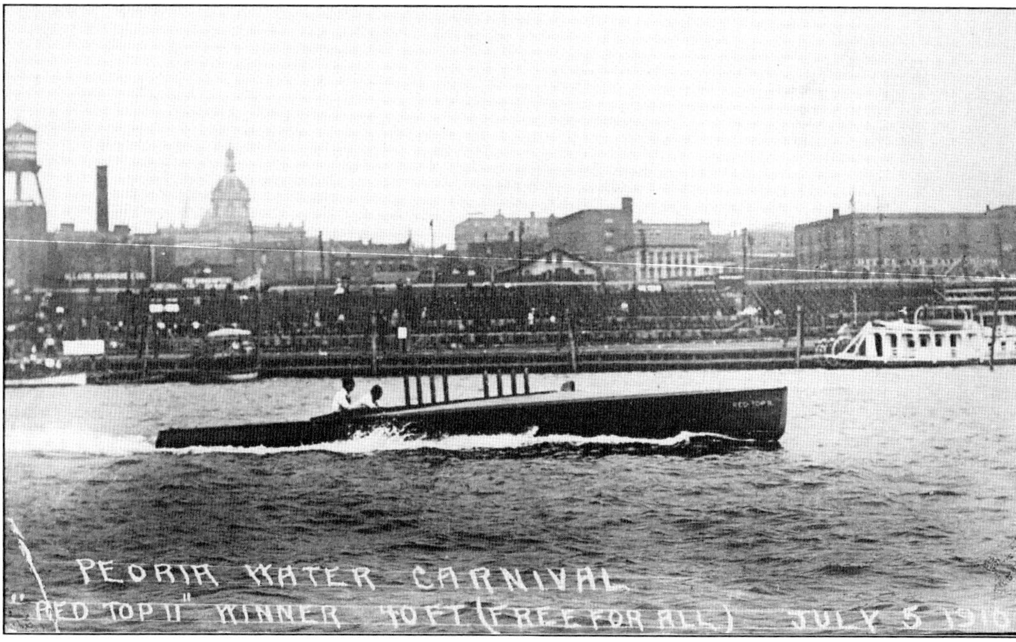

Peoria's early joint venture with the Peoria Water Festival began on the Illinois River in 1906. This annual event was under the auspices of the Peoria Regatta Association and the Peoria Association of Commerce and was often referred to as the "water carnival." The winner of the 40-foot free-for-all held July 5, 1910, was *Red Top II.* This vessel proudly parades in front of the water grandstand. Visible in the background is the county courthouse.

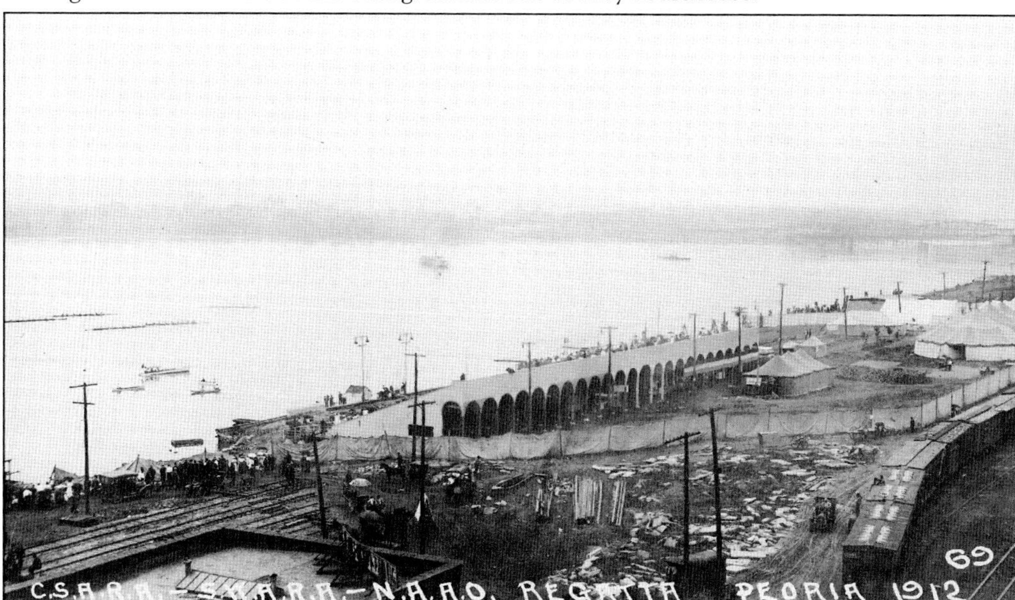

Lake Peoria was again the scene for Peoria's water festival for the Central States Rowing Association, the Southwestern Amateur Rowing Association, and the National Association of Amateur Oarsman Events. The grandstand was re-erected at the Pleasure Boat Landing. Events were scheduled from August 5 to August 10 of 1912. The newly opened Jefferson Hotel Gold Room served as the scene of the annual convention headquarters.

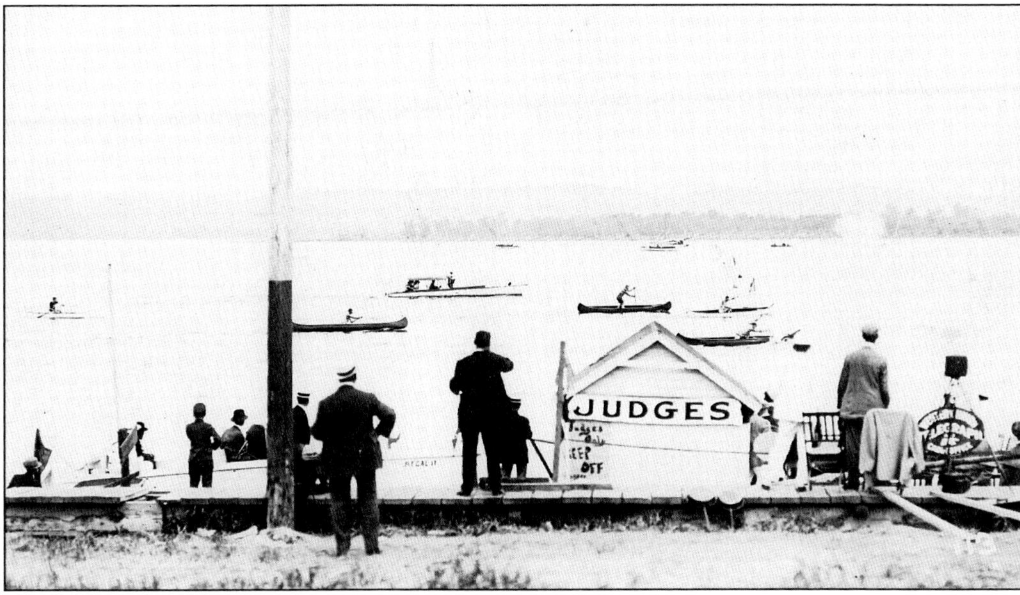

The judge's stand was hastily assembled in front of the grandstand. W.E. Hull, a future Congressman from Peoria, was chairman of the finance committee and judges. This event attracted such world-wide appeal that Western Union Telegraph installed a location next to the judge's stand as seen above. Spectators must have been a problem since there is a painted sign proclaiming "judges only; KEEP OFF."

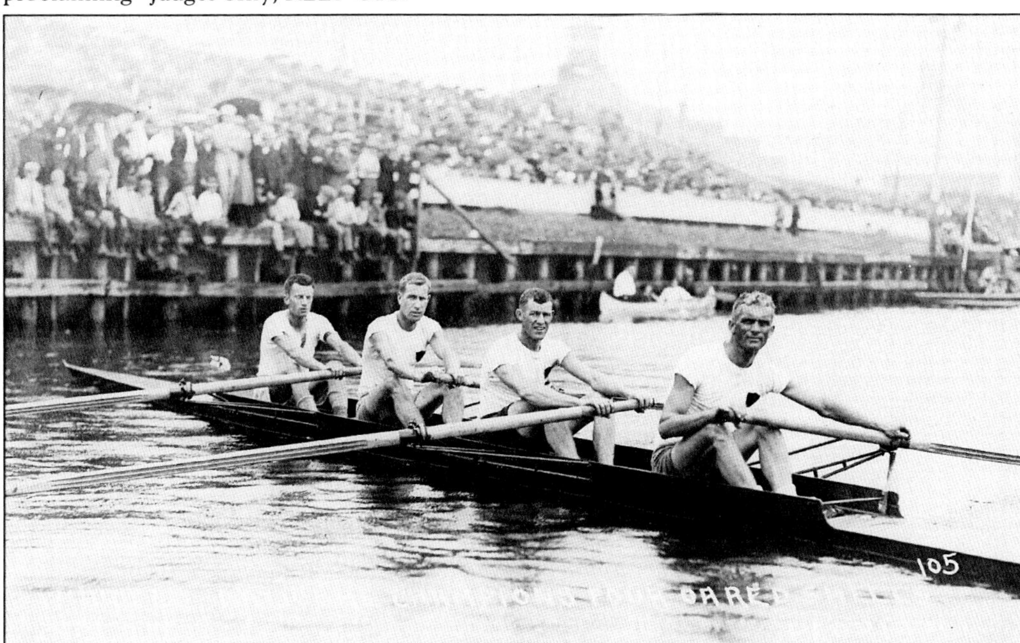

Proud-but-exhausted oarsmen from Winnipeg, Canada, were declared winners and new champions for the Four-Oared Shells, senior class. The event began at 2:20 p.m. on Friday, August 9, 1912. The National Association of Amateur Oarsmen sponsored this next-to-last day's event. The day ended with a band, parade, and concert, and in the evening fireworks were displayed opposite the grandstand on the other side of the river.

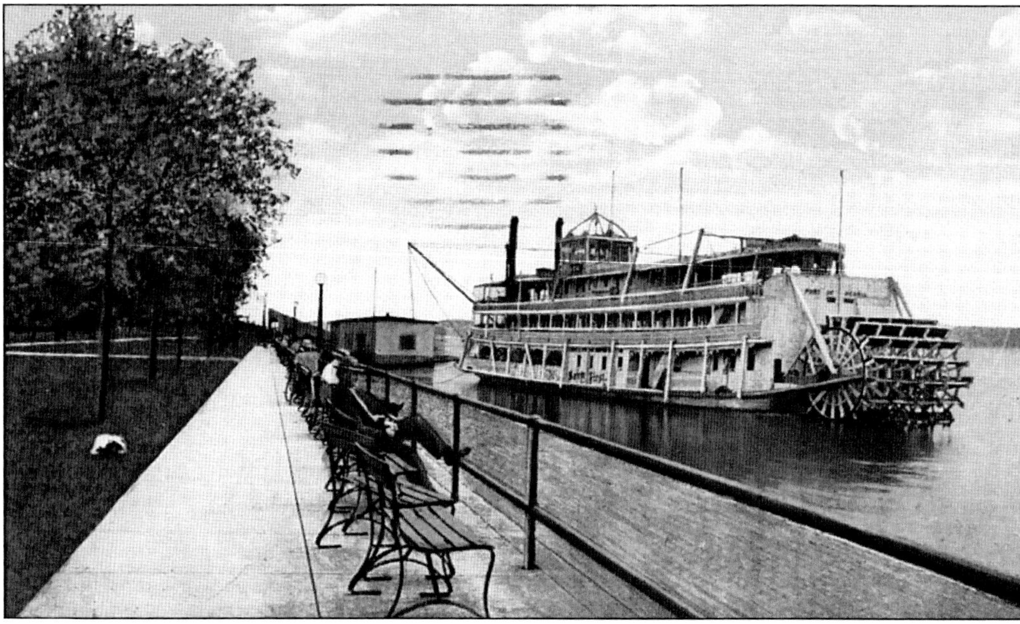

Peoria's Pleasure Boat Landing is shown here in May of 1921. In the far middle background may be seen the permanently erected grandstand for the water festival during the regatta. The docked steamboat was assigned to the Port of Peoria. However, the name of the steamer is not visible in the postcard. It appears to have been an excursion boat journeying up and down the river from this port.

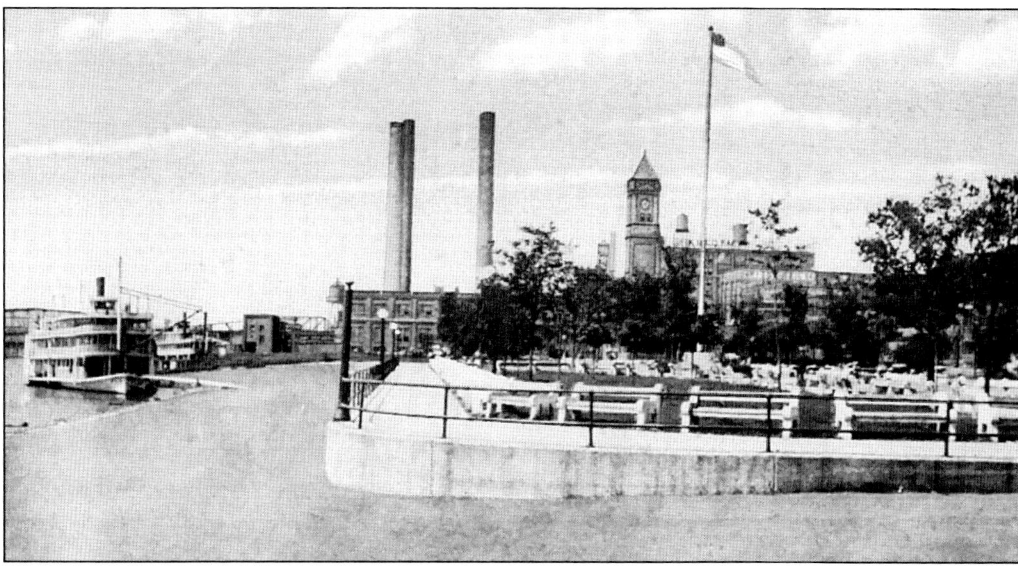

Eckwood Park, a named derived from the first syllables of the last names of City Commissioner S.W. Eckley and E.B. Woodruff, was developed in 1912—perhaps to accommodate the Peoria Water Festival of 1912. It was first known as Levee Park, and the dedication was in June 1915. It contained about 10 acres complete with an amphitheater at its lower end and was developed at the cost of $100,000, with a drinking fountain and many trees and flowers. Today a mere ghost of the park exists, with that area being used mostly for parking space for riverfront activities.

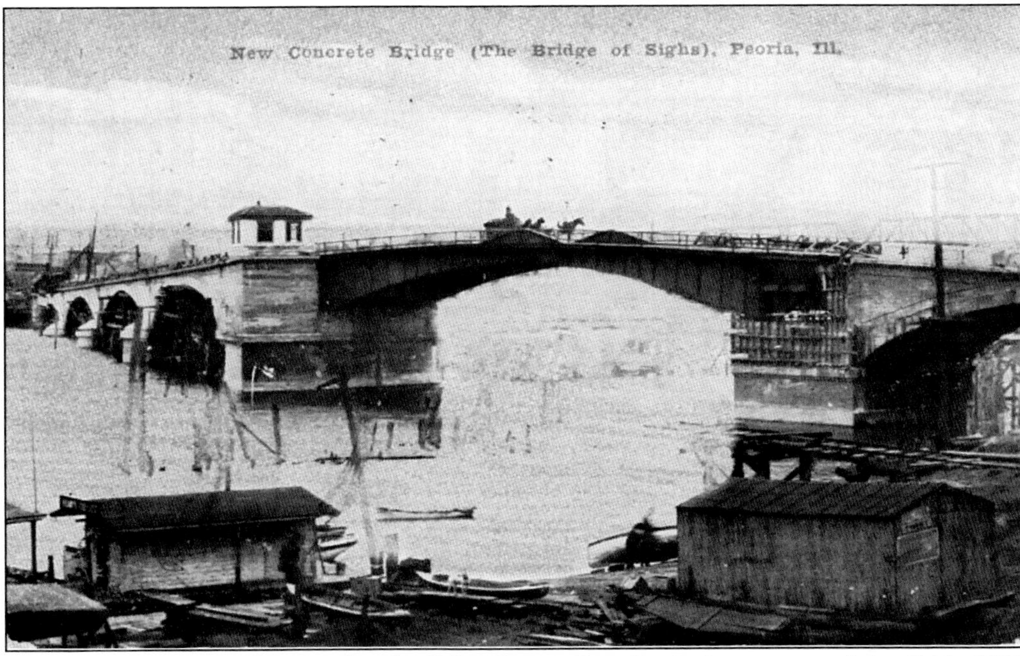

The ribbon-cutting ceremony for the "New Lower Free Bridge" commenced April 11, 1909. The first car to cross was that of the Peoria mayor. A string of dignitaries would follow, and the nickname "The Bridge of Sighs" stuck. Joseph H. Cody, of Cody and Sons boilermakers and smokestacks, turned over its newest complcted bridge to the city. Later, part of the bridge would become known as the Franklin Street Bridge.

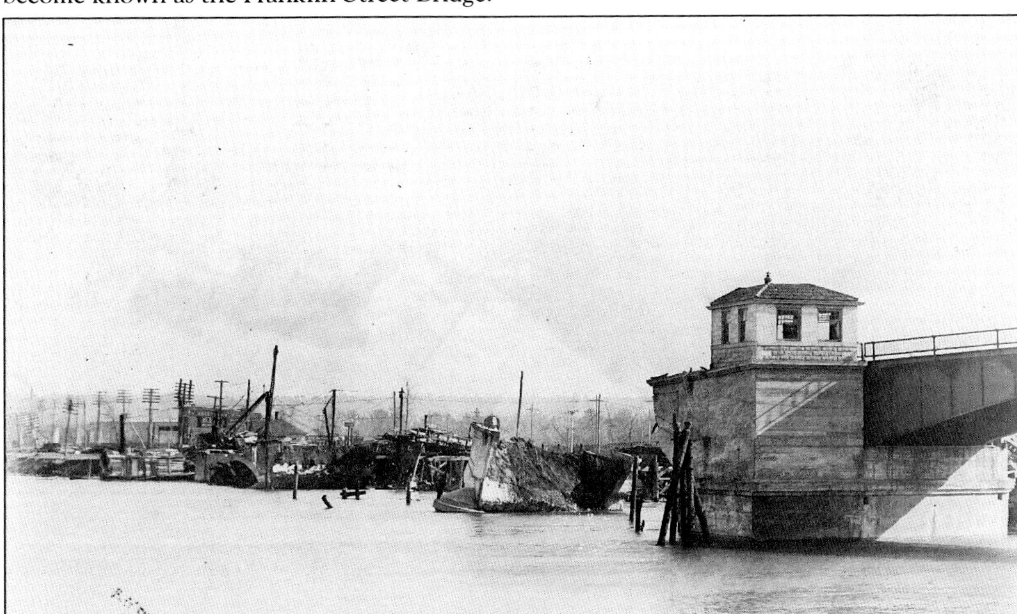

This location was the site of two previous bridge collapses. Rumors circulated that the bidding for the new bridge was never open for public scrutiny. A closer inspection of the bridge by a city engineer caused it to be closed to traffic. Police stood at each bridge entrance to assure that it was not used.

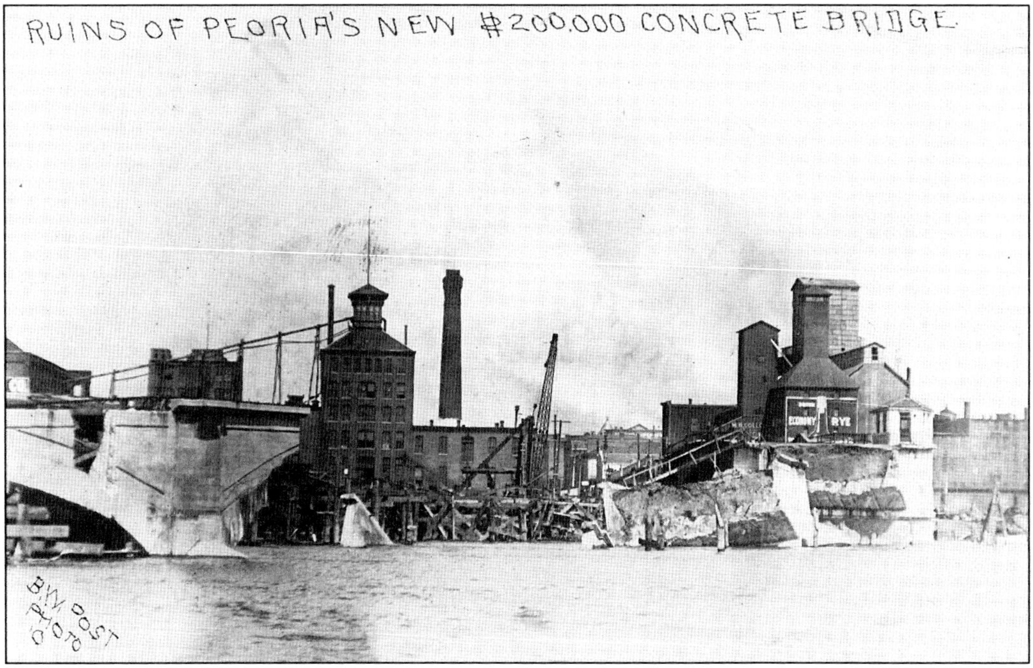

There were additional checks by several city engineers to determine how structurally deficient the bridge actually was. The supporting structure was faulty—while the work was underway, this concrete span, just 20 days old, collapsed. Three spans fell into the water at 5:50 a.m. on May 1, 1909. The city had remitted full payment for completion of the bridge just days before it fell into the river.

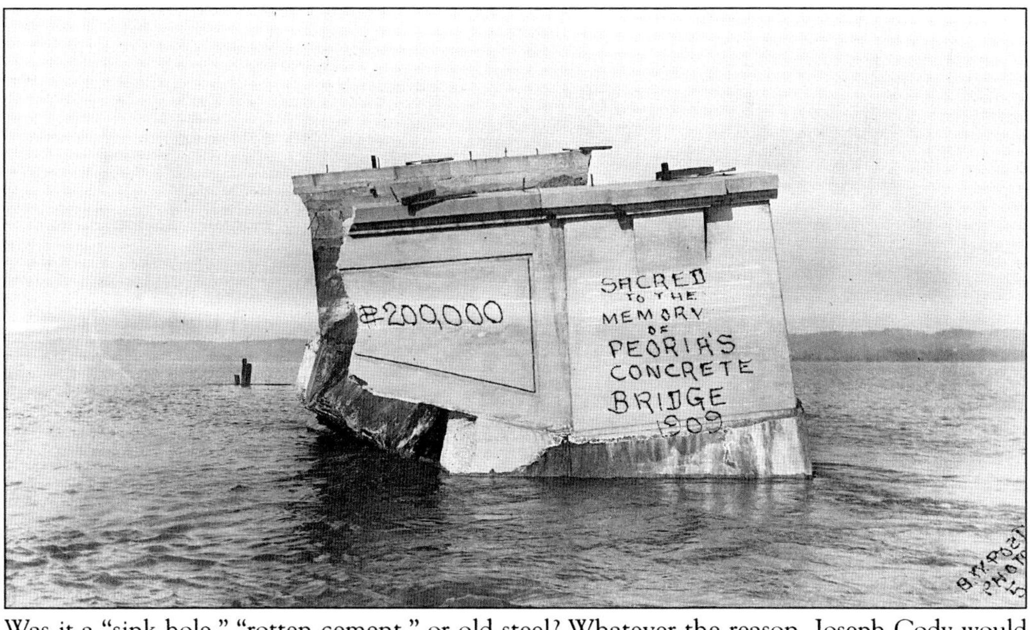

Was it a "sink hole," "rotten cement," or old steel? Whatever the reason, Joseph Cody would collect a settlement from one supplier for the collapsed bridge. This final card appears as a memorial to this tragic story. Two hundred thousand dollars was the amount paid for the collapsed bridge.

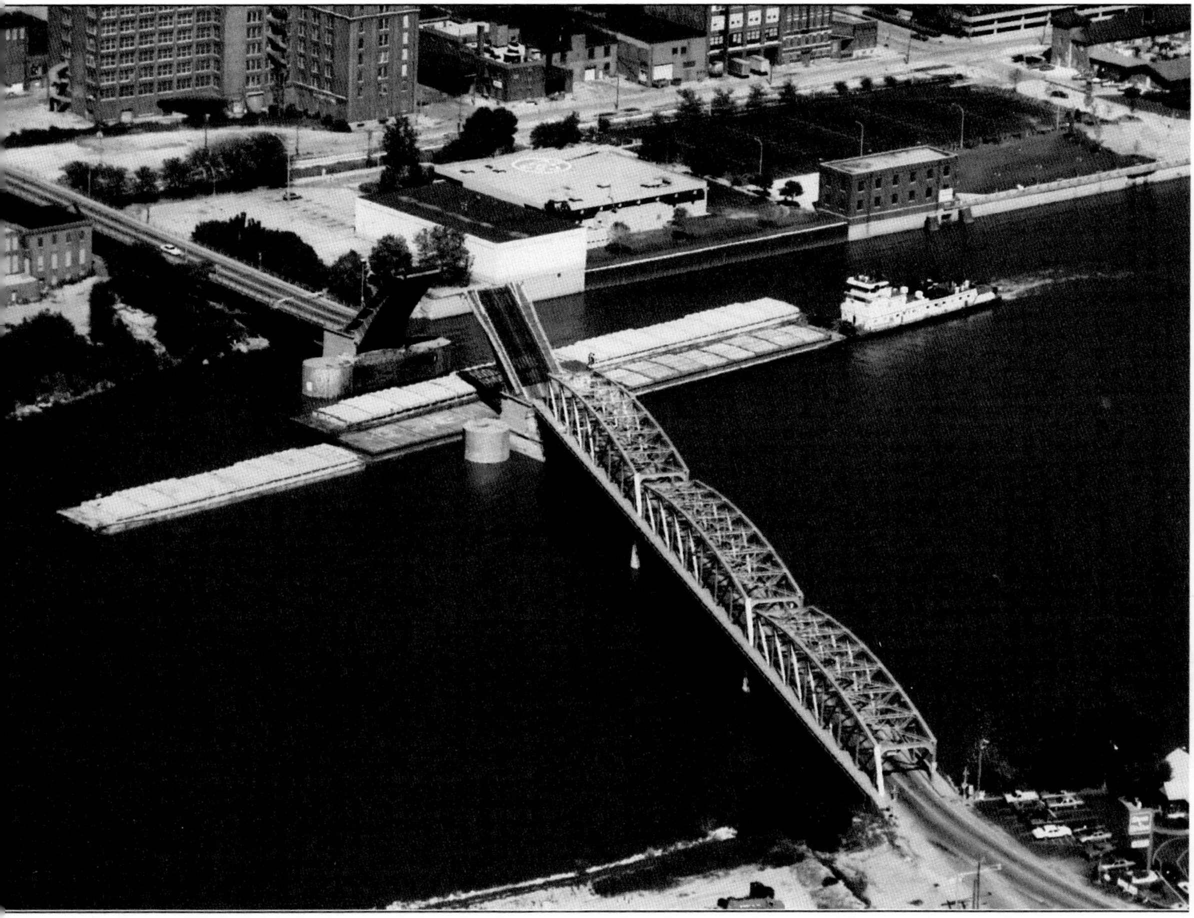

The above illustration is one of the final photos taken before the Franklin Street Bridge was demolished. This steel span was the answer to the city's problem of salvaging what remained of the Franklin Street Bridge after the 1909 collapse. Photographer James P. Carr knew the value of pursuing a photographic view of the draw bridge just before it was removed in the mid-1990s.

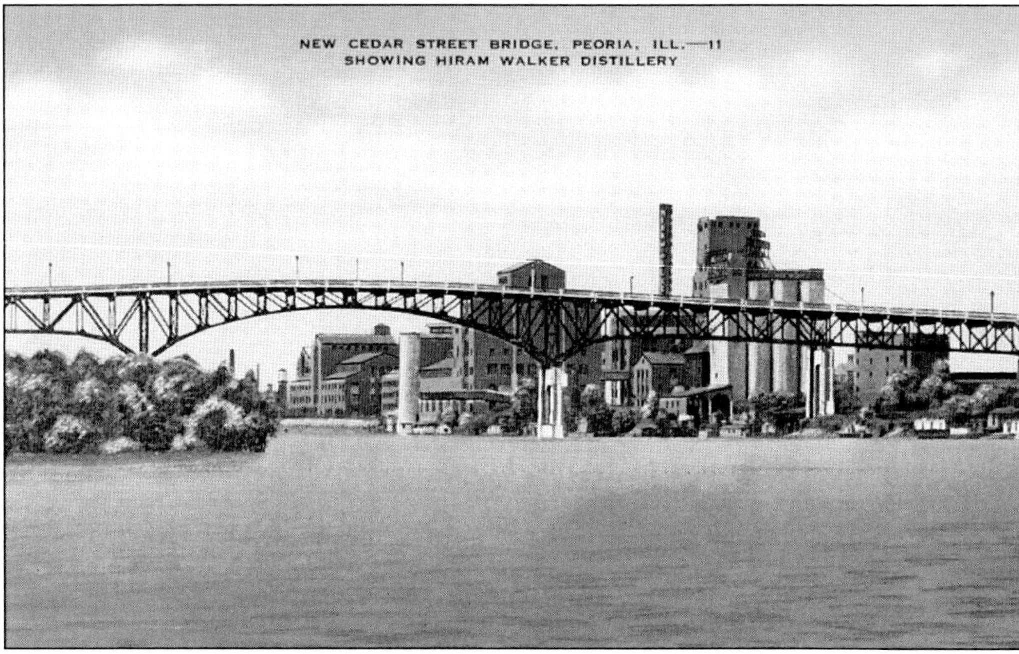

The above postcard was taken shortly after the renaming of Cedar Street to honor General Douglas MacArthur on June 2, 1942. This city ordnance did not address the naming of the bridge. Thus, today the bridge is the Cedar Street Bridge and the approach highway is MacArthur. This span was completed in January 1933, after years of long delays and legal battles.

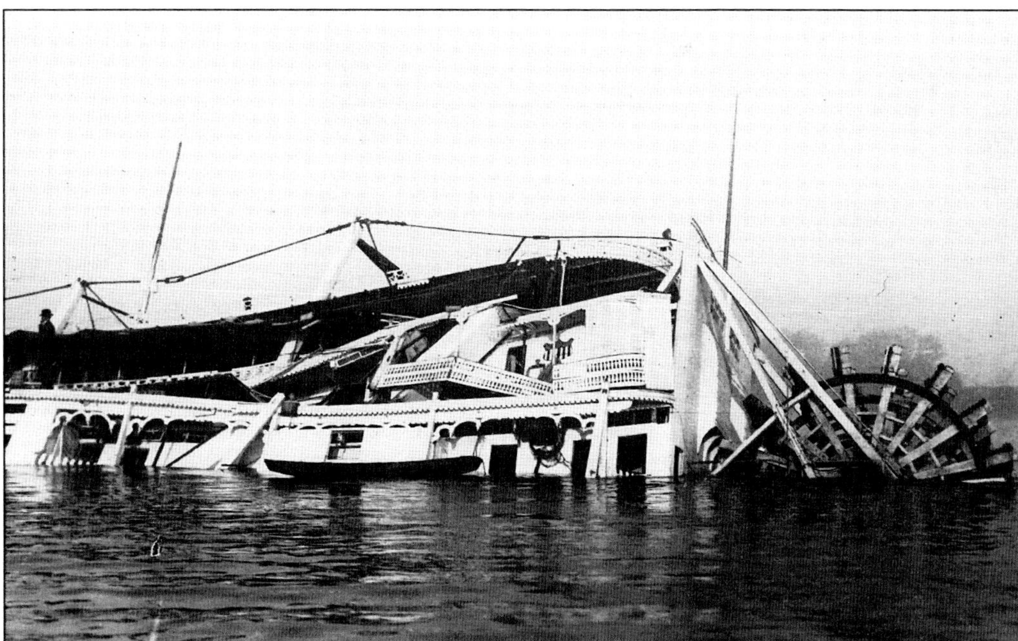

Kingston Mines and Pekin were the pickup points on July 5, 1918, for the ill-fated *Columbia* steamboat. This was to be a round-trip and a day affair, complete with band, food, and dancing. The South Side Social Club would list this trip as one of their most popular.

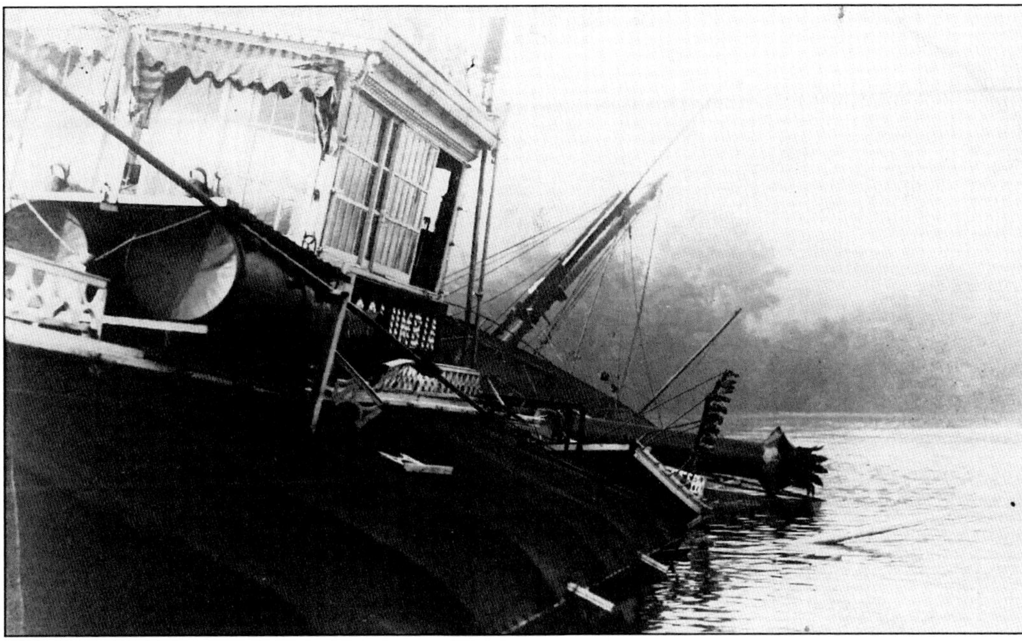

The return trip was rather short, with over 550 people enjoying the day at Peoria's famous Al Fresco Park. At a point about even with Wesley City, an object protruding from the water tore a hole in the shallow water craft. Reverse movement, as ordered by the captain, caused the vessel to collapse, and as the above picture indicates, it sank partially.

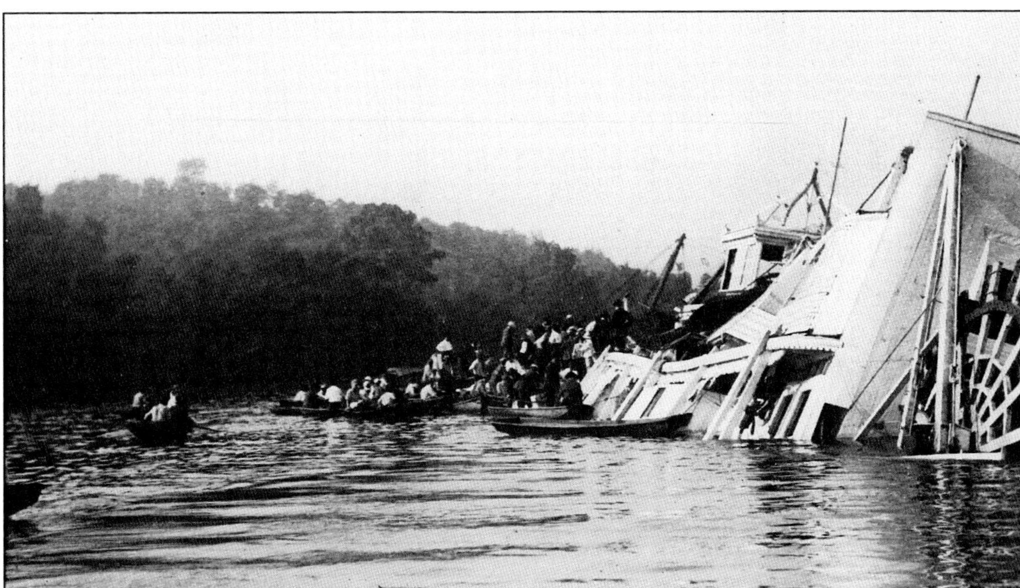

The destruction was soon complete. Salvage was limited to only a few souvenirs found by the reserve parties that night and the following morning.

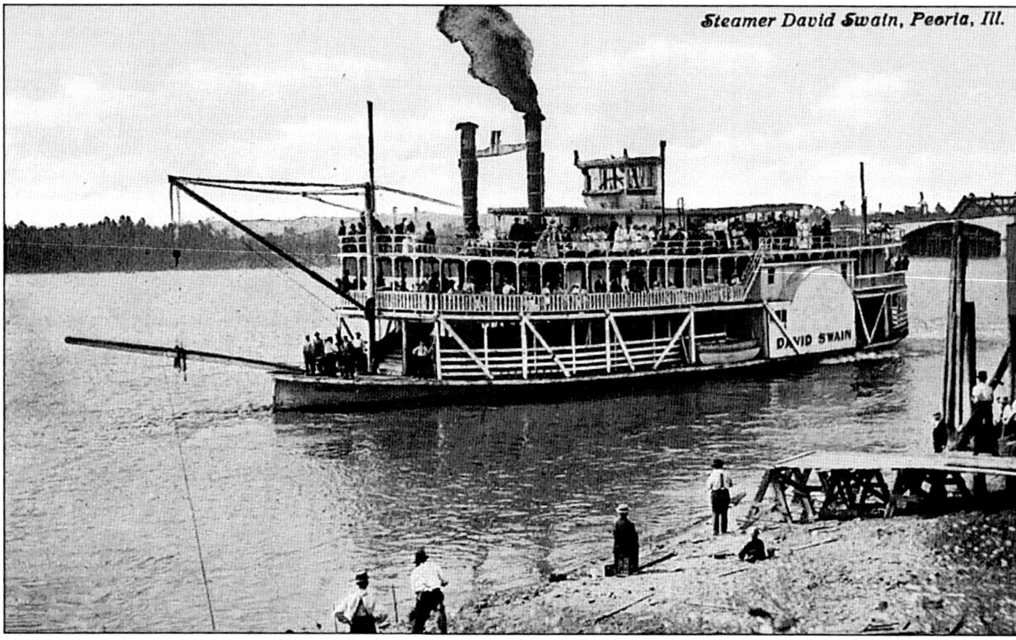

Beginning in May 1890, David Swain and his sons, Perry and Verne, initiated a packet (steamboat) line and began offering service between Peoria and La Salle. In all, the Swains operated ten steamboats. By 1922, the packet business was eliminated. The excursion trade would last two more years and then be discontinued.

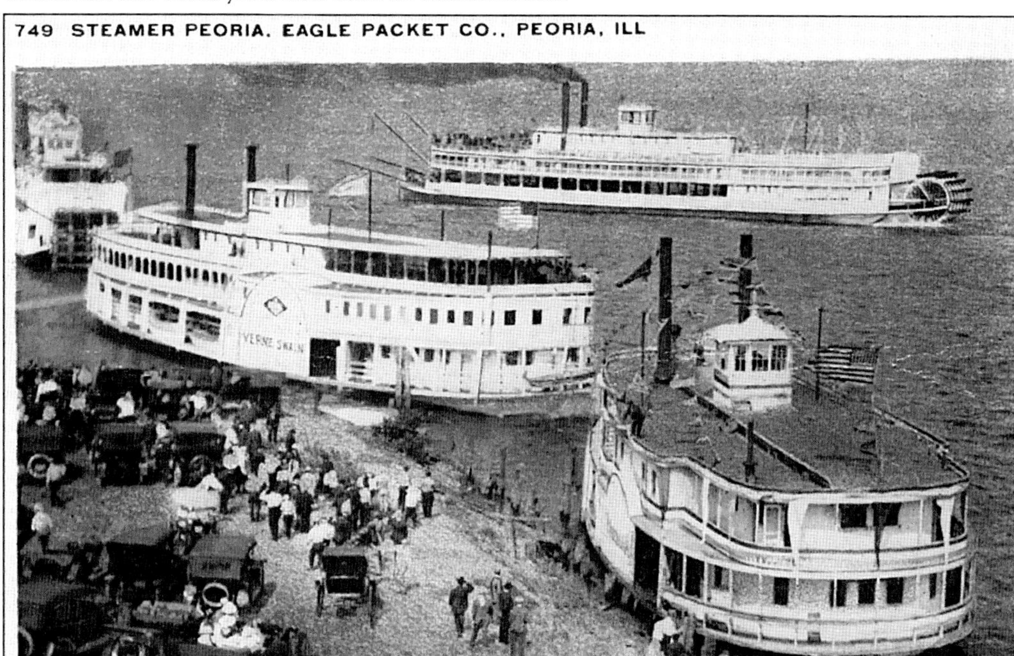

Pictured above are the riverboats *Peoria* and *Verne Swain*. The Eagle Packet Company was the last of the river lines to provide service between Peoria and St. Louis. This service began in 1891 and ended in 1935, when the Illinois River became controlled by a series of locks and dams.

Two

Peoria's Downtown

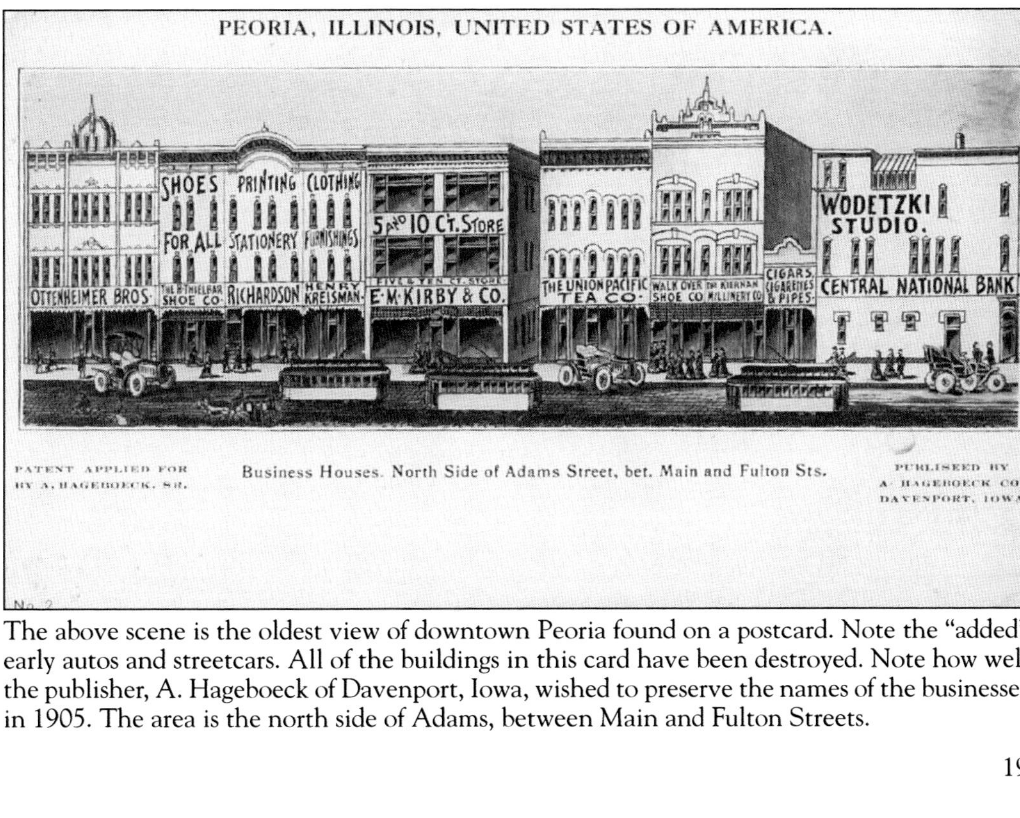

The above scene is the oldest view of downtown Peoria found on a postcard. Note the "added" early autos and streetcars. All of the buildings in this card have been destroyed. Note how well the publisher, A. Hageboeck of Davenport, Iowa, wished to preserve the names of the businesses in 1905. The area is the north side of Adams, between Main and Fulton Streets.

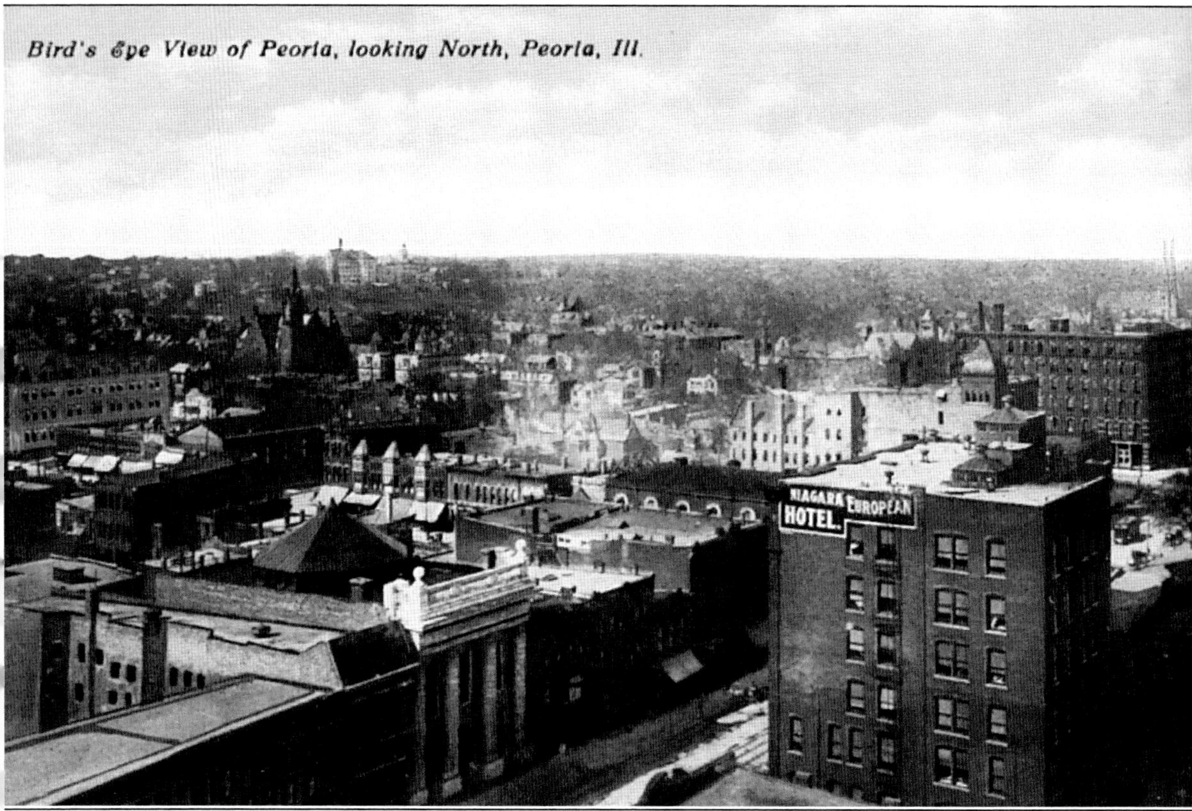

This rare, double card displays a downtown view of the courthouse. Adams Street is to the right and Jefferson Street is to the left. Main Street is in front of the center buildings. This street

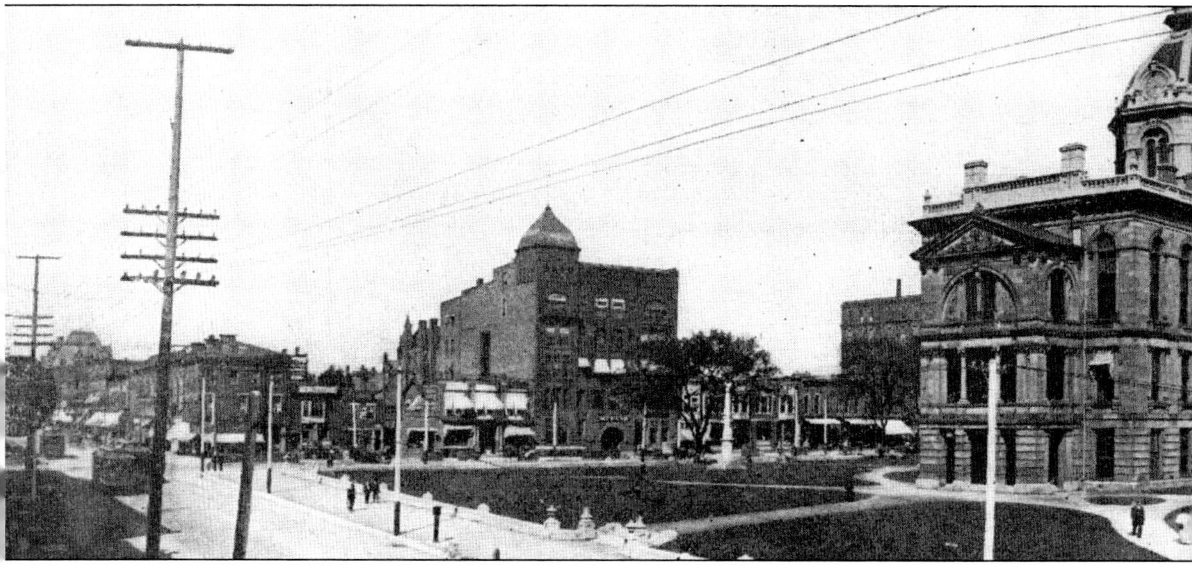

Here is the panoramic view of the downtown, with the courthouse in the center. This building was completed in 1878, at a cost of $248,000. The YMCA building to the left was lost in a fire

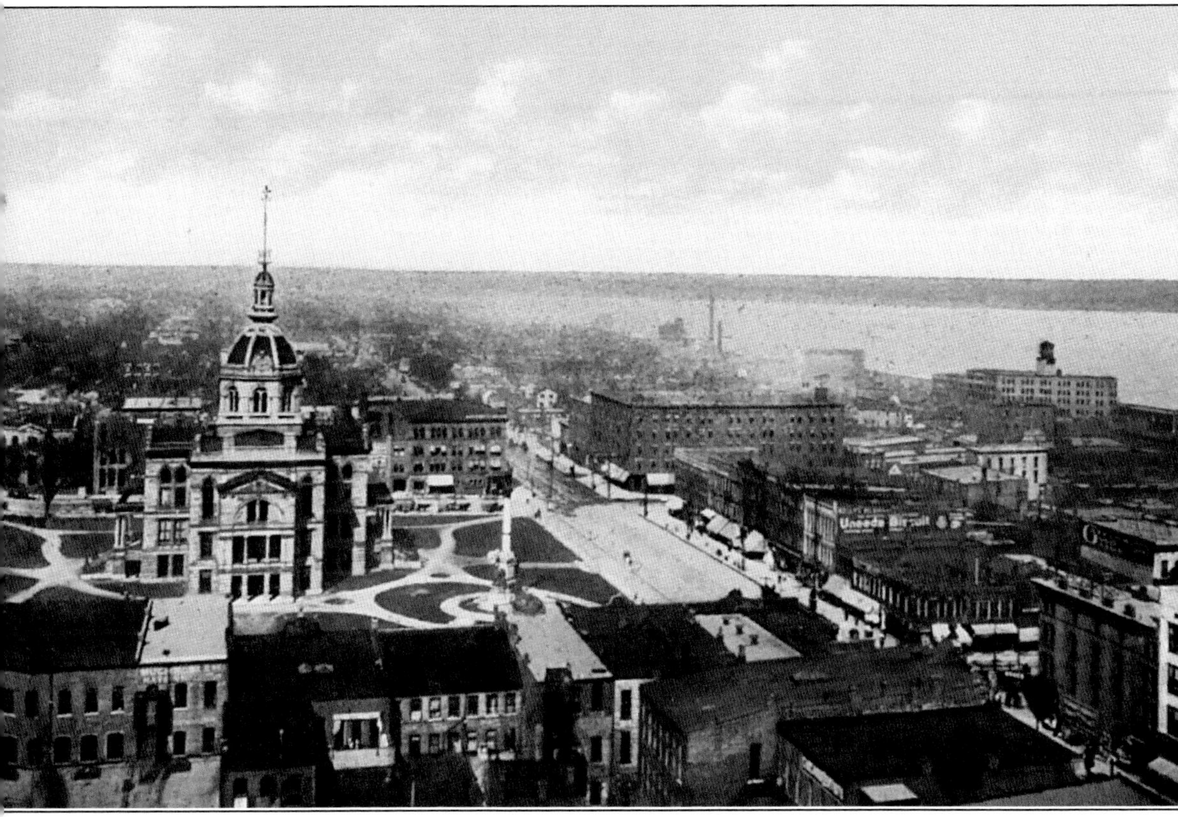

scene was taken in 1907.

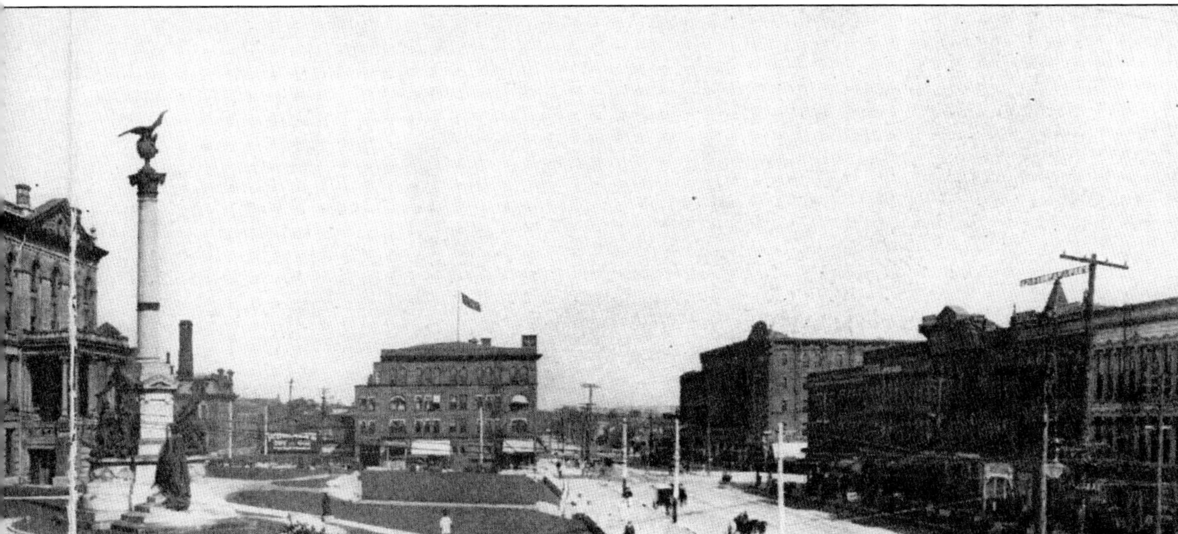

in 1915. To the far right, on Adams Street, is the Mayer Hotel, built in 1907 and destroyed by fire in 1963. This 1910 postcard was mailed in 1911.

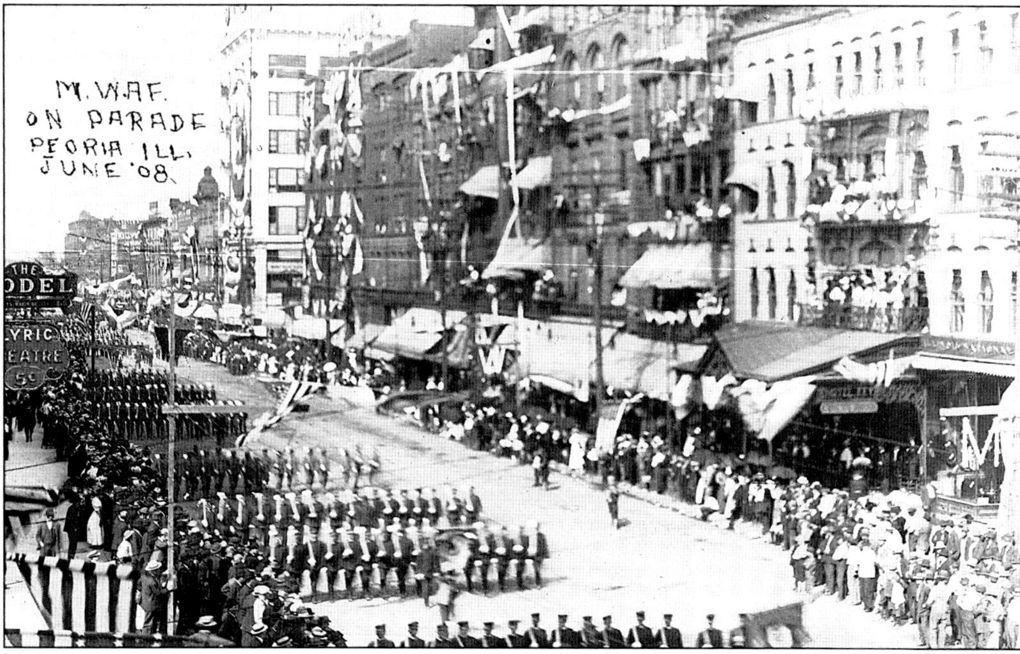

To commemorate the Modern Woodmen of America meeting held in Peoria, this large parade was held on June 10, 1908. Peoria had six camps at the time, providing plenty of marchers. Note the Fey Hotel to the far right. Schipper and Block, located near the middle of this image, was built in 1905.

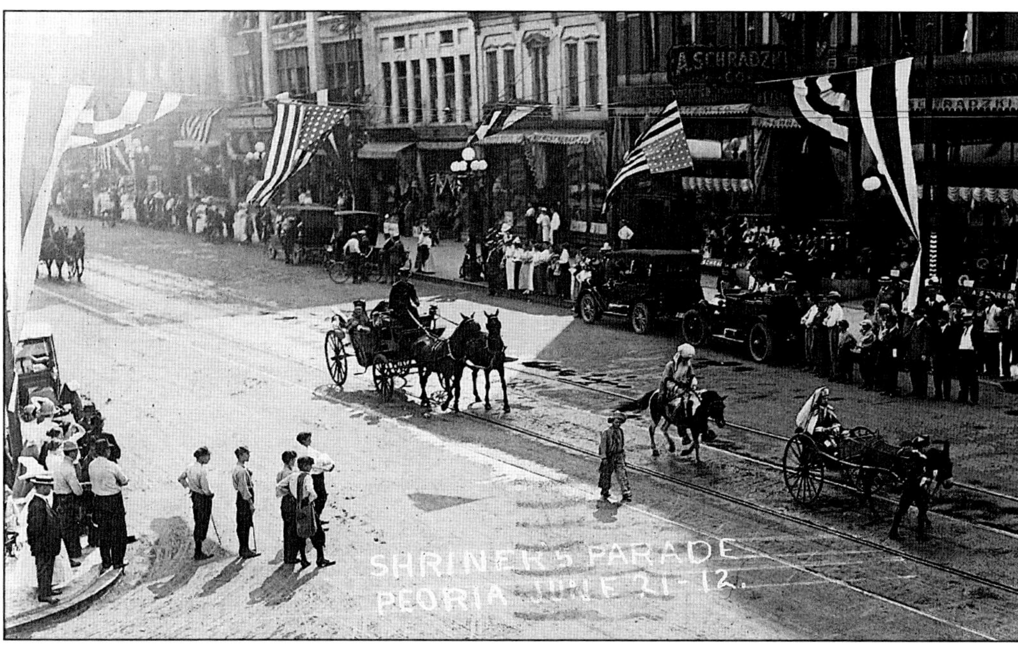

Peoria has always been a city of parades and conventions. It has the distinction of hosting the nation's oldest Santa parade, begun initially in 1888 by Schipper and Block. The above parade was the finalist for the Shriner's parade held on June 12, 1912.

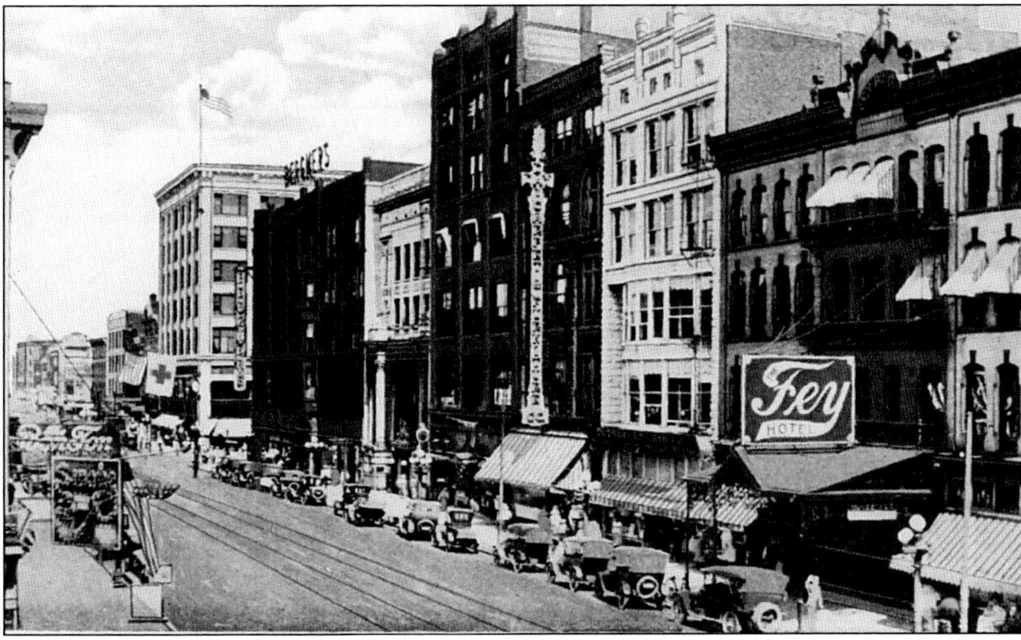

Downtown Peoria, in the early 1920s, was photographed from Adams Street looking north from Liberty. The Fey Hotel on the right was built in 1885 and razed in 1935. Note the stone front to the Bergner Store. Later, this was double-faced with metal to hide the original look. Next to Bergner's was the First National Bank, which was later used as the men's department for Bergner's.

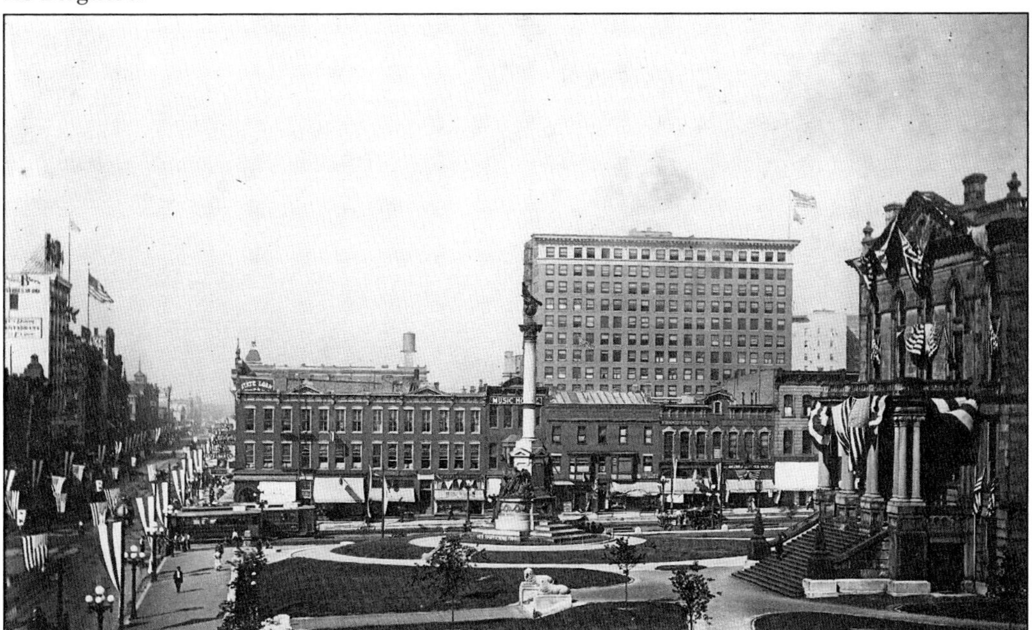

This 1910 view of the county courthouse was taken on the Fourth of July. The courthouse, as pictured here, was built in 1878 and would be razed in 1964. The American flags were probably draped just before the parade. The view is from Hamilton Boulevard looking southwest on Adams. The picture was taken from the Mayer Office Building.

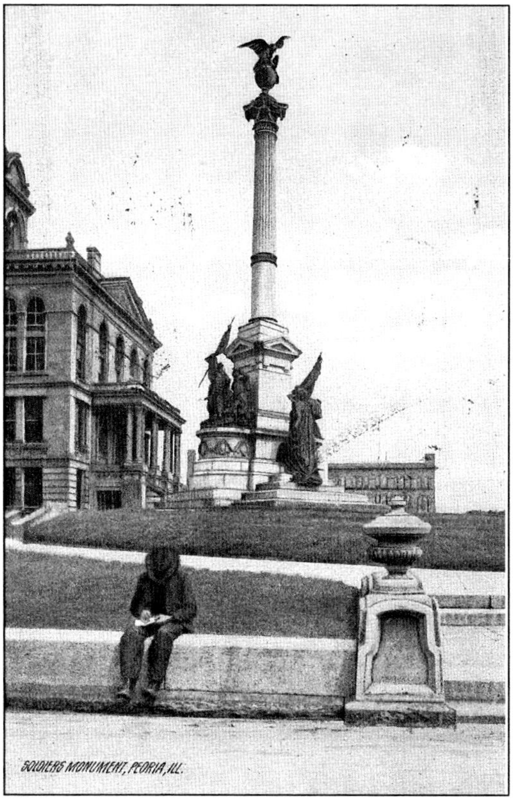

Sculpted in Pistogo, Italy, the Soldiers and Sailors Civil War Memorial was just eight years old when this picture was taken. The Mayer Office Building may be seen in the background to the left. President McKinley would be present at the dedication on October 6, 1899.

The horse and wagon days are clearly represented in the postcard below, taken in 1901. The place is Adams Street, north of Main Street. None of the buildings survive today.

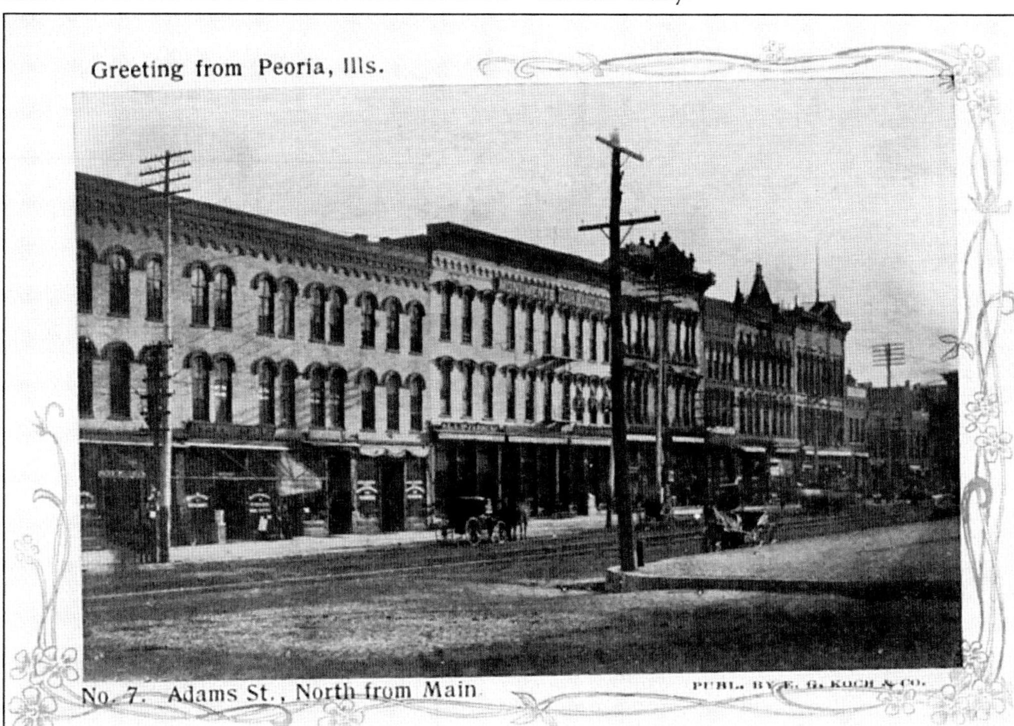

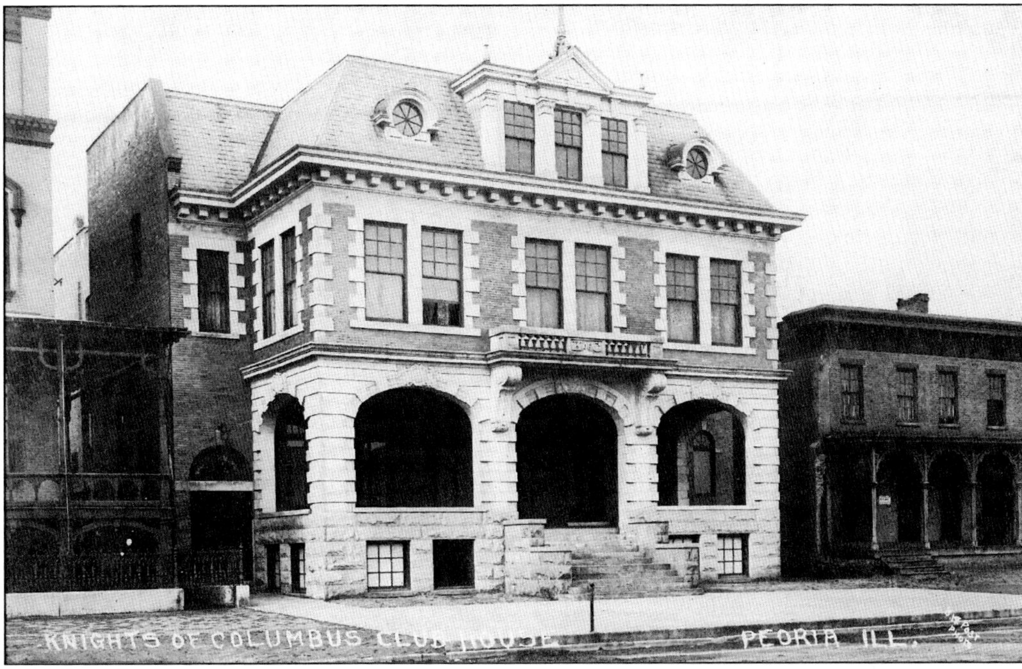

Peoria had another presidential visit in 1910. The occasion was the dedication of the Knights of Columbus Club at 227 North Jefferson Street. President Theodore Roosevelt's visit also included a stop at the Peoria Country Club and a reception with Archbishop John Lancaster Spalding.

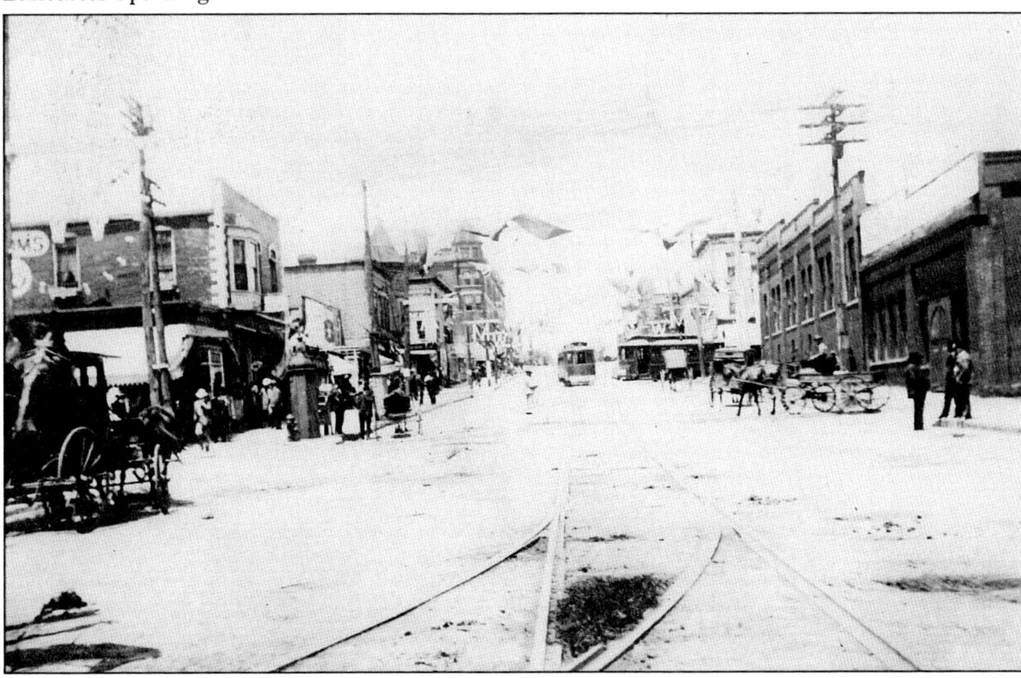

The entrance to the Franklin Street Bridge is pictured above in 1909. The building to the left survived until it was destroyed in order to widen the street to accommodate the new Bob Michael Bridge.

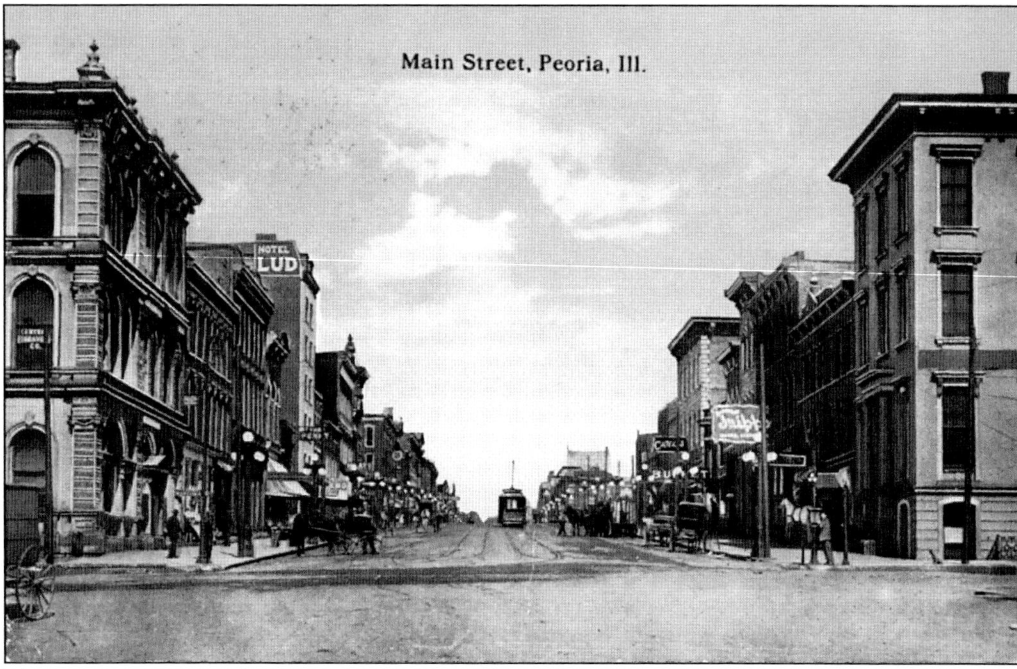

This is a 1914 view of Main Street from Washington Street. There are as many as 40 different postcard views of Main Street. The buildings to the right would be razed for the world headquarters of Caterpillar, Inc. Redevelopment to the left occurred in the late 1960s.

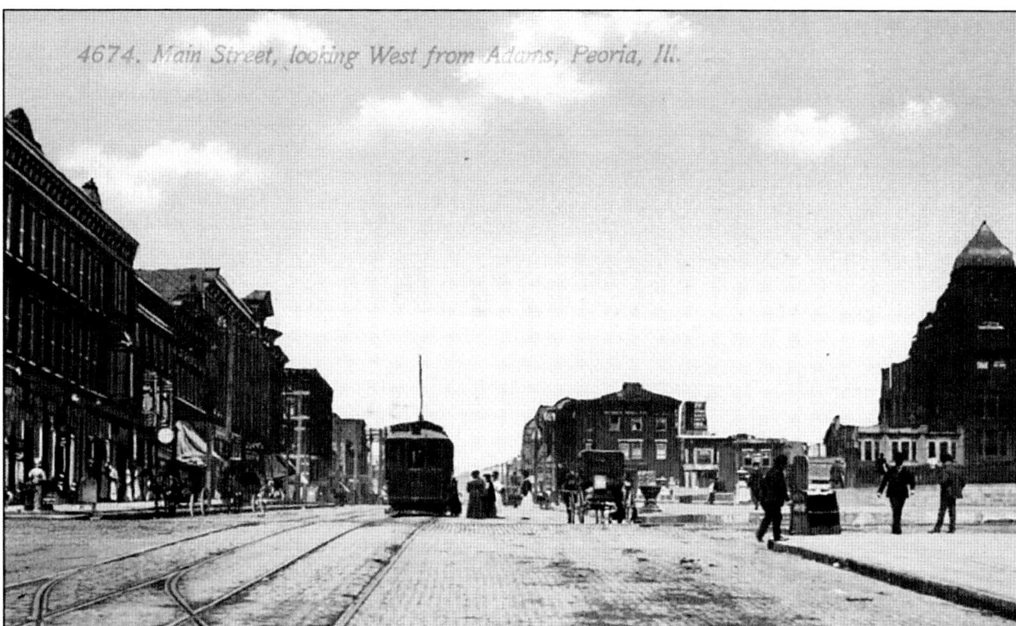

Pictured is a stroll further up Main Street in this 1910 postcard. The YMCA building, erected in 1890, later became the German Insurance Fire Company, and was eventually destroyed by fire in 1915. In the upper center stood the Rouse's Opera Hall, later known as the Main Street Theater. These buildings were razed in 1917 to make way for the Peoria Life Building.

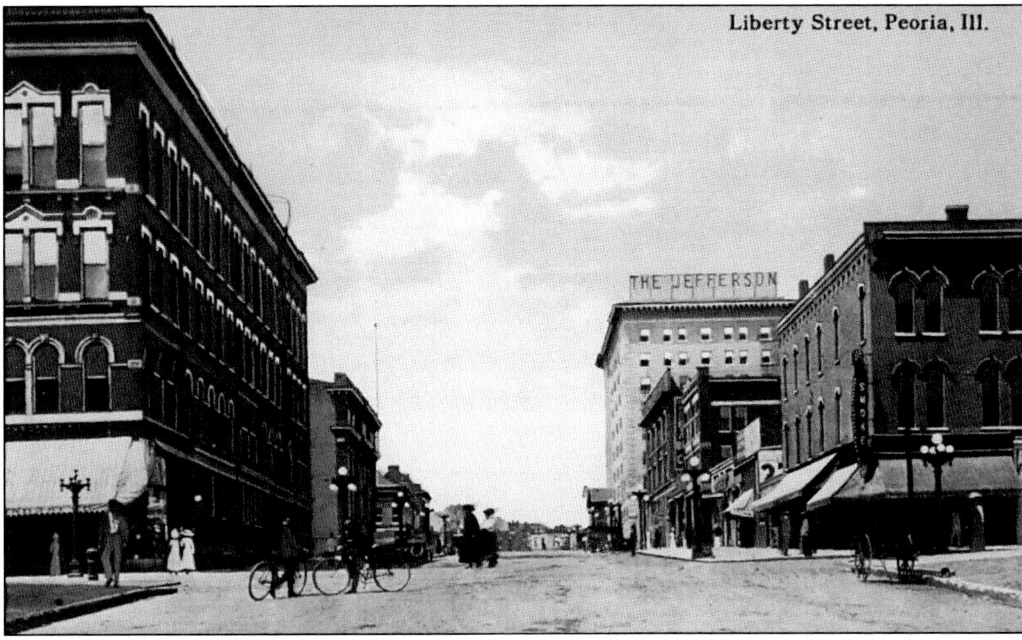

This was a scene at Liberty Street looking up to Adams Street in 1913. The building to the right was eventually razed, and CILCO came to occupy that space. To the left was the Schrodzki's, which would later burn down; today the site is occupied by the First of America Bank Building. The Jefferson Hotel, which opened in 1912, is in the background on the right.

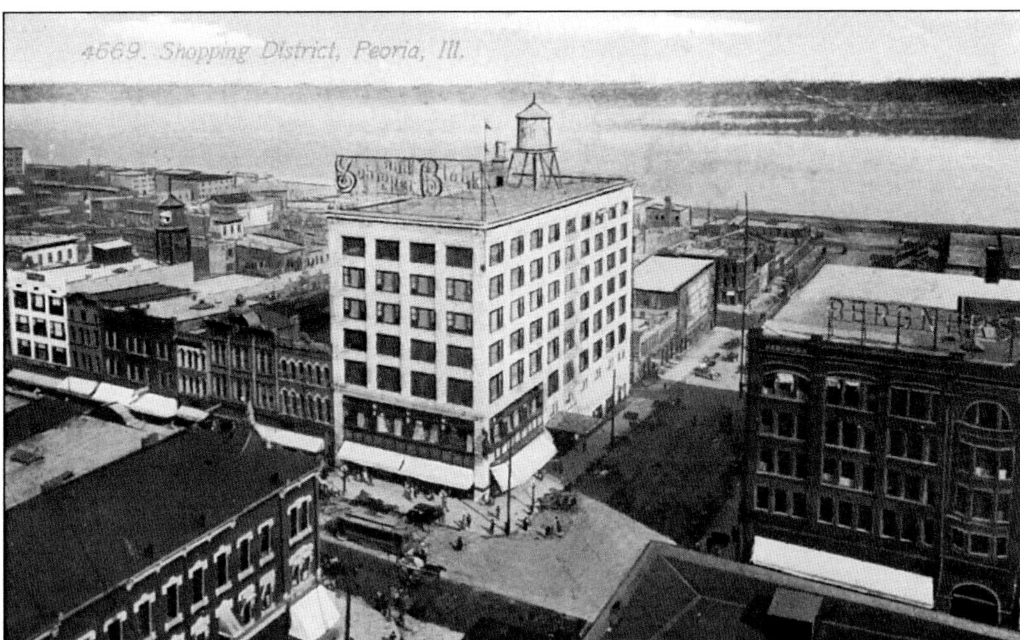

This view of the central shopping district was taken before 1914. The area was a large part of the great white way for Peoria's patrons. Note the absence of bridges on the Illinois River.

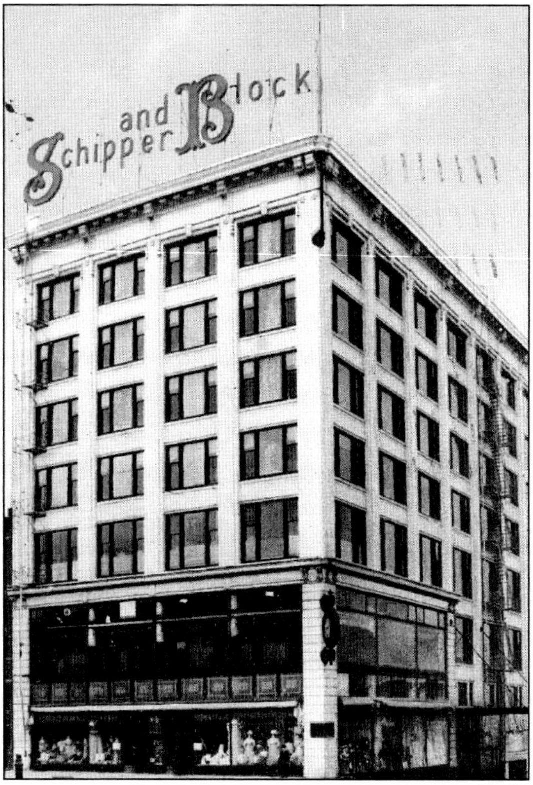

This picture was taken in 1908 at the corner of 124 South West Adams and Fulton. The corner has been a commercial location since 1869. There were seven retail businesses here before 1904, with only a one year absence due to the construction of this building. Schipper and Block were there in 1905, Block and Kuhl in 1914, Carson Pirie Scott in 1959, Jefferson Bank in 1978, and Bank One in 1992.

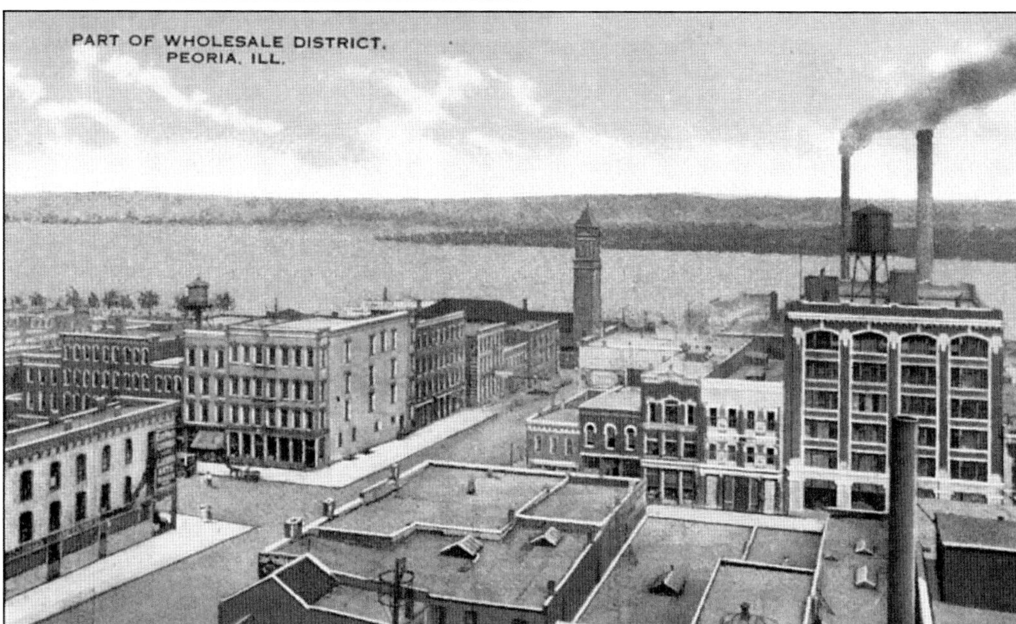

With a population base of 66,950 by 1910, Peoria exploded as a distribution center. Wholesale houses were once located along Washington and Liberty Streets. This postcard was taken between 1910 and 1915. Note that the Rock Island Depot is pictured before the removal of the clock tower.

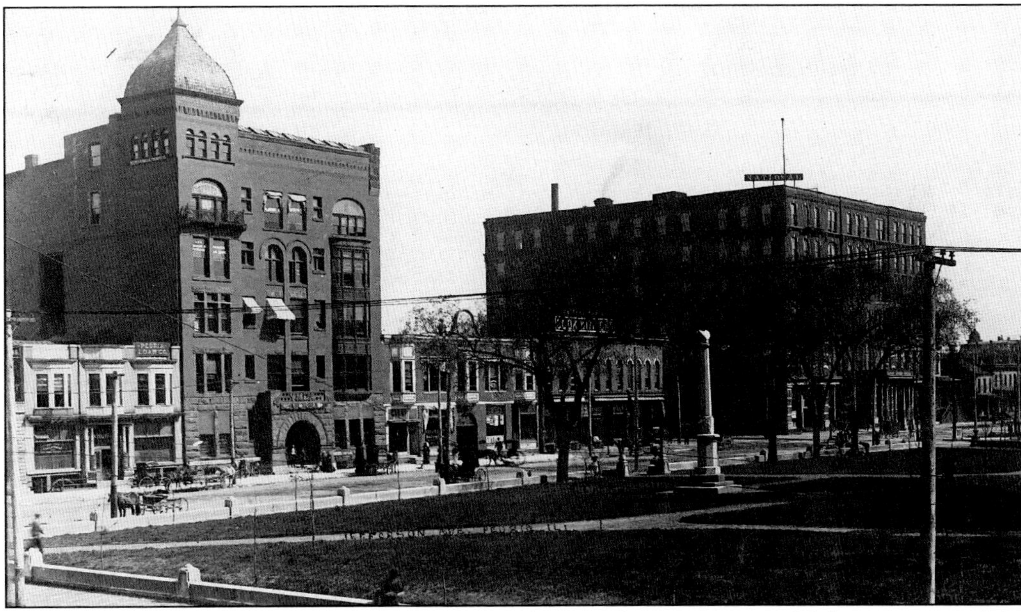

This 1909 view of Adams Street is across from the courthouse. Fire would destroy most of this block, and part of the next block, shortly after this picture was made. The YMCA building, or German Fire Insurance Building, was destroyed by fire in 1915. The National Hotel to the right was destroyed in 1911. The Civil War Memorial in the center of the picture would remain until the new courthouse was constructed in 1964.

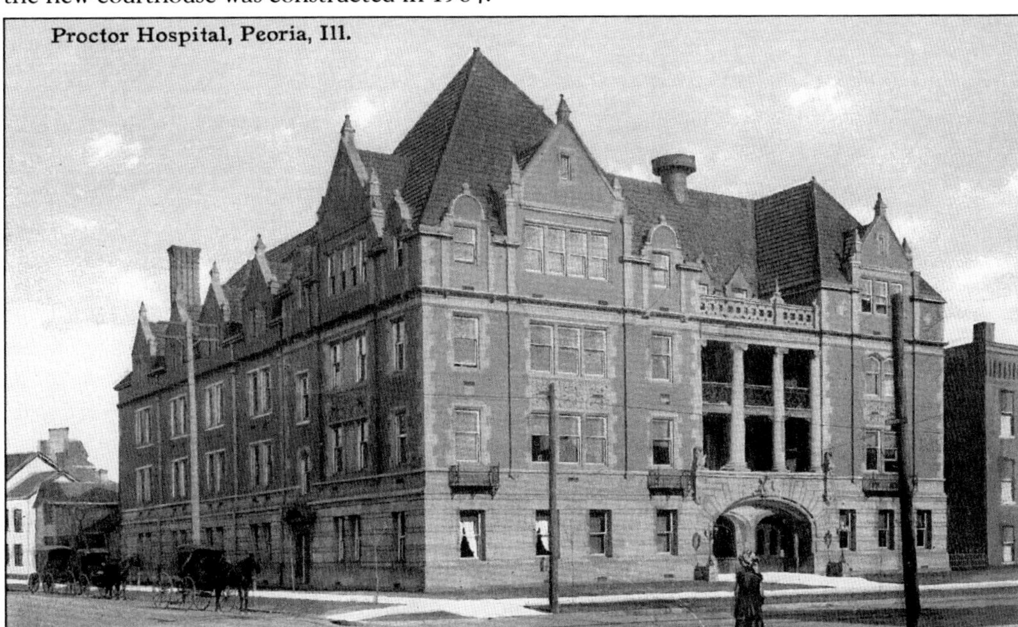

The above building was the second one constructed at Second and Fisher Streets. The first was the Cottage Hospital and was erected in 1893. The next building, pictured above, was completed in 1902 at a cost of $85,000. At the death of John C. Proctor in 1907, the name was changed to honor the chief benefactor of this institution. Proctor Hospital erected, beginning in 1959, a new complex on Knoxville.

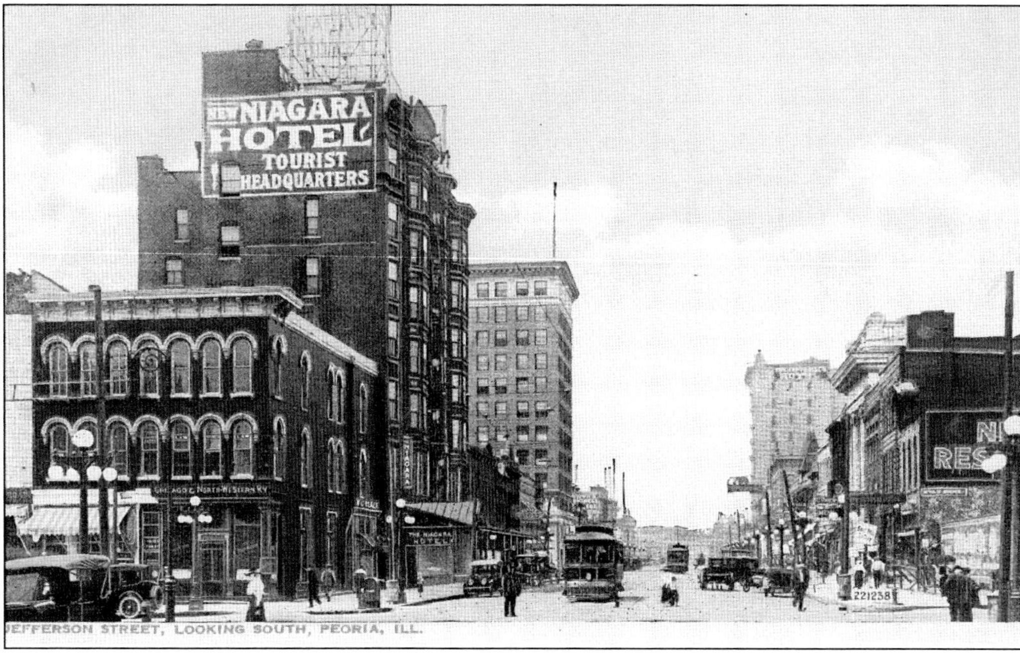

A stroll down Jefferson recalls two large hotels—the Niagara (on the left), razed in 1968, and the Jefferson (to the right), which was destroyed in 1979. In the center of the card is the Jefferson Building, which remains standing to this day. All the other buildings have been removed.

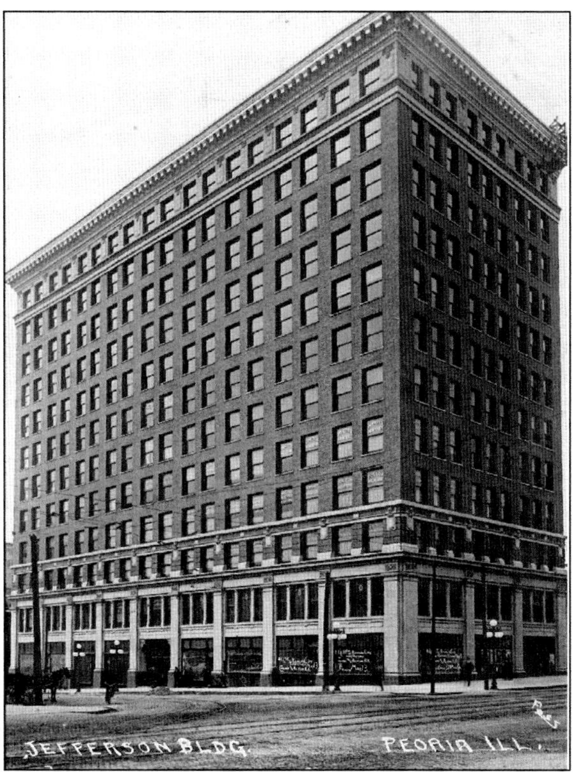

The Jefferson Building, also known as Peoria Savings Plaza, was designed by William I. Jenney in 1910, and was the largest building in Peoria. This is a classical-style building, complete with friezes and terra-cotta molding. It was also one of the first buildings in Peoria to be built with steel frame and brick. In 1980, an extensive remodeling occurred, preparing the building for the next 50 years.

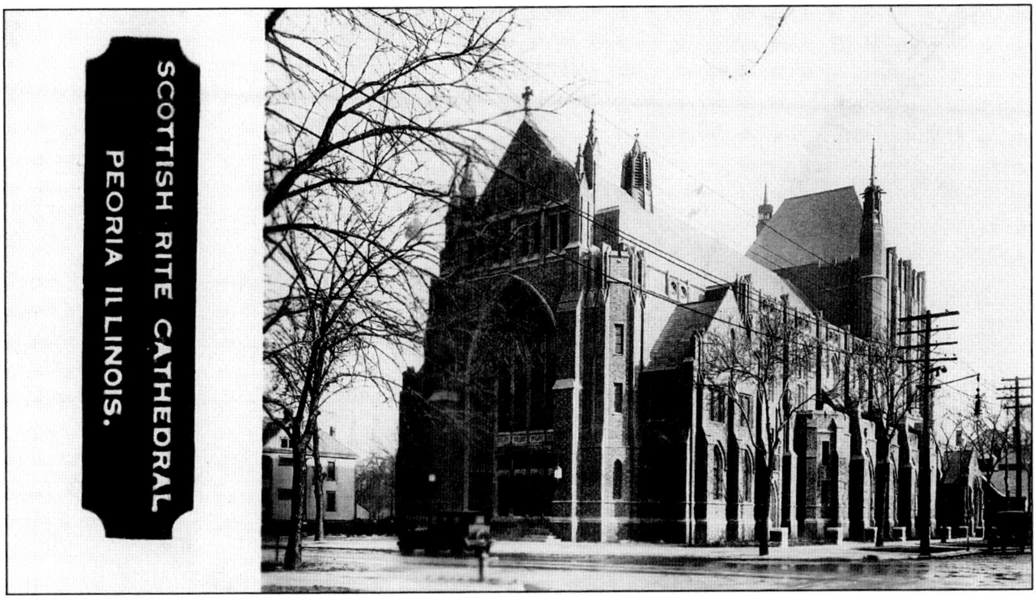

The Scottish Rite Cathedral at 400 Northeast Perry is pictured above. The building was constructed in 1924. The inspiration for the design of this building was found in Scotland. It still stands at the Perry address.

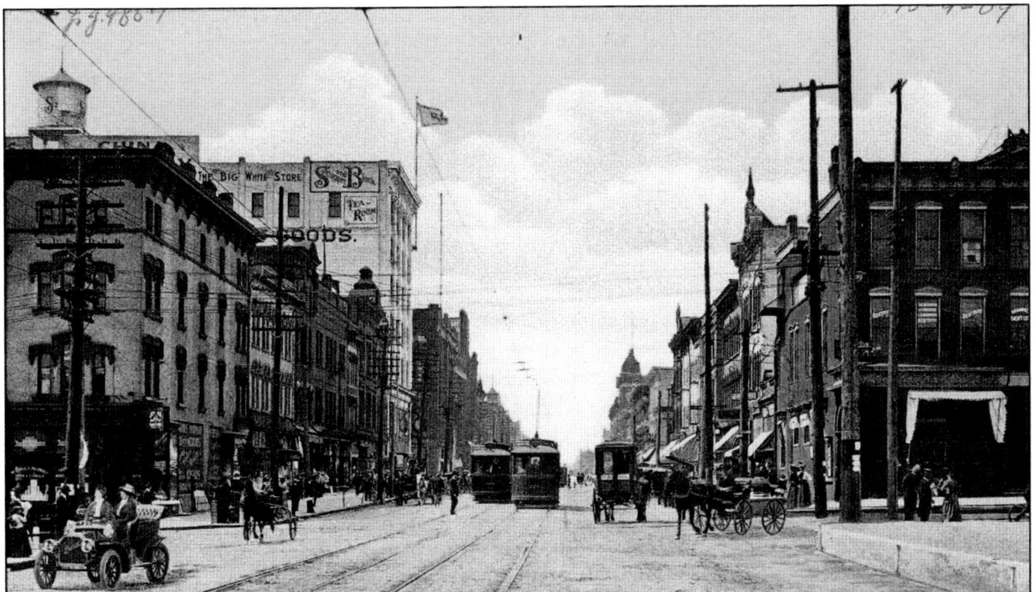

It appears the creator of this card may have tinkered with the photograph by adding automobiles and wagons. This same 1909 postcard of Adams Street has since been reproduced without many of the people and objects.

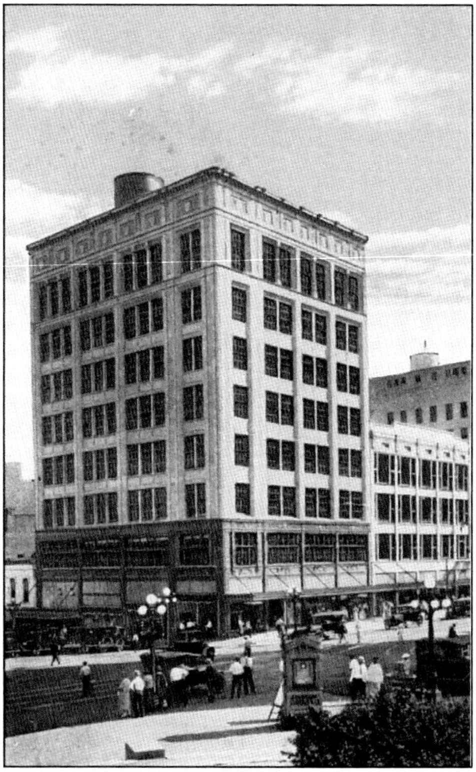

The Clarke Building, previously located at Main and Adams, was completed in 1928. This company was a leading dry goods company until 1944, when it was sold to the St. Louis firm Ely-Walker. The lease was lost, and Clarke closed in 1951. That year the building was renamed the Citizens Building, with office space for sale to the community. The building was razed in 1981 by Caterpillar, Inc., for a new parking lot.

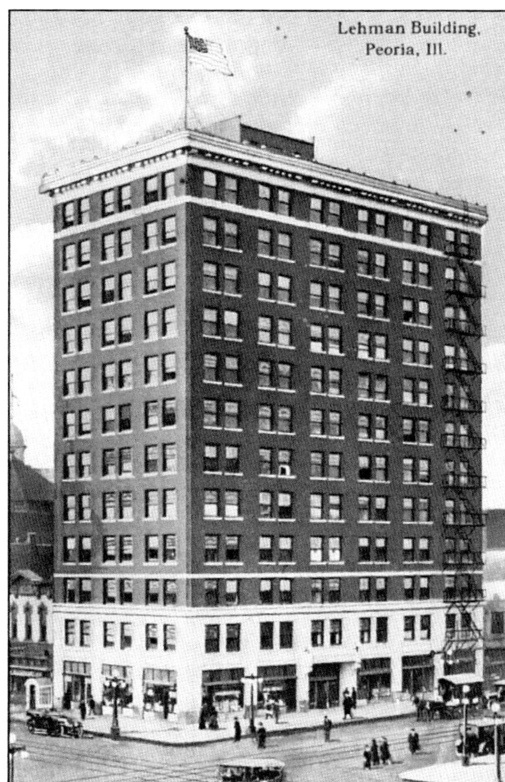

Named after distiller Arthur Lehman (who financed the building along with William E. Hull), the Lehman Building was built at 405 Main Street in 1916. Hull would later have his congressional office located here. The building attracted the medical professions, and many doctors chose to located their offices here. After being vacant for a number of years, the building burned and was razed in the early 1990s. The Becker Building occupies the site today.

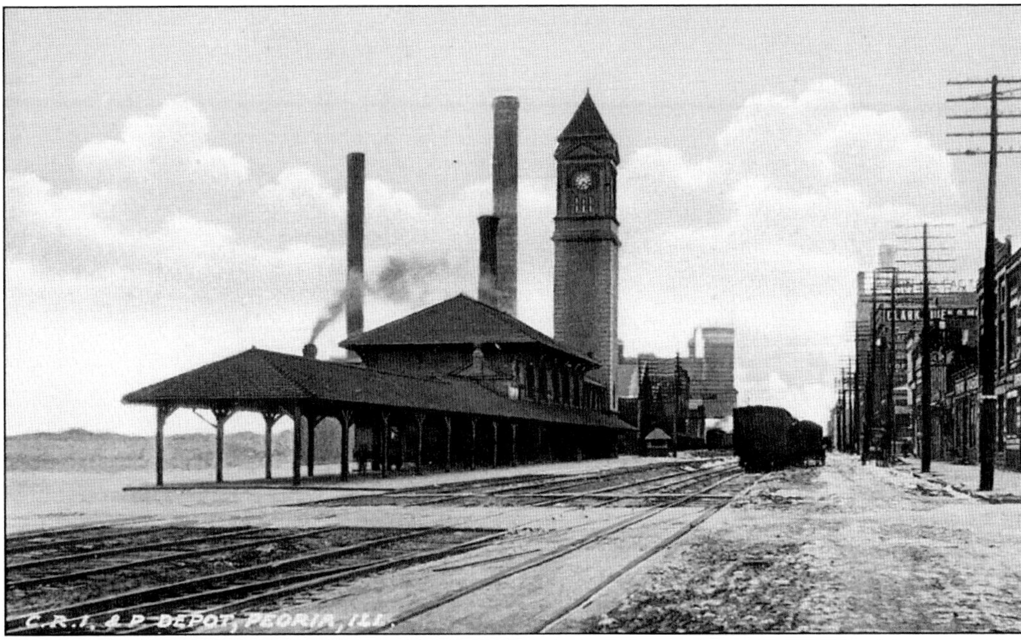

The Chicago and Rock Island Railroad completed the above Neo-Classical building in 1891. By that time, railroads had largely replaced steamboats as a mode of transportation by allowing cheaper, faster, and safer trips. The depot had a freight house added in 1899. In 1939, the clock tower was removed. Today the River Station Restaurant occupies the building.

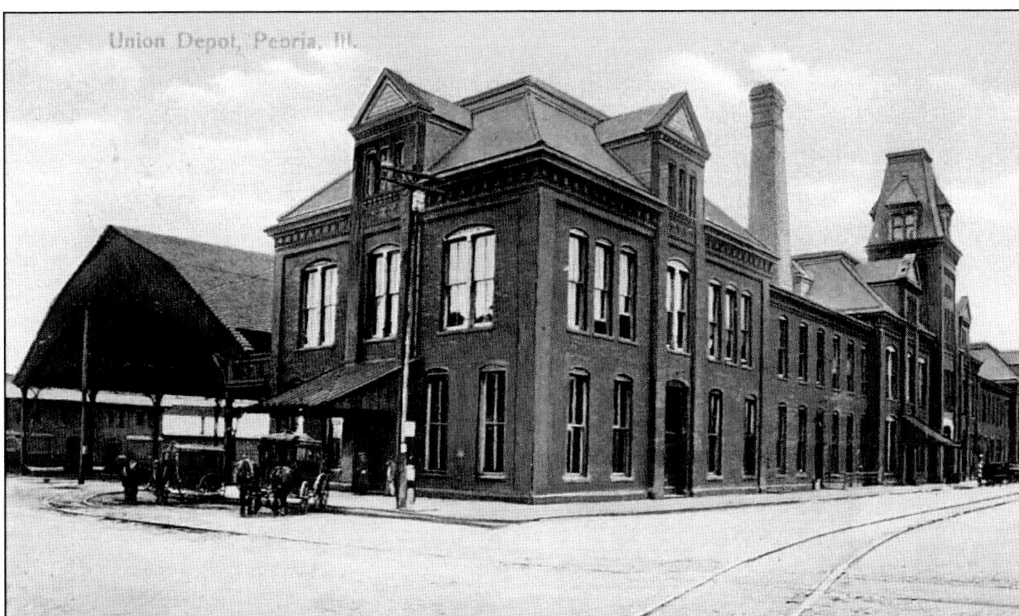

The Union Station opened in 1882 at State Street. This depot would serve as the fourth-largest rail hub in the U.S., accommodating 15 railroads and over 70,000 rail miles. The building was destroyed in 1963 by fire.

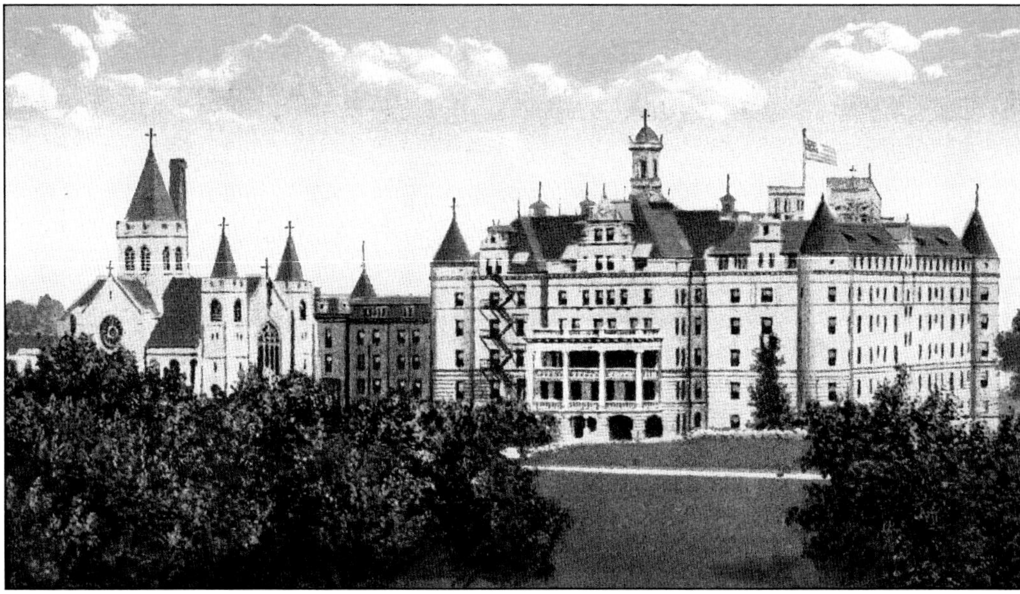

The Sisters of St. Francis, newly arrived from Germany, founded the St. Francis Hospital in 1876. Bishop Spalding arrived in 1877. He came to take charge of the new Diocese of Peoria. He initiated a monument to improve the new hospital. From a lone house, formally known as the Isaac Underhill Mansion, St. Francis grew. The above card shows the extent of the growth by the 1930s. St. Francis was one of the first hospitals in central Illinois and is still found at the original location.

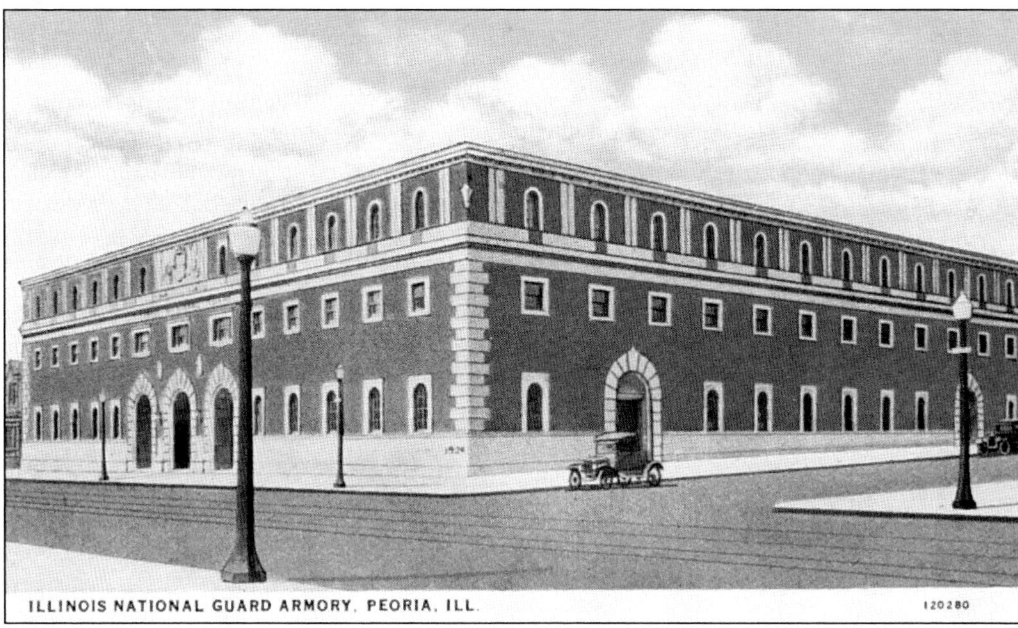

The Illinois National Guard Armory was constructed in 1924 at the corner of Adams and Hancock. Prior to the armory, this site had been the location of the old coliseum, which was built in 1901 and which burned in 1920. Prior to the coliseum, it was the residence of Valentine Jobst. Bradley basketball would use the building until 1949, when the games moved to Main Street at the campus. Today the building still stands, awaiting a new use.

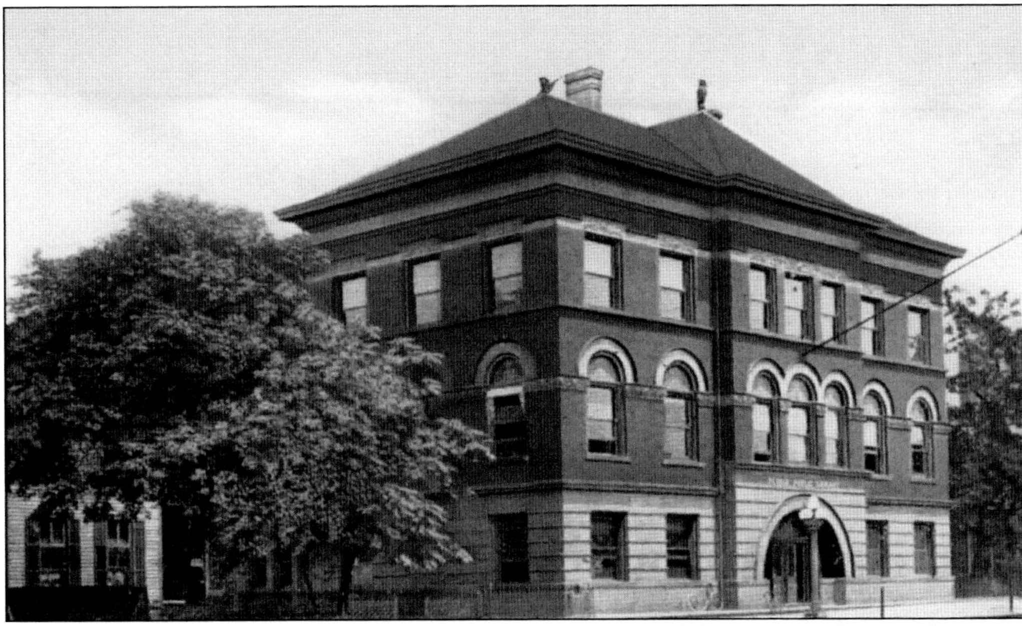

The Peoria Public Library was established in 1880. Several businesses, along with a great number of book donations, encouraged the city council to build a home for the library. The above building was the result. It opened in 1897 on Monroe Street. That building was replaced with a new one in 1967.

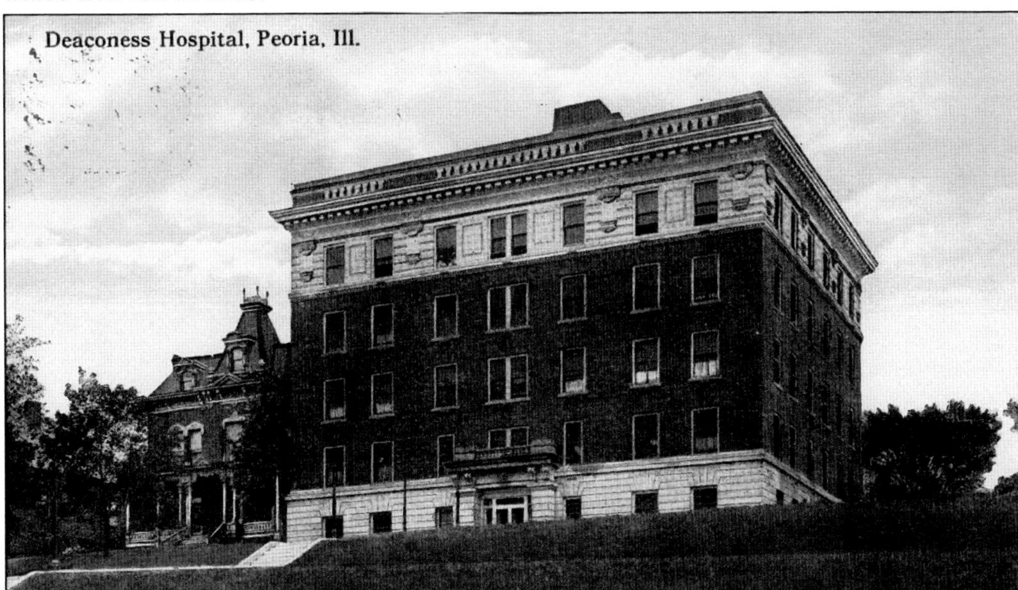

The above postcard captures the beginning of the Methodist Medical Center in Peoria. This institution was founded as the Deaconess Home Hospital Association in 1900 by acquiring the John H. Bunn home at 221 North Glen Oak (as shown to the far left in the above card). The building to the right was completed in 1911. In 1917, the name of this institution was changed to Methodist Hospital. The Bunn house was removed in 1925 and this institutional continues to expand near the original location.

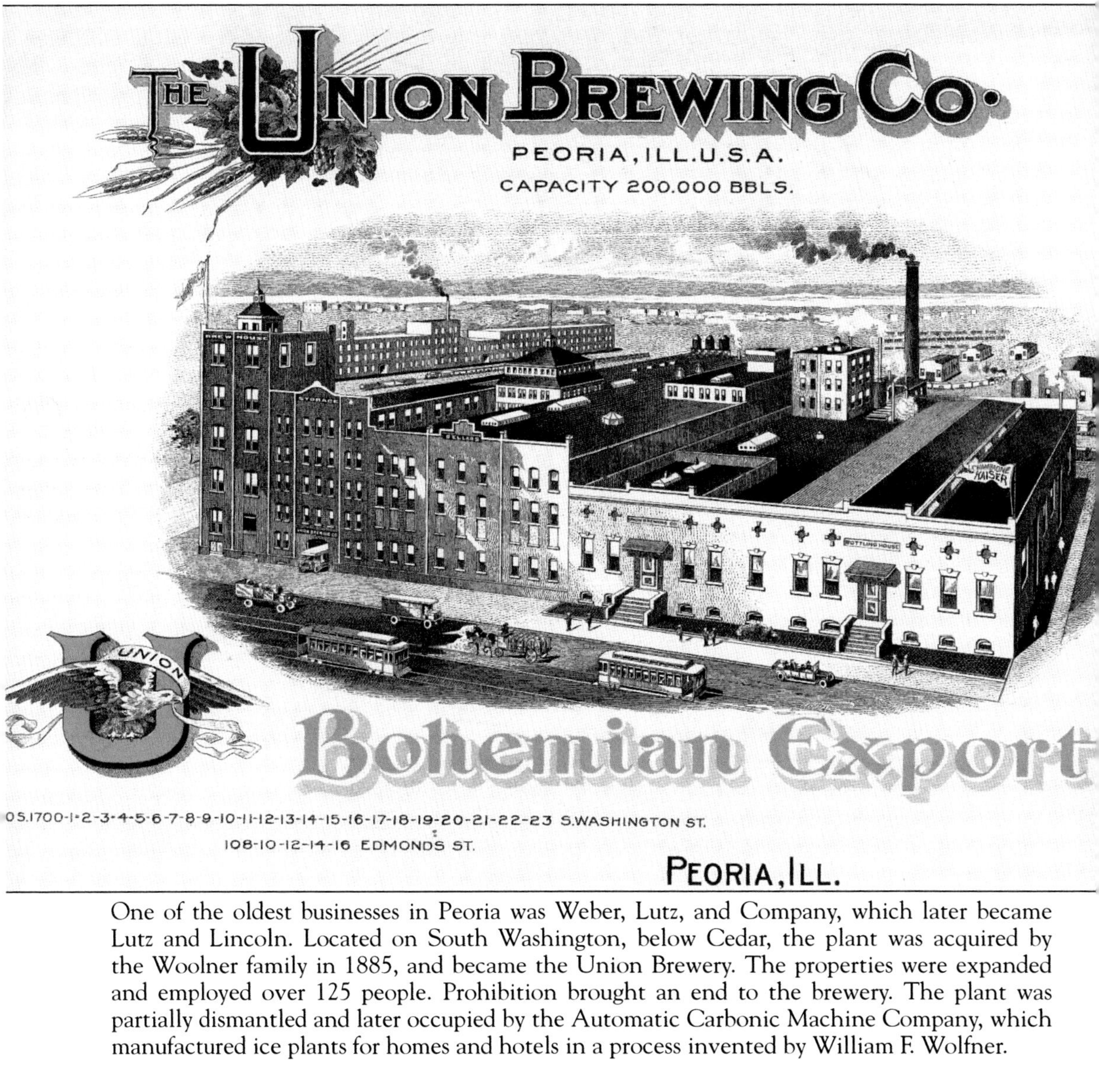

One of the oldest businesses in Peoria was Weber, Lutz, and Company, which later became Lutz and Lincoln. Located on South Washington, below Cedar, the plant was acquired by the Woolner family in 1885, and became the Union Brewery. The properties were expanded and employed over 125 people. Prohibition brought an end to the brewery. The plant was partially dismantled and later occupied by the Automatic Carbonic Machine Company, which manufactured ice plants for homes and hotels in a process invented by William F. Wolfner.

Three

WEST BLUFF

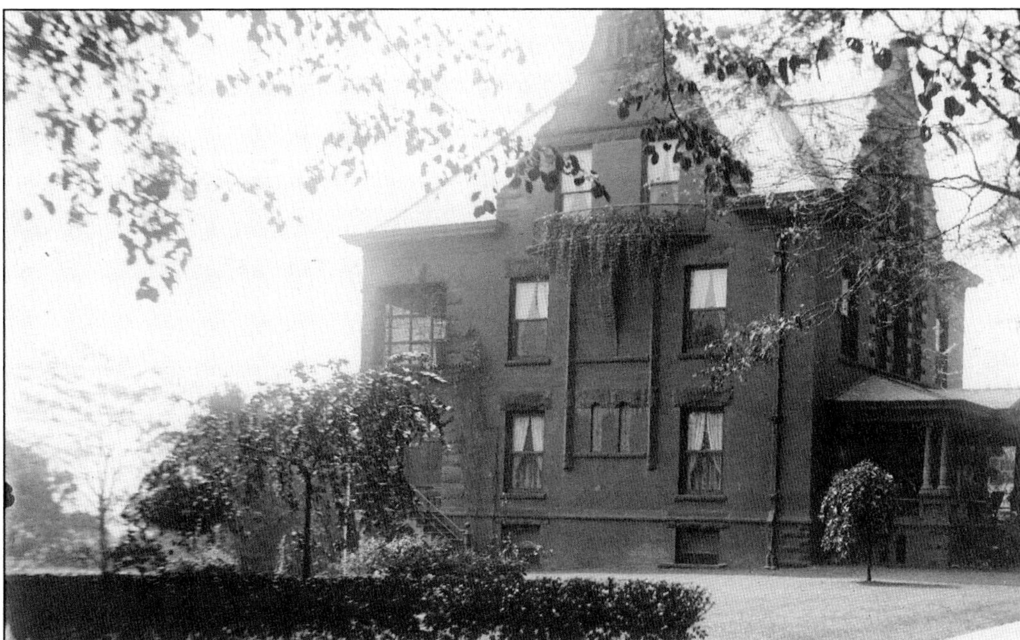

Shown from a side view, the above postcard is the home of Richard W. Kempshall. This Flemish, Renaissance-style home was built in 1894 and is located at 518 High Street. So many barons of the whiskey business constructed homes on High Street that it earned the nickname "High Wine Street." The Kempshalls owned the home until 1967, when it was first sold. The builder, Richard W. Kempshall, was an insurance representative who became influential in many circles of Peoria life. The home is under careful restoration, along with a new garage that fits the period and grounds.

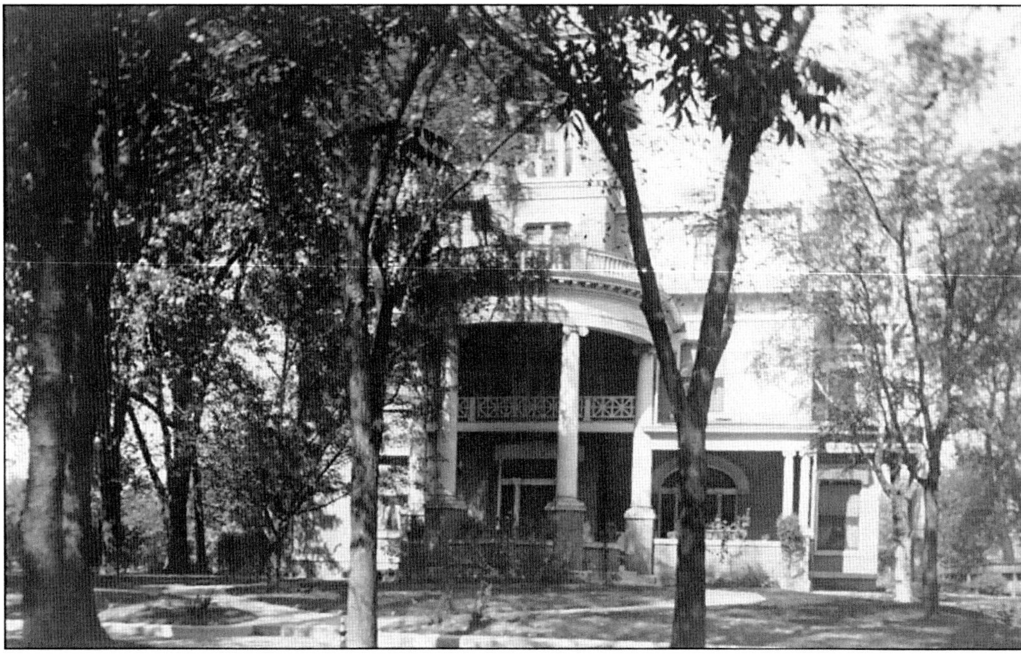

The Erastus D. Hardin home, pictured above, was erected in 1859. Located at 511 High Street, this building was originally constructed with a three-story, Second Empire-style facade and a central tower portraying a view of downtown Peoria. Around 1900, a remodeling took place with the addition of columns, a portico, and changes to the mansard roof windows. It was tastefully converted into upscale apartments, and the home and grounds are now in a state of careful restoration.

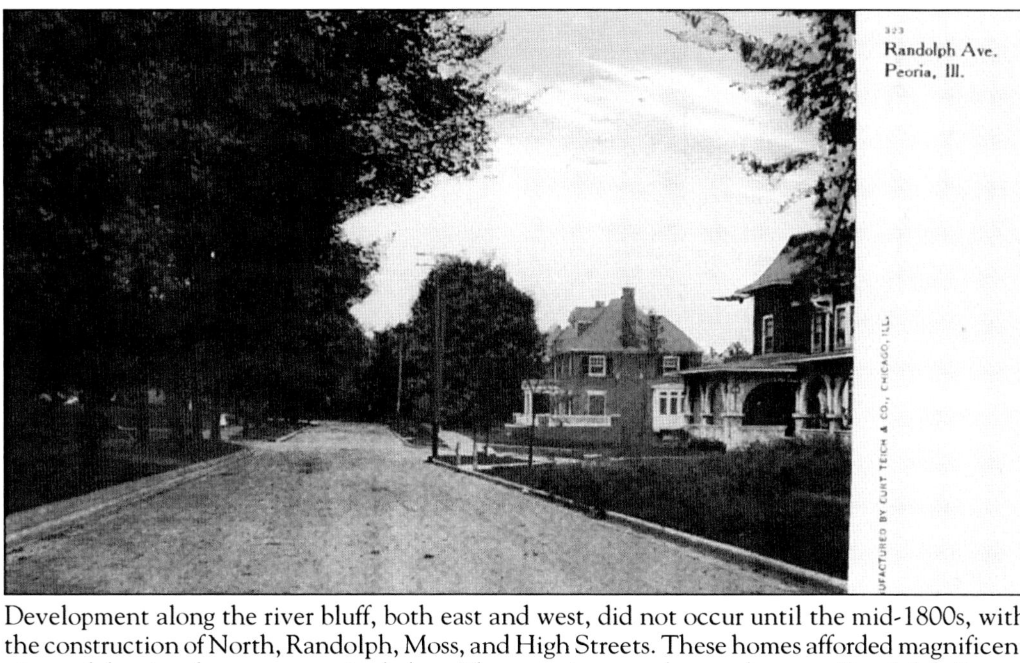

Development along the river bluff, both east and west, did not occur until the mid-1800s, with the construction of North, Randolph, Moss, and High Streets. These homes afforded magnificent views of the riverfront community below. The mansions, as shown above on Randolph Street, were described as princely residences with landscaped grounds.

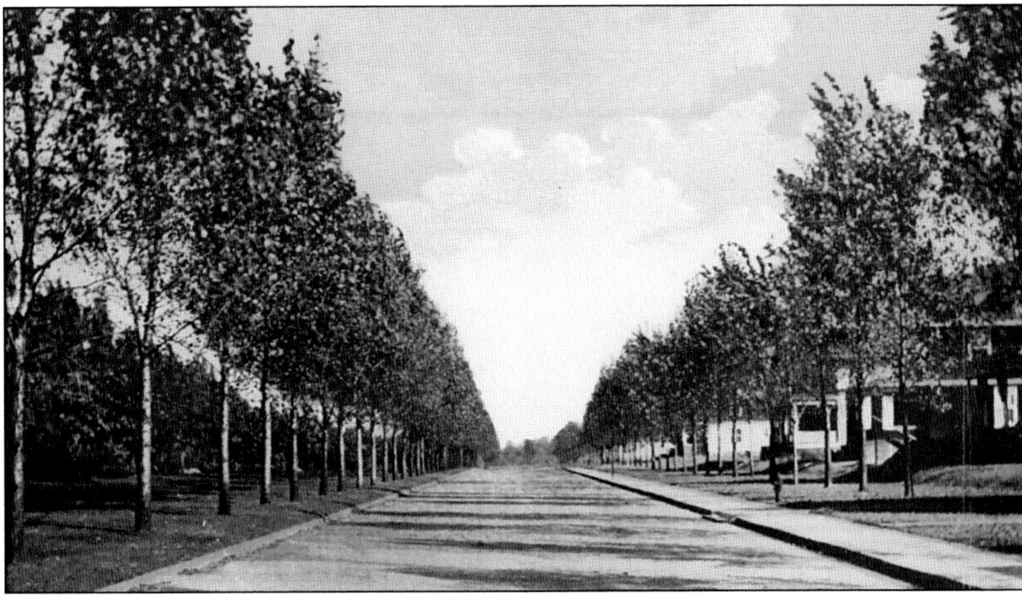

The postcard above shows the Park Side Drive entrance into Peoria's first planned subdivision. Laid out in 1902, the Uplands is an outstanding example of preservation in Peoria. Park Side Drive (the street that overlooks Bradley Park) boasts many homes that have changed little from the design of the original builders.

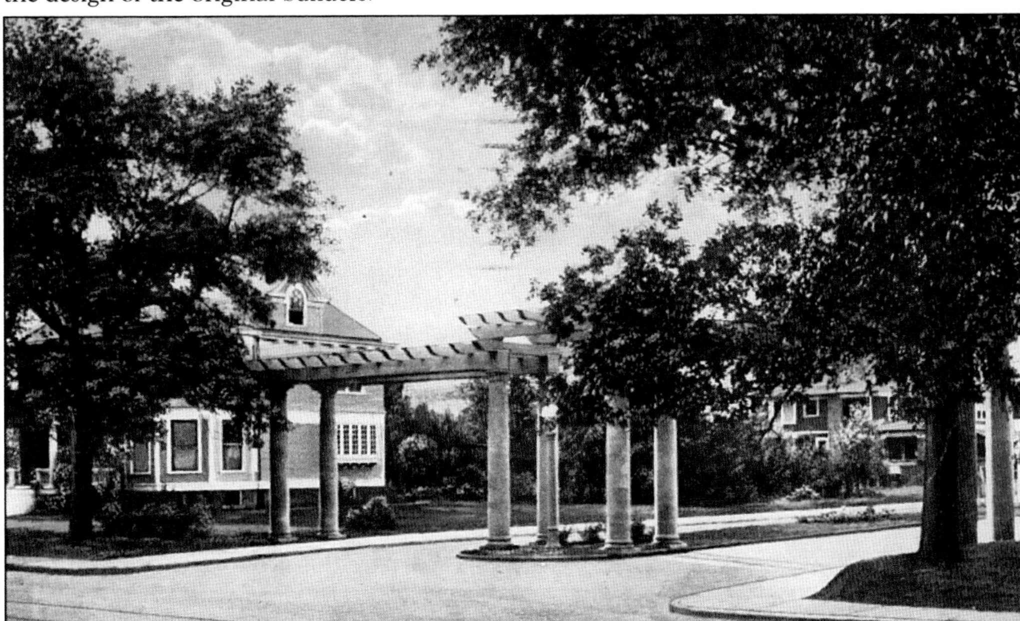

The Bradley West neighborhood has two streets that have boulevards, which were made available when the lots were laid out after 1900. To entice purchasers to acquire the lots, two very attractive Pergola Gates were installed. The one pictured above stood at Bradley and Rebecca Streets. The City of Peoria removed this gate in the early 1970s. Its twin, presently located at Main and Rebecca, still marks the entrance to the subdivision. Today the gates are known to many simply as the arches.

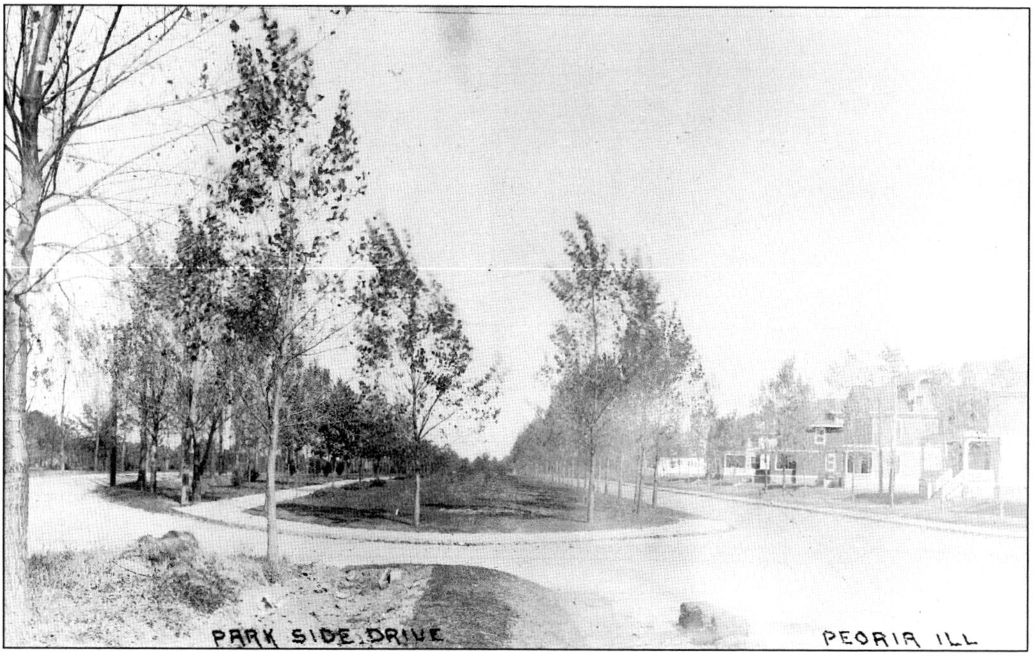

Bradley Park was seven years old when the above card was mailed in 1908. The street to the right is Park Side Drive, and the street to the left was the original entrance, which has been removed.

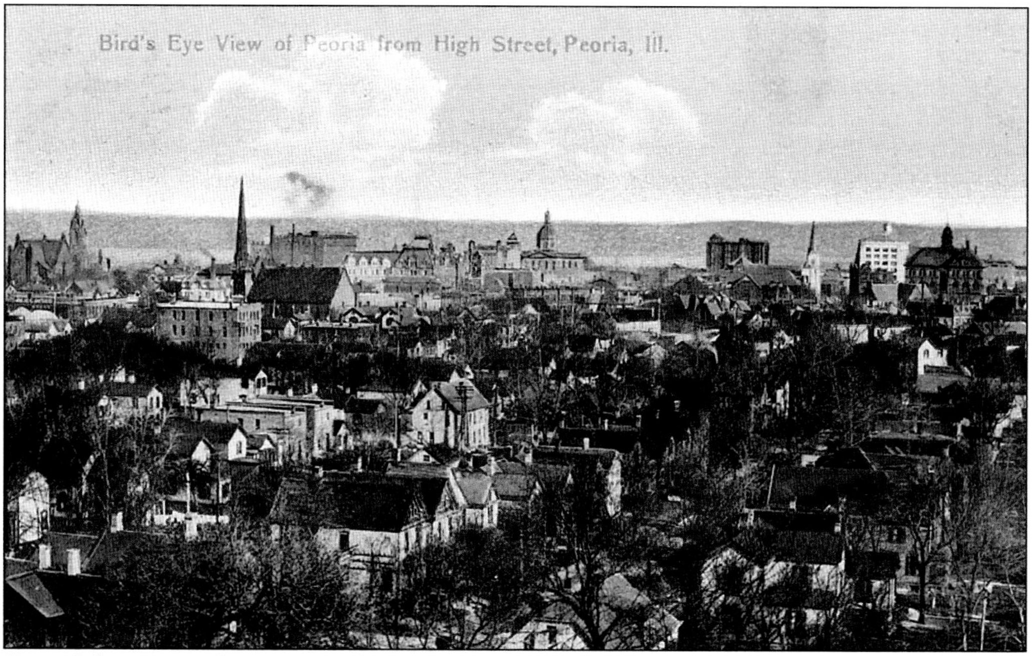

One of the principal reasons High Street was developed was the view allowed of the river and the valley below. This card, mailed in 1909, displays a panoramic view of downtown Peoria. Note the courthouse (in the far center), and the new Schipper and Block store to the right, completed in 1905.

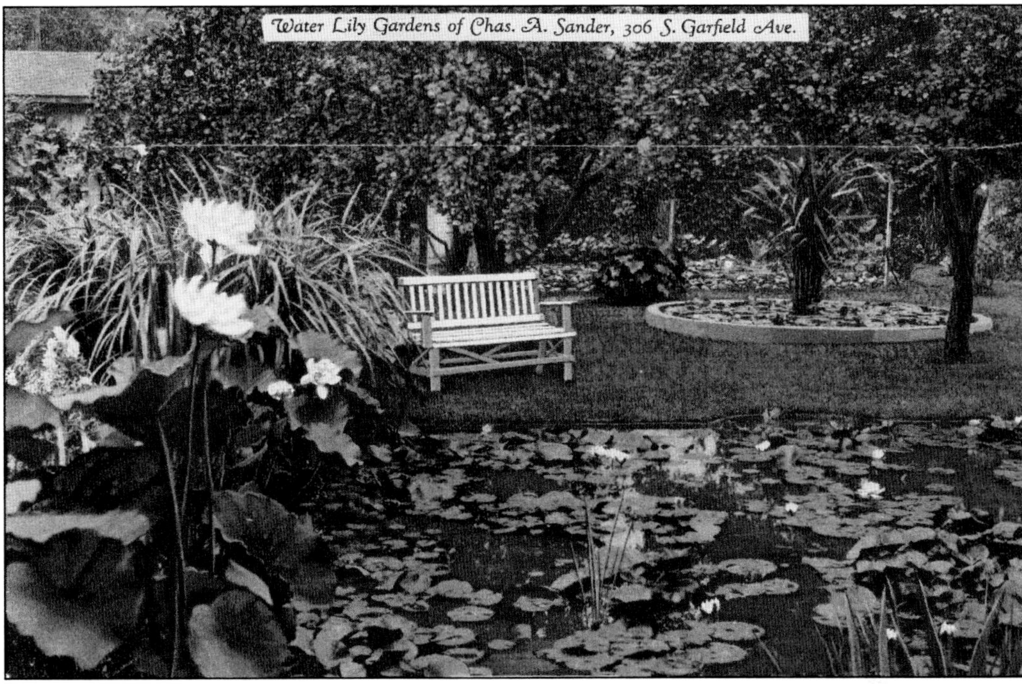

Many postcards displayed throughout this book were the works of the Sander Bros Post Card Company. One of the partners, Charles A. Sanders, used his backyard garden for this card. The garden was filled with exotic plants and contained a water lily garden. Sanders lived at the above address from 1906 to 1949. The house remains, but the garden has long since vanished.

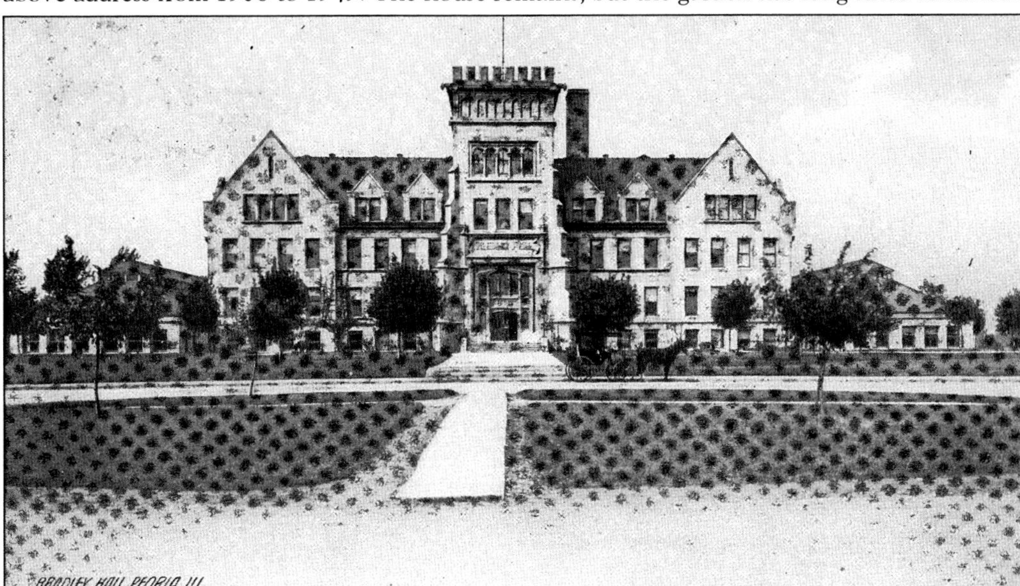

Mrs. Lydia Bradley decided on two plans to dispose of her large holdings. One was to establish a park. The other was the establishment of a school to honor her husband, the late Tobias S. Bradley. Construction began on the above building in April 1897. Ed O. Sisson was appointed director of the institute. One hundred and five students were admitted for the first class on October 4, 1897.

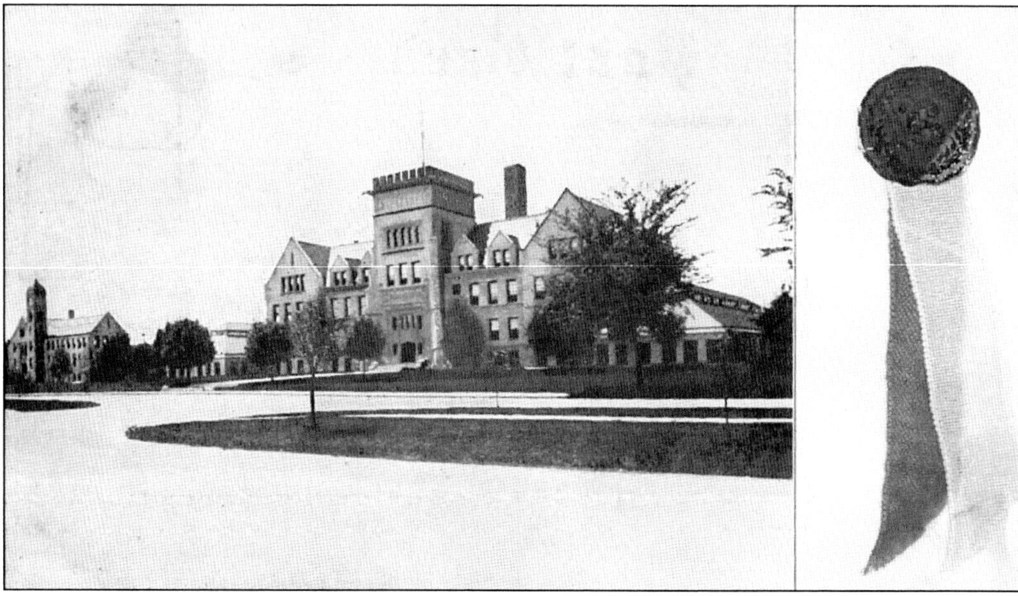

The above card is very unusual because the school colors, made of ribbon, are attached. Founders Day was held October 8, and a similar event is still held annually. The original name, Bradley Polytechnic Institute, became Bradley University.

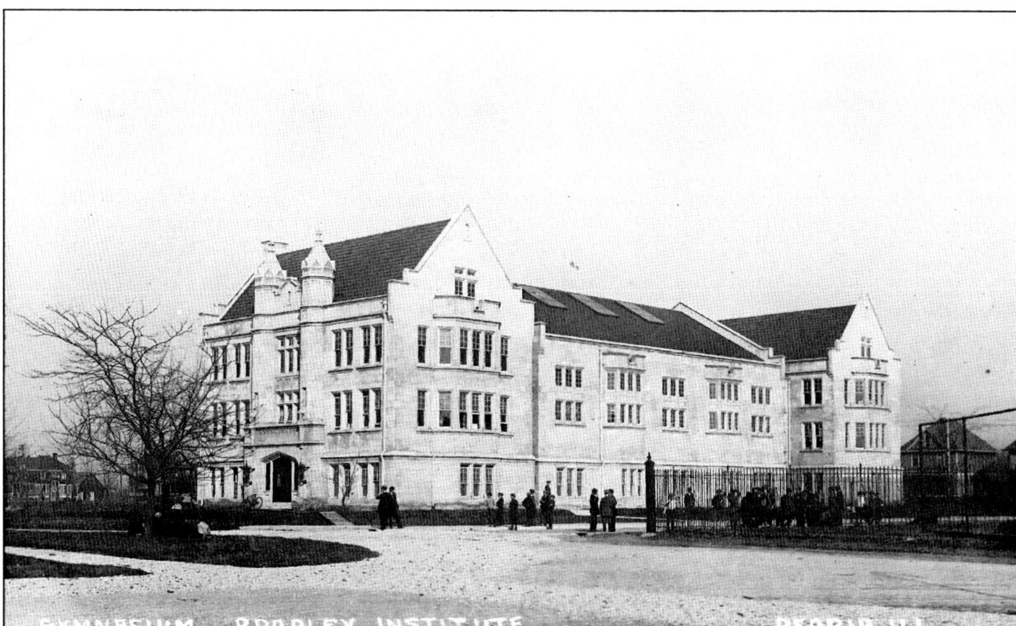

A reorganization in 1946 created a new and final name—Bradley University. The above building was only one year old at the time this card was mailed in 1910. It was then the gymnasium. The building still stands in a state of excellent repair.

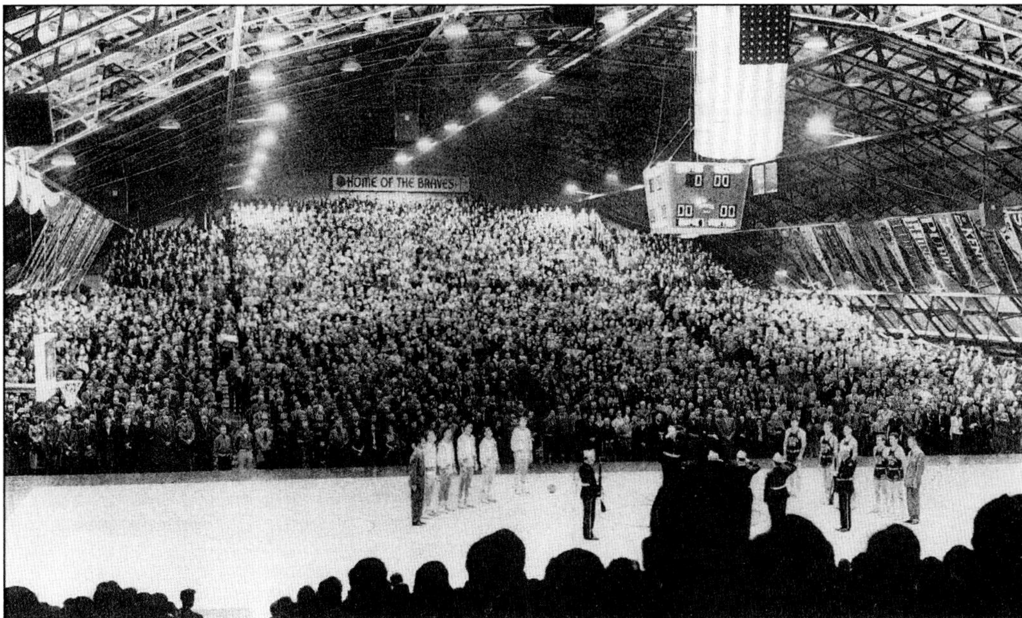

Robertson Memorial Field House BRADLEY UNIVERSITY Peoria, Illinois

The famous Bradley University Braves basketball games were held at the downtown armory until moving to the above facility, known as the Robertson Memorial Fieldhouse. In 1949 this building accommodated 7,000 fans for both basketball and other events for the university. It was named in honor of coach A.J. Robertson.

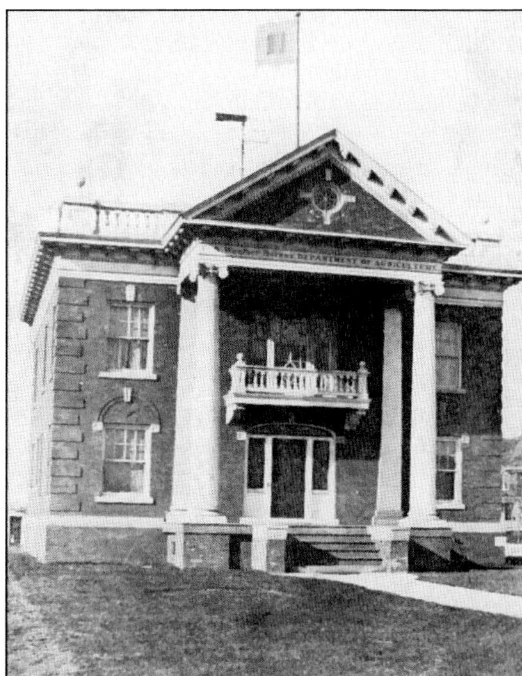

U. S. Weather Bureau Station, Peoria, Ill. Peoria Souvenir Co., Box 36

Bradley University, or Bradley Polytechnic Institute, granted the United States Department of Agriculture a location for a weather bureau station at Main and Institute, facing east. The above building was dedicated in 1905. This location served as a weather station until 1944, when the station was moved to the Peoria airport. The building then became the North and Alumni Halls. It was destroyed in 1957 to make way for the new Baker Hall.

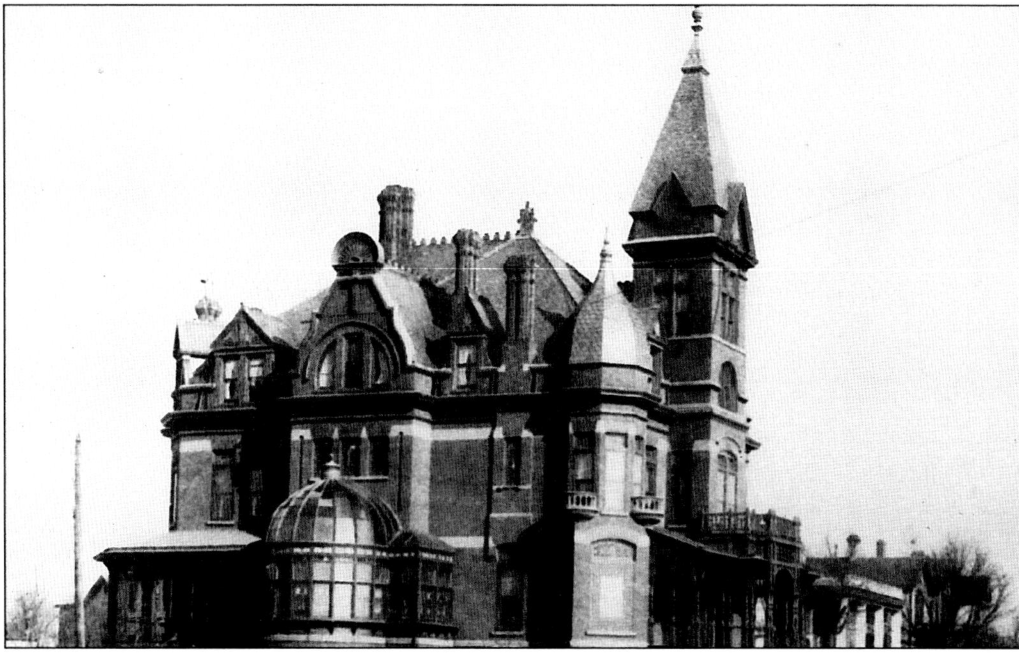

The above house was built as a residence for Peoria's most prominent citizen at that time, Joseph B. Greenhut. Erected in 1884 at the cost of $50,000, this 35-room mansion had multiple porches, sun rooms, and balconies. Mr. Greenhut could see his many investments from the huge tower. President McKinley was entertained here in 1899.

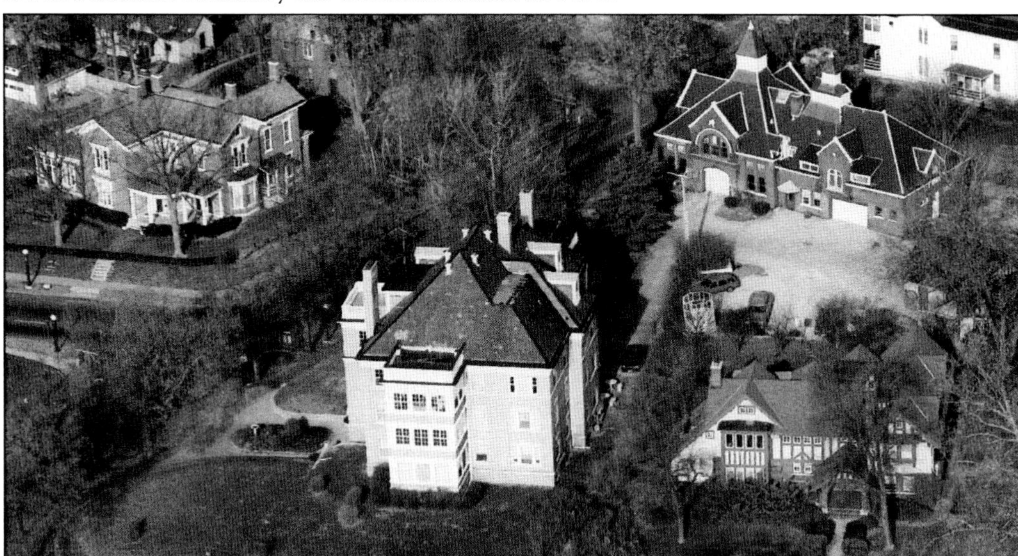

The Greenhut Mansion is shown here as it appears today. Greenhut sold his home after relocating to New York. His brother-in-law, William F. Wolfner, purchased the house in 1912. Between 1916 and 1917, the house was converted to three flats known as the Wolfner Apartments. A later conversion created ten apartments in the main house. Also in the picture is the coach house for the Greenhut Mansion, built in 1886, and the Douglas Bethard residence at 611 High Street, built in 1909. In the upper left corner is the William R. Bush home, at 703 West Moss Avenue, constructed in 1858.

Four

Hotels and Restaurants

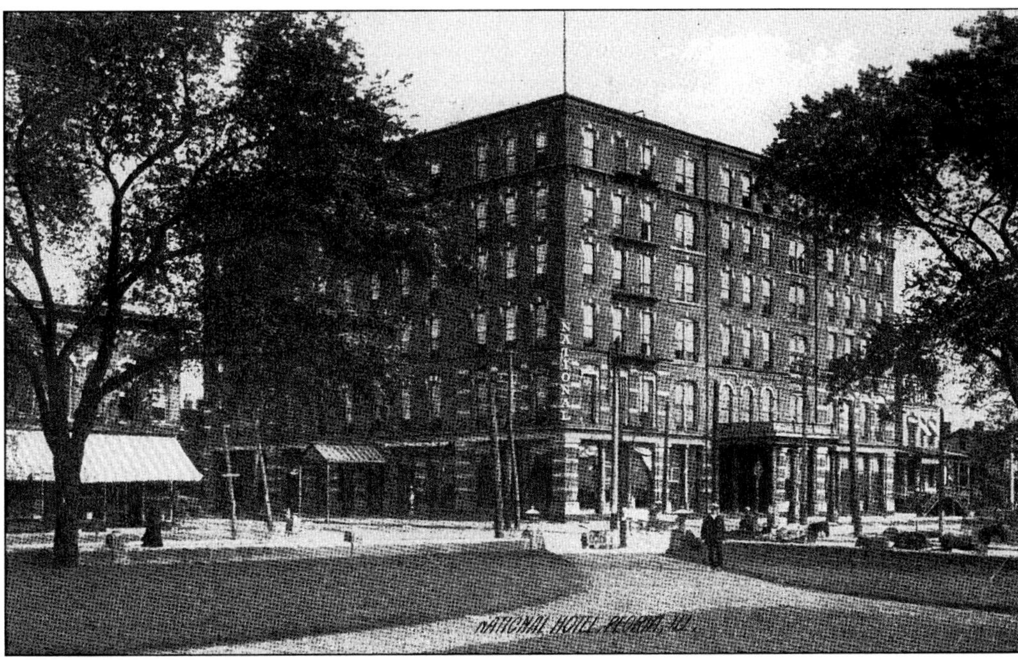

On October 30, 1883, the National Hotel at the corner of Hamilton and Jefferson Streets opened. It was constructed at a cost of $325,000. This hotel immediately became a favorite stopping place for the social elite as well as important visitors. The building was destroyed by fire on the night of November 12, 1911.

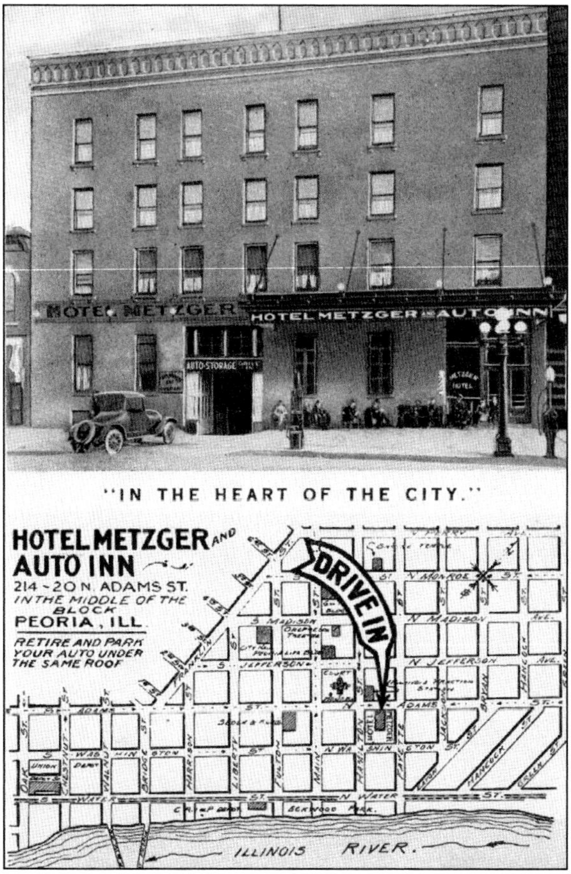

The Metzger Hotel, located at 214 North Adams, was converted from the Palace Livery Stable by Dave Mayer in 1919, thus creating one of Peoria's first auto inns. The motto of the hotel was "Retire and Park" under the same roof. The name was changed to the Milner Hotel in later years. It was destroyed in 1956 to accommodate the building of the Sands Motel.

The new National Hotel was one of the largest conversions from residence to commercial use in Peoria's history. When the National Hotel burned in 1911, the former residence of Colonel Robert G. Ingersoll, built in 1875, was remodeled into this new National Hotel. The building was razed on July 23, 1970. Today the site is a parking lot known as 217 Northeast Jefferson.

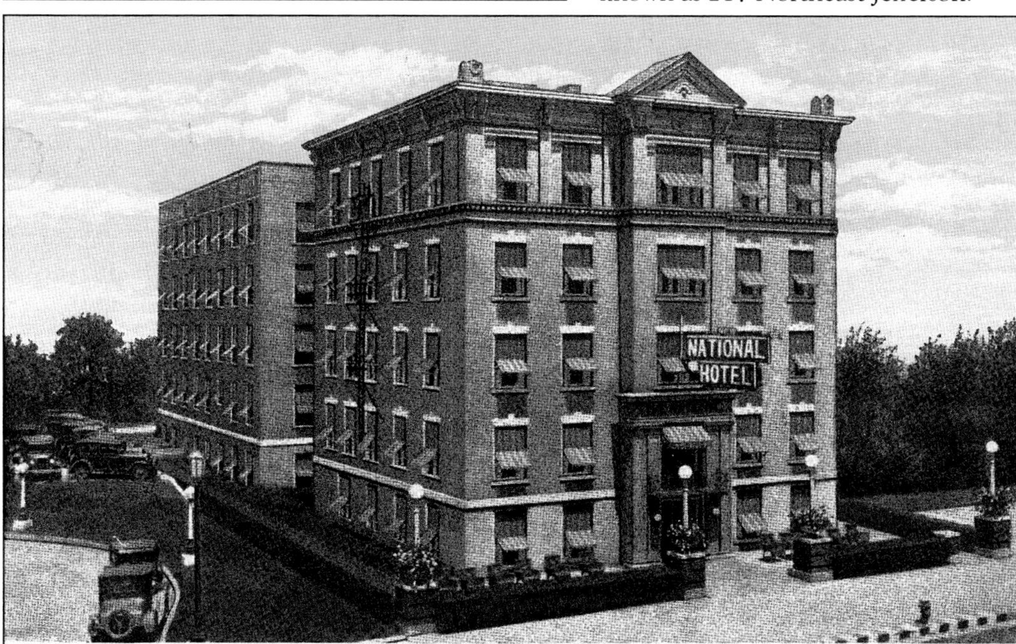

THE NEW NATIONAL HOTEL, PEORIA, ILL. 3393.

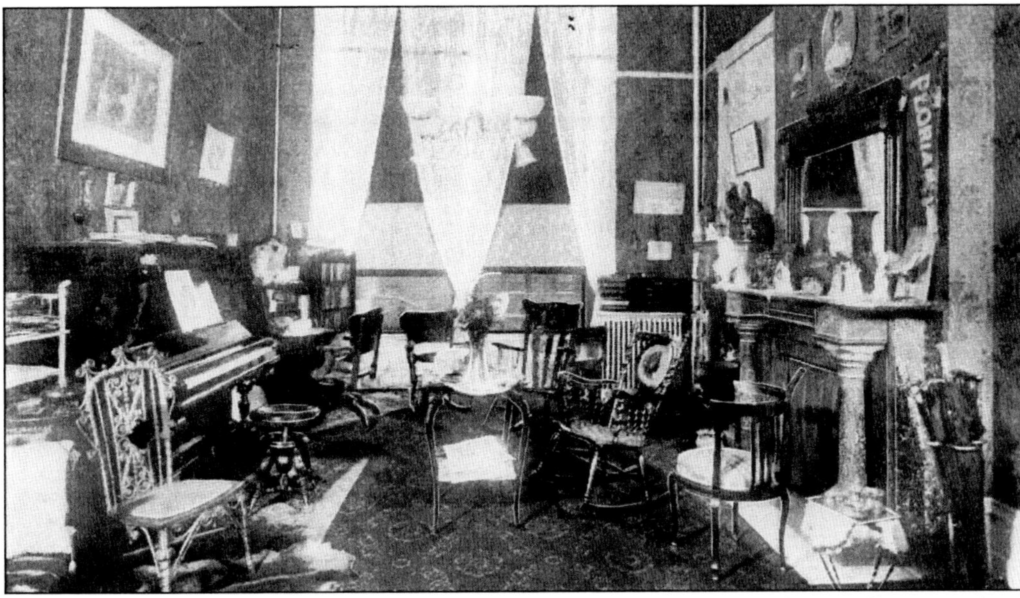

The Colonel Ingersoll house was moved to the near center of the block on Jefferson and was used as a factory for the production of cigars, known as the Lewis Single Bender Cigar Factory. Later it reopened as "The Ingersoll" hotel. Pictured here is Parlor "A," with furnishing as it may have looked at the time this was a residence.

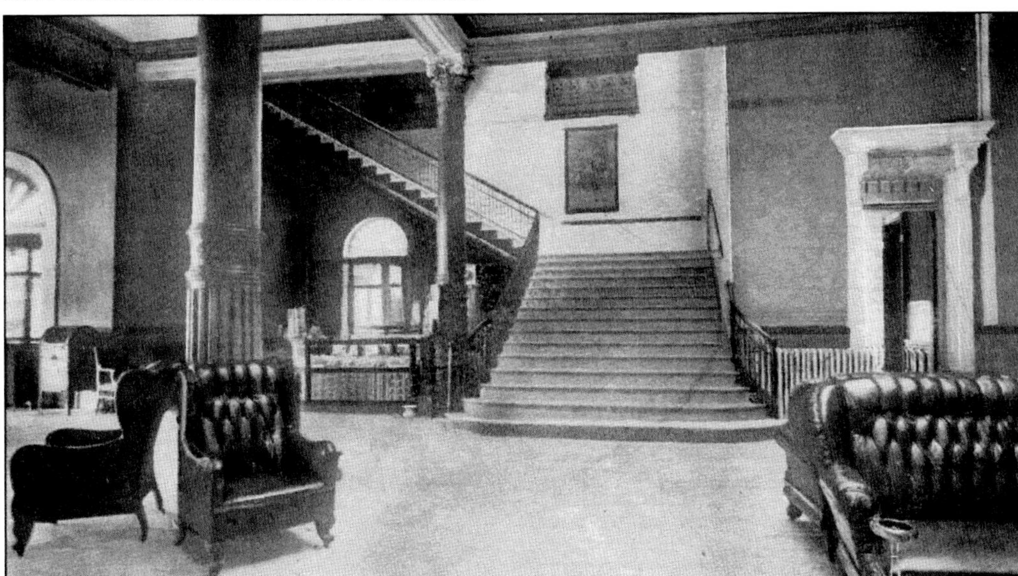

In 1868, Washington Cockle erected a brick-and-stone dwelling costing over $50,000 on the northwest corner of Jefferson and Hamilton Streets. Years later, the First National Bank acquired the property and, shortly thereafter, transferred title to Colonel Robert G. Ingersoll. He was the bank attorney at that time. After Ingersoll left Peoria for Washington, D.C., the house was outfitted as a hotel and called "The Ingersoll," opening for business in 1879. The property was sold to the National Hotel Company, which moved the building to the third lot on Jefferson. It was later occupied by the Cattle Feeders and Distillers Trust, the Peoria Club, and the Frank P. Lewis Cigar Company.

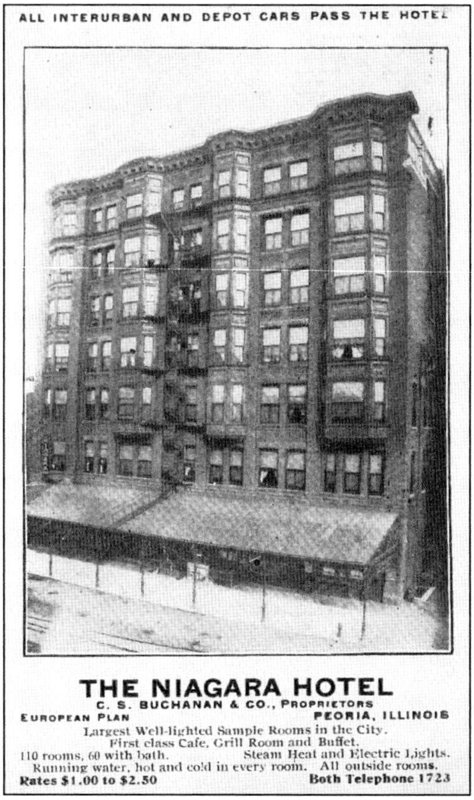

The Niagara Hotel was one of the leading hostelries in the early 1890s. The original structure at the site was erected as a livery stable in 1875. Subsequently, a three-story office building was constructed and known as the Niagara Building. In 1893, four more stories were built, along with an elevator, by William F. Becker. The dining room of the Niagara Cafe was a favorite night spot for after-theater crowds. The hotel changed hands many times. In August of 1968, the owners razed the building floor by floor.

By 1913, the Niagara Hotel dining room had become a favorite night-time eating place for patrons of the vaudeville circuit in Peoria. Later, the basement would be occupied by the Combo Club, and by the Niagara Cafe at the time the hotel was closed.

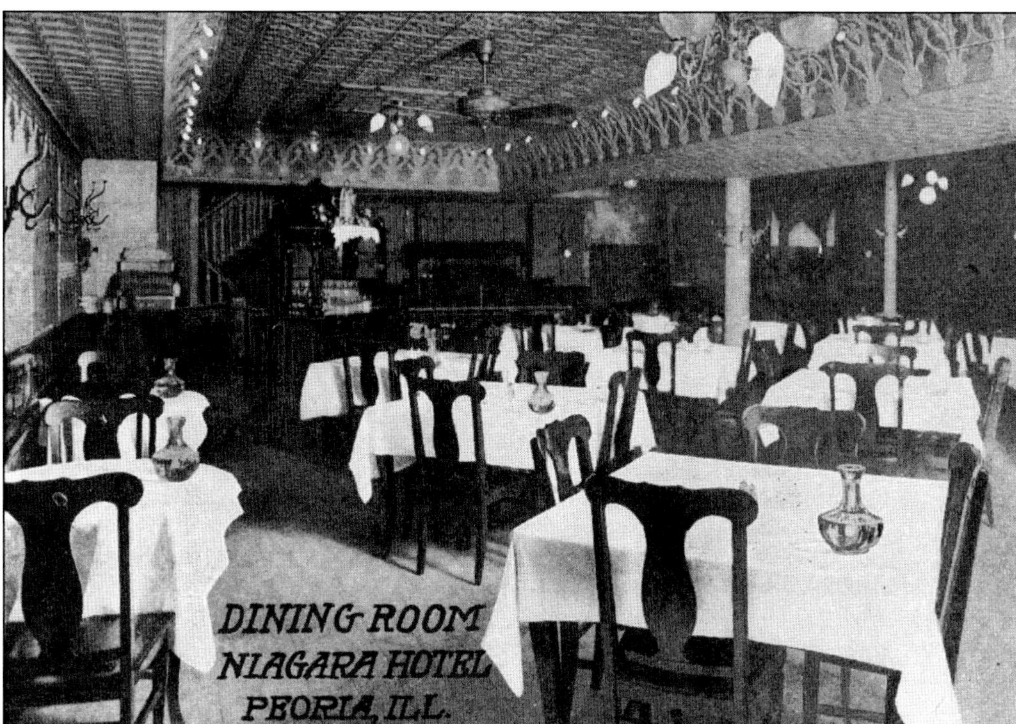

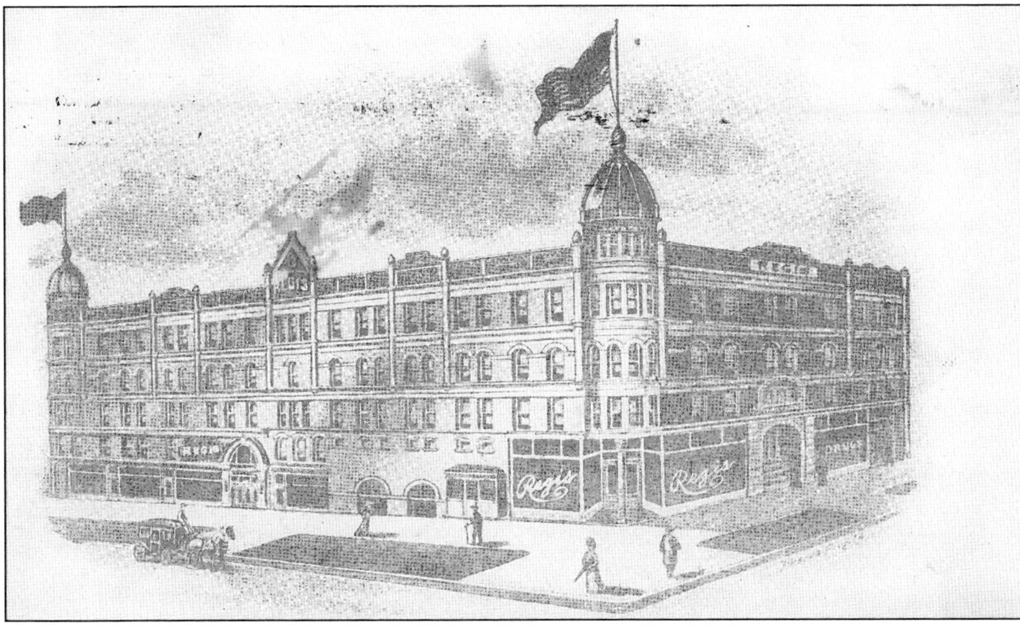

In 1899, Dr. John Wesley Van Sant, a Peoria dentist, erected a three-story brick building on the corner of Adams and Chestnut Streets to accommodate his eight-chair dentist office. In 1903 a new floor was added. Dr. Van Sant had such wide appeal that clients would journey here from as far away as several hundred miles. Not only was professional service accorded, but overnight accommodations as well.

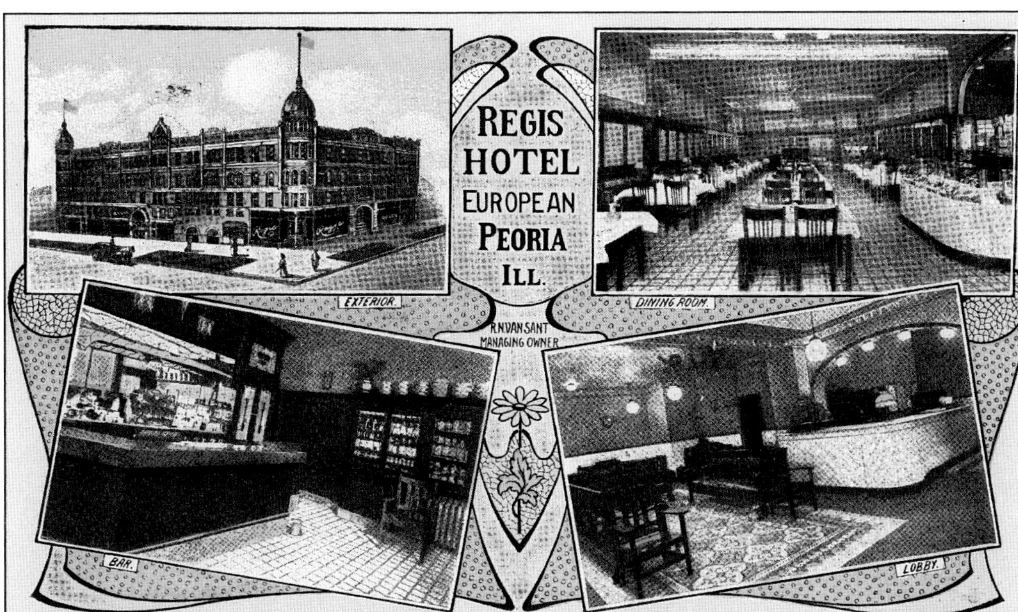

Dr. Van Sant's professional service began to decline, and by 1909 he converted the building into a hotel and renamed it Regis Hotel. Van Sant must have had a liking for European style, as the furnishings radiated that taste. Van Sant's two sons, L.R. and R.H. Van Sant, managed the hotel, and R.H. Van Sant would continue to do so until 1917, when the name would be changed to the Grand Hotel.

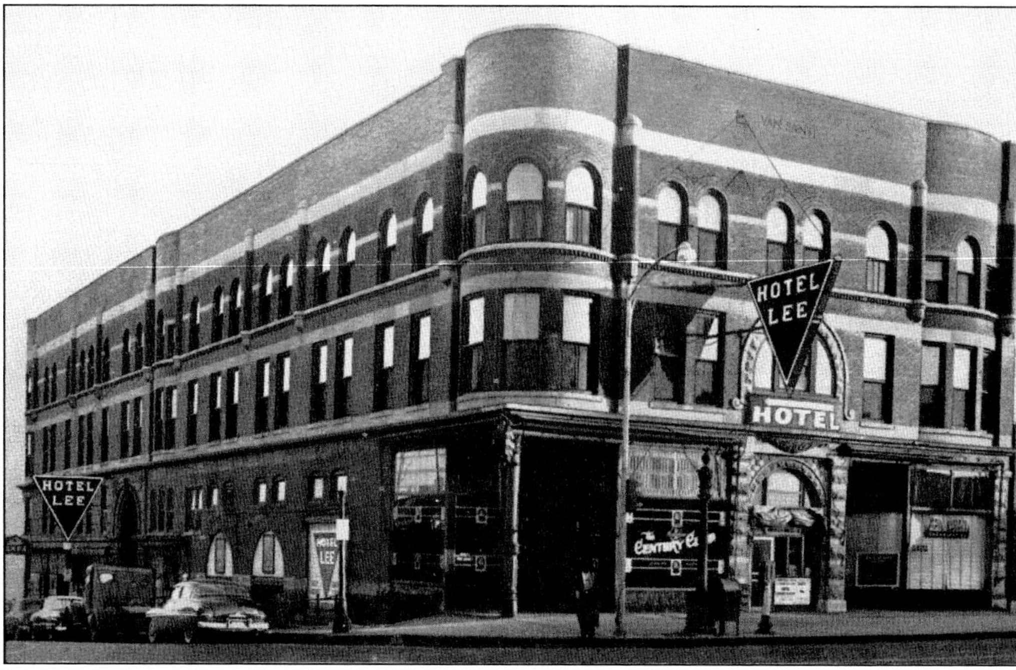

Its proximity to the railroad station established the Grand Hotel as one of the finest "One Dollar" hotels around. The graceful 97-room limestone-and-brick building was remodeled in 1933. Another name change occurred and it became known as Veterans Hotel. The hotel burned September 20, 1991.

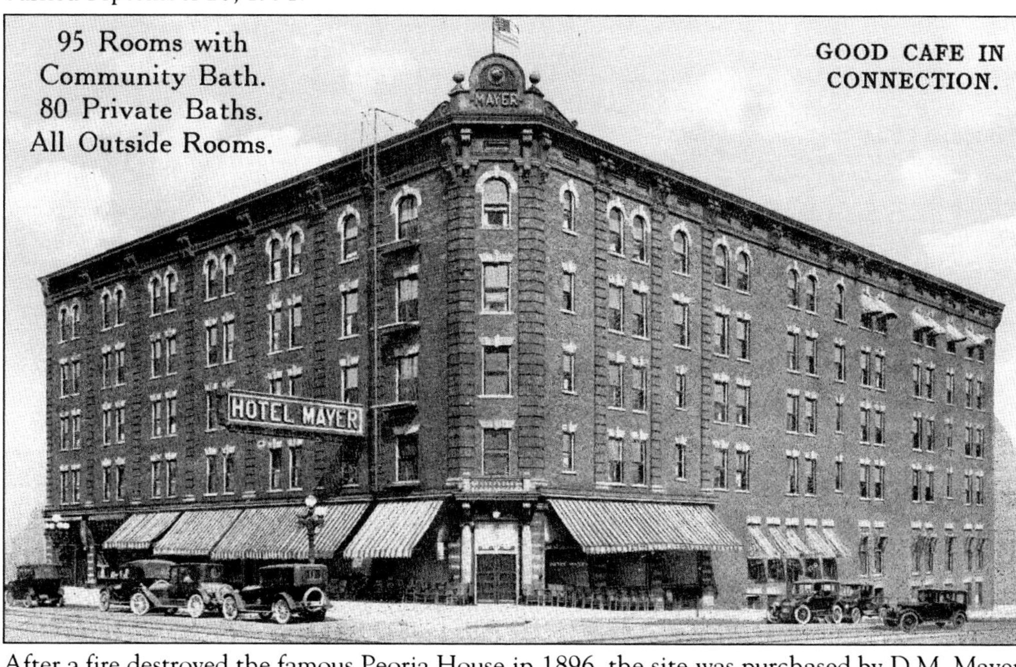

After a fire destroyed the famous Peoria House in 1896, the site was purchased by D.M. Mayer, who built this five-story hotel, which featured 158 rooms and a basement. The location was the northeast corner of Hamilton Boulevard and Adams Street. By 1930, the Mayer was remodeled and additional rooms were added, bringing the room total to 168.

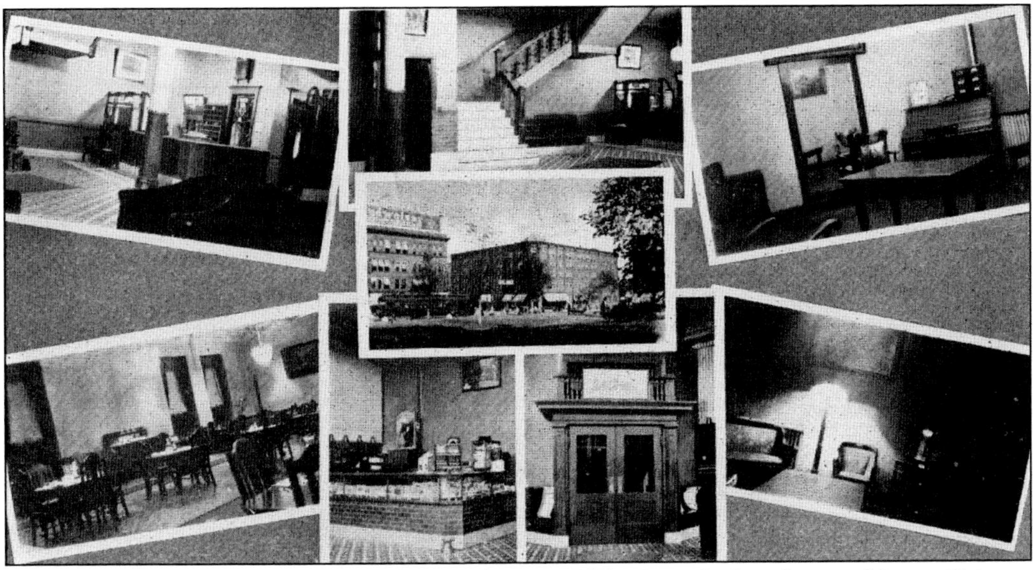

The Mayer Hotel passed out of local ownership in 1955, when the hotel was sold to a Chicago firm for $210,000. This hotel, as with many others, was 30 percent occupied by resident guests. it was destroyed in a spectacular fire that occurred on February 14, 1963. Three people were killed and eight others were injured. Shortly thereafter, the Security Savings built their headquarters on the site. When this institution closed, the building was sold to Caterpillar Co., and today it serves as an office annex.

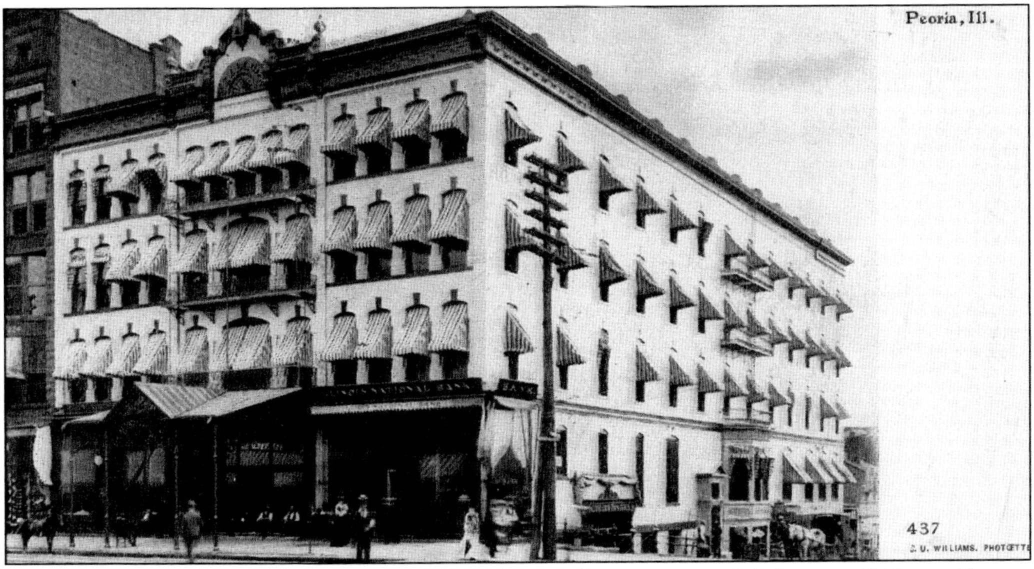

In 1885, a four-story building was erected on the northeast corner of Adams and Liberty Streets for various business uses. Its builder, David Fey (a jeweler), converted the building to a hotel in 1892. The hostelry remained in operation until December 1935; the property remained in the hands of the Fey family from 1866 to 1934, when it was sold to Henry W. Voght. He then sold the building to Montgomery Ward, which razed the building in 1936. Montgomery Ward erected their building in its place, where it remained until 1971. At that time the company relocated to the Northwoods Mall. Remax Realtors and the Princeville State Bank Mortgage Operation occupy the building today.

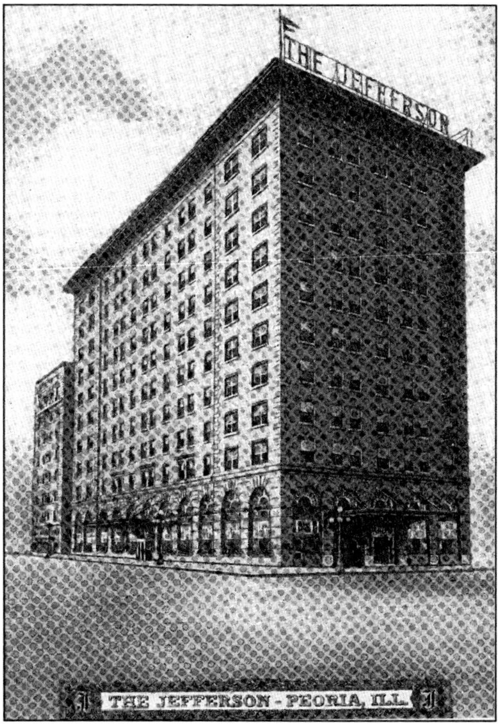

The original Jefferson Hotel, which served as a safe house in the Underground Railroad, was operated by Moses Pettengill, who eventually sold this property in 1874. The property changed hands several times before 1910, when the Jefferson Hotel Company was formed. When these promoters failed to make progress, William E. Hull was approached to complete the enterprise. From this beginning, the hotel was finally completed and it opened its doors on February 6, 1912. This postcard was mailed only three months after it opened.

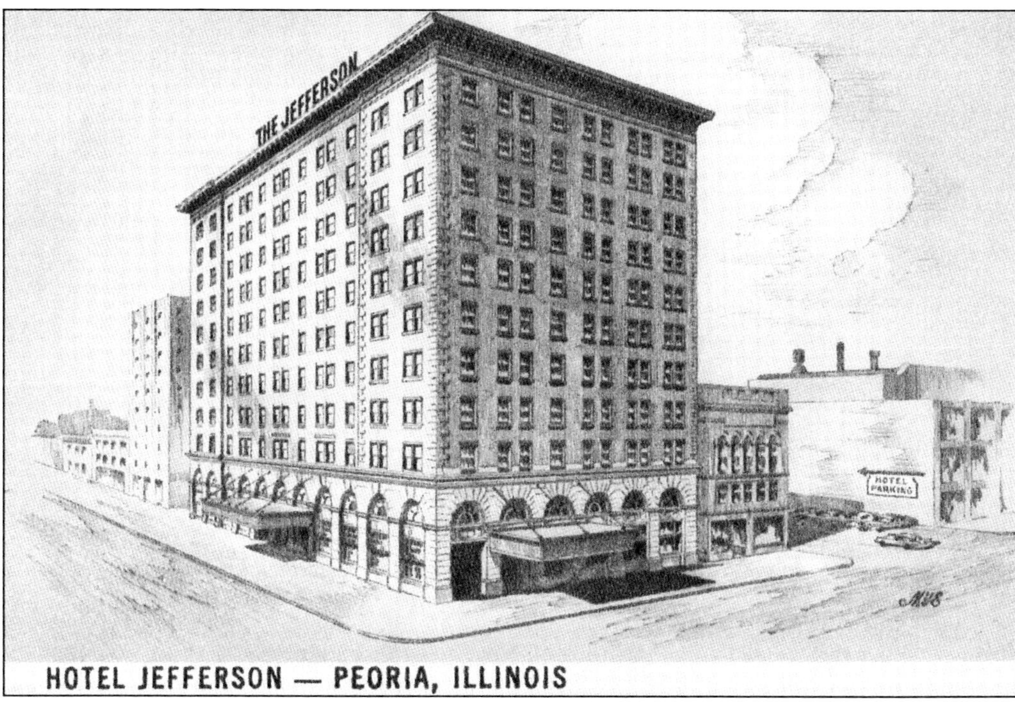

The final count of guest rooms was eventually brought to four hundred. However, a new concept was beginning in the 1930s that would last until the end of the decade—resident guests. By 1933, the hotel's principal promoters, William E. Hull and Arthur Lehman, had made changes that would bring the splendid hotel successfully through the Depression.

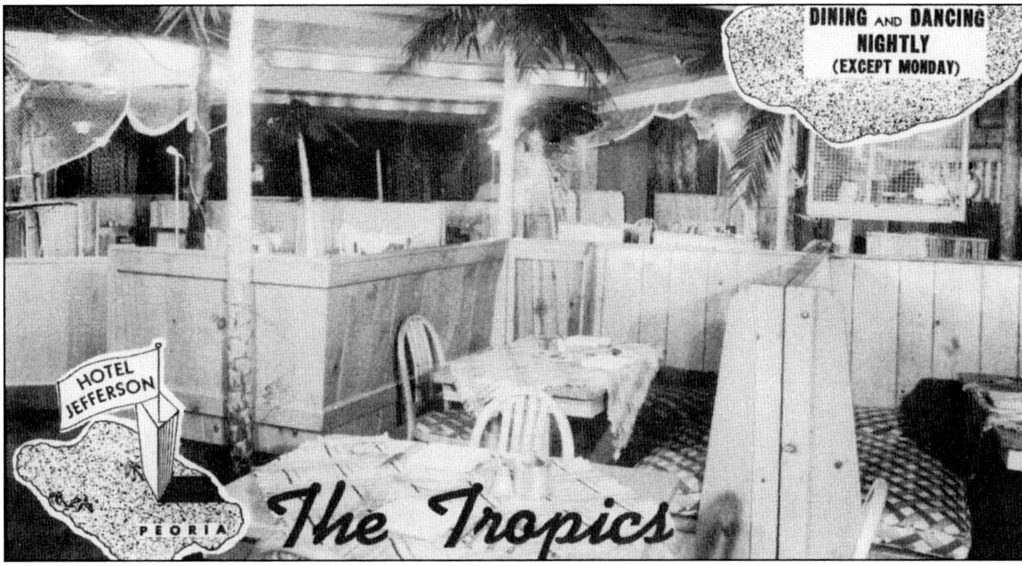

The Jefferson Hotel's then-famous dining and dancing room, "The Tropics," sponsored many shows, including the "Four Rockets." The Jefferson was long known as "Peoria's Friendly Hotel." The hostelry was well located for viewing the river from many rooms and was famous for the "Sunday Smorgasbord and Coffee Shop." It was destroyed by explosion in 1979, and spectators from all around came to see the historic event. The hotel was razed to make room for the civic center.

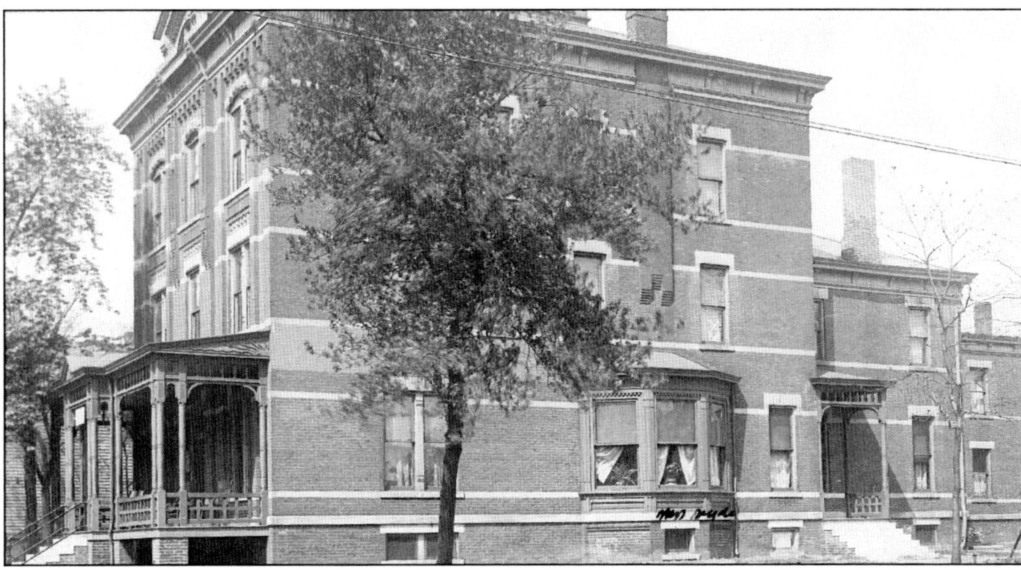

Edward and Sarah Easton, wealthy distillers and grain brokers, established Edna Home as a memorial home to their daughter Edna, who died at an early age. It was a home for working girls and women. In 1888, Mr. Eaton erected the above building of 20 rooms at 203 Third Avenue. This site was the family's former residence. The Eatons would later live at Main and High Street. After 12 years the Edna Home closed, and the property was eventually sold and proceeds given to the Women's Christian Home mission. The Alton Hotel opened around 1909, which is when the above picture was taken. Later, the hotel became the Bawin Hotel. It was eventually destroyed.

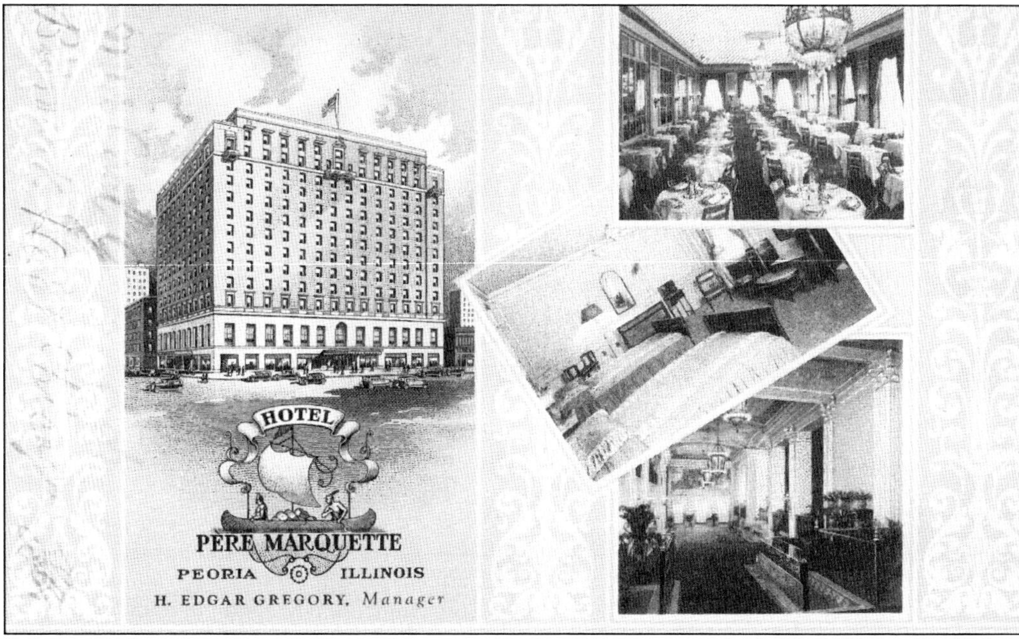

Father Jacques Marquette was the first white man to set foot on the present site of Peoria in August 1673. For this reason, Mrs. H.M. Kipp, of 218 North Street, submitted the name "Pere Marquitte" for Peoria's grandiose hotel in a 1925 contest. Her name was chosen, and she won a $50 cash prize for its submission. Stock in the hotel was purchased by the Peoria Life Insurance Company and some of its offices. The hotel, 13 stories high, was constructed by V. Jobst and Sons at a cost of more than $2,000,000.

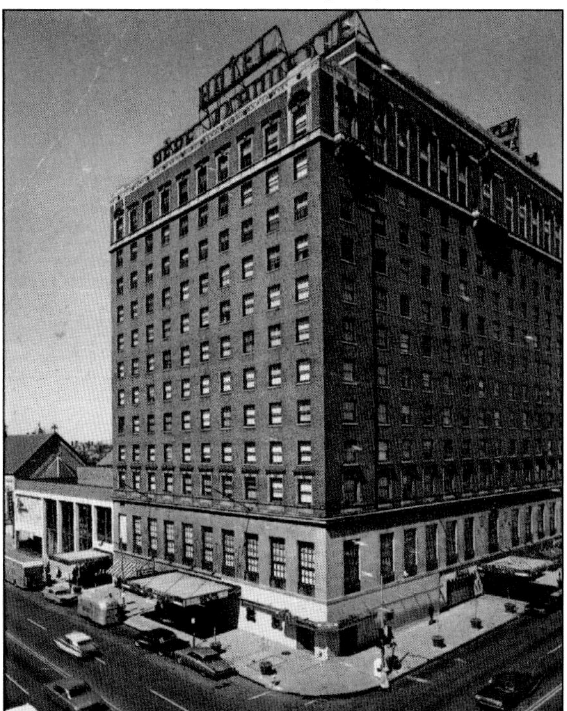

The hotel Pere Marquette opened on January 5, 1927. An addition was added in 1930, bringing the number of rooms to five hundred. This hotel was one of the first to have air conditioning. The Pere Marquette would later add a motor entrance and additional deck parking that adjoined the building. Thus, central Illinois gained its finest hotel. However, this large hotel would be a victim of a changing downtown. Several owners would attempt to revive its charm, including a well-known hotel chain. The hotel eventually closed, but again reopened in the 1980s. Today, the hostelry is still one of best in central Illinois.

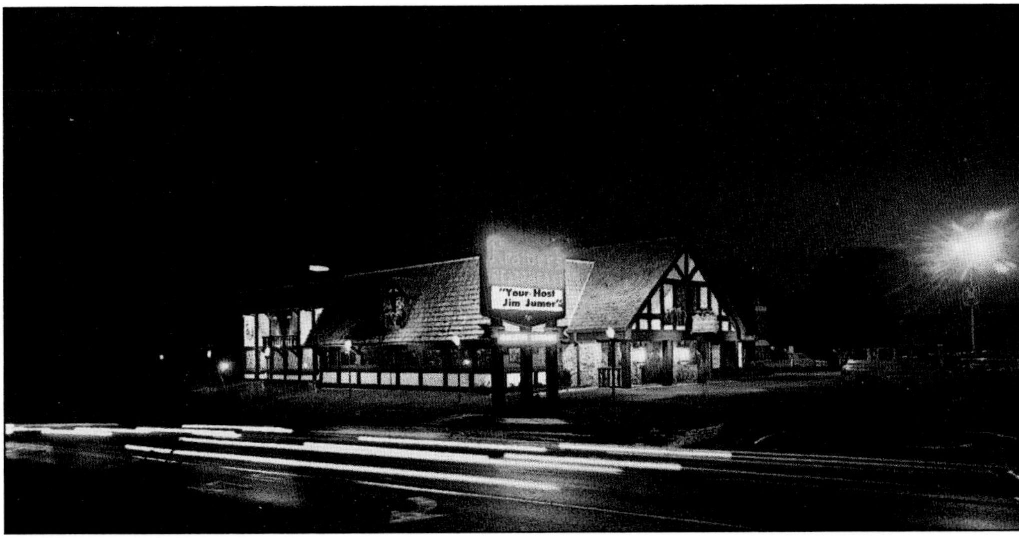

The above postcard shows how elaborate the Kramer drive-in on Western had become since its move from the downtown location. It replaced Hunt's restaurant, which had moved to Farmington Road by the mid-1930s. This business grew out of small building which sold, in 1937, hamburgers, sodas, and sundaes. The next expansion was to the familiar log-cabin design, along with the inclusion of curb-side service. Erwin Kramer, the owner, sold the business to Jim Jumer in 1960. Jumer would operate the restaurant until 1970, when he erected the now-famous Jumer's Castle Lodge.

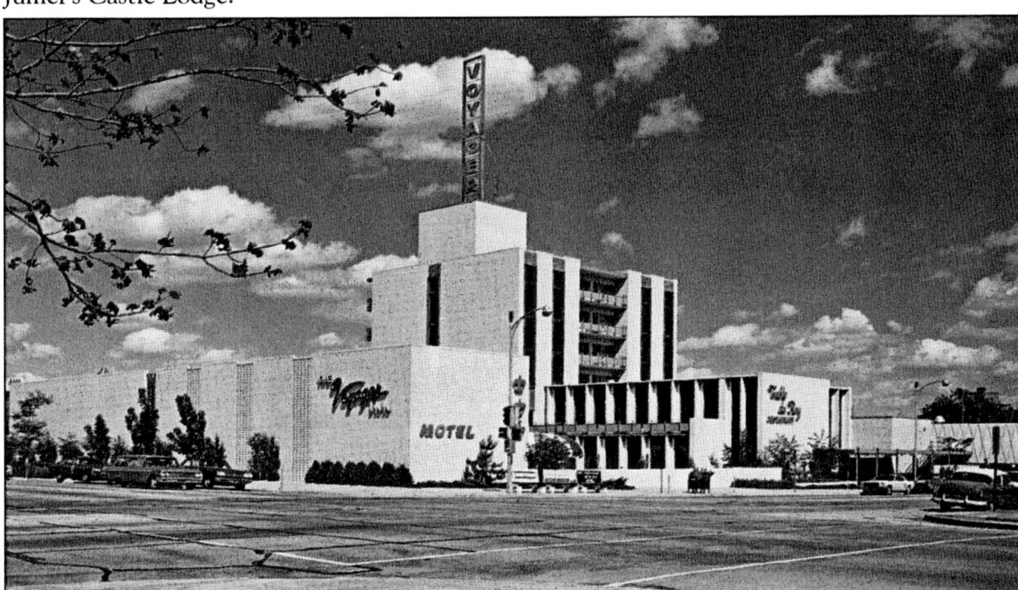

Boss Hotels, Inc. of Des Moines, Iowa, operators of the Pere Marquette, realized the need for motels in downtown Peoria. Plans were announced September 22, 1957, for a 70-unit luxury motel. All units would face an open court that allowed for maximum privacy. Complete guest services were afforded, along with much-needed parking. The name Voyager Inn was selected to tie in with the French theme and atmosphere of the motel. Voyager comes from the French word "Voyageur," meaning explorer. It gave honor to the first white explorers in the region.

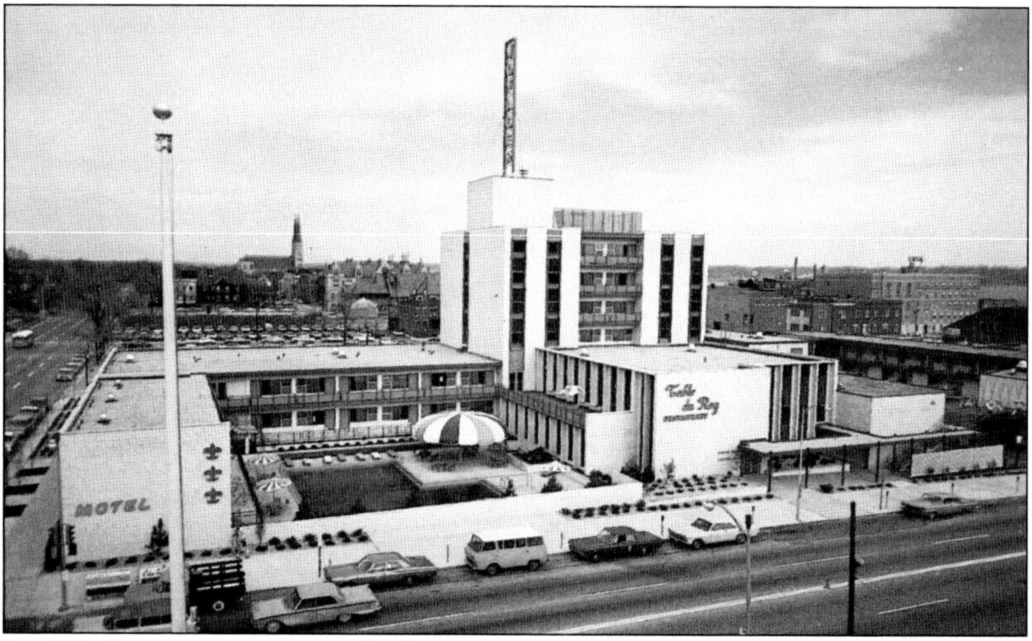

In 1958, the opening ceremonies for the Voyager included a parade complete with a stagecoach surrounded by attacking Native-American warriors, followed by antique and new cars carrying hundreds of people to the new hotel. A tower and restaurant were added in 1966, bringing the number of rooms up to 175. Also, one of the tables in the restaurant was a reproduction of the famous Table De Roi in Paris. To complete the block, plans were drawn for a seven-story office building and parking deck. The hotel was reworked and expanded to become the Continental Regency in the early 1980s. Today the hotel is the Holiday Inn Downtown.

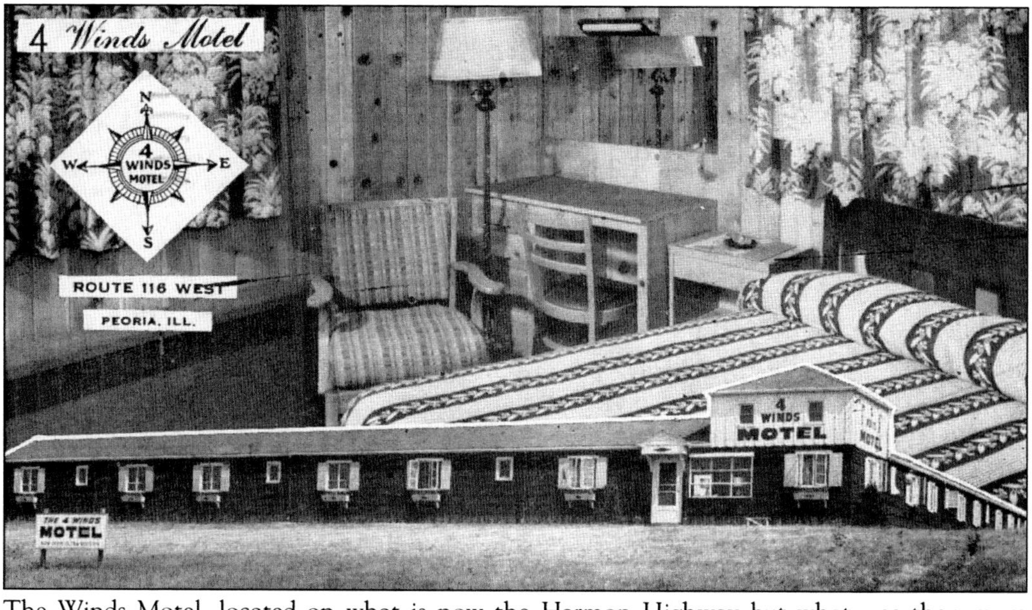

The Winds Motel, located on what is now the Harmon Highway but what was then more commonly known as Route 116, was an early example of suburban motel design. This motel opened in the mid-1950s and was razed in 1974.

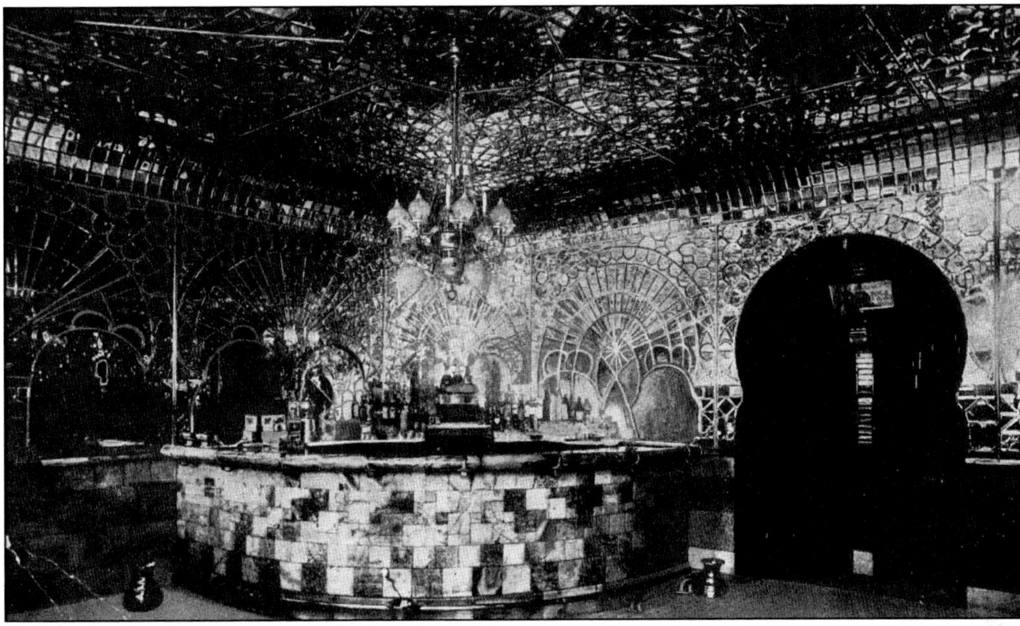

In the 1920s, there was a great deal of activity in an area referred to as Niagara Place. The location was the alley between Jefferson, Adams, Main, and Fulton. One of the main attractions was the Alcazar, owned and managed by W.A. Schmitt. Ten thousand pieces of beveled, French plate-glass mirrors and imported, black, English plate-glass mirrors were used in its construction. There are upwards of one thousand pieces of Mexican onyx near the bar.

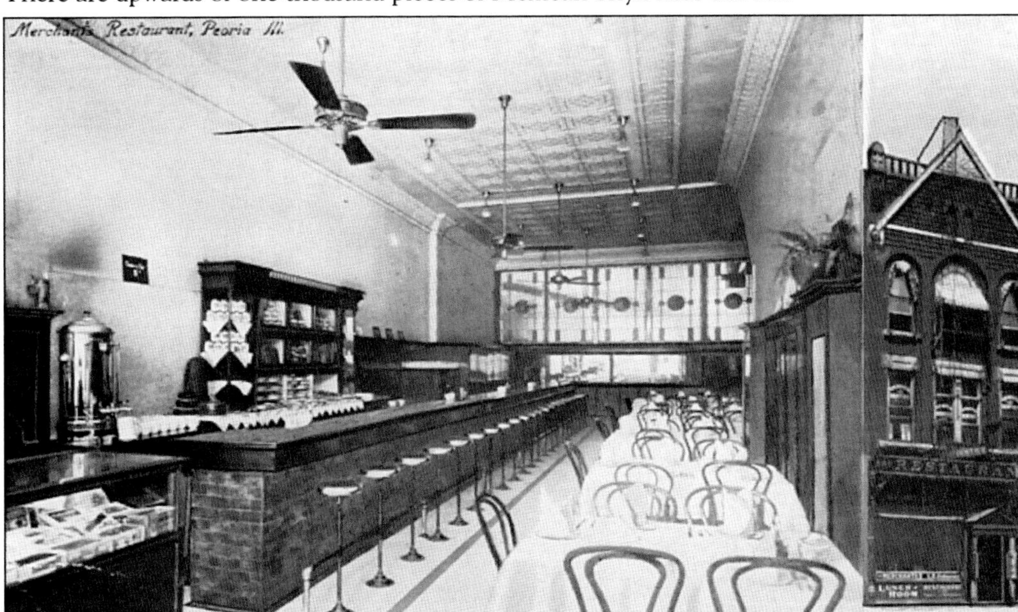

The above interior shot of merchants was taken during the late 1930s. The name was derived from the former use of the building as the Merchant's National Bank. On January 1, 1930, the Merchants Bank merged with the Illinois National Bank. Later, the name again changed to Commerce Merchants National Bank, which was later sold to the Commercial National Bank. The building formerly stood at the 300 block of South Adams.

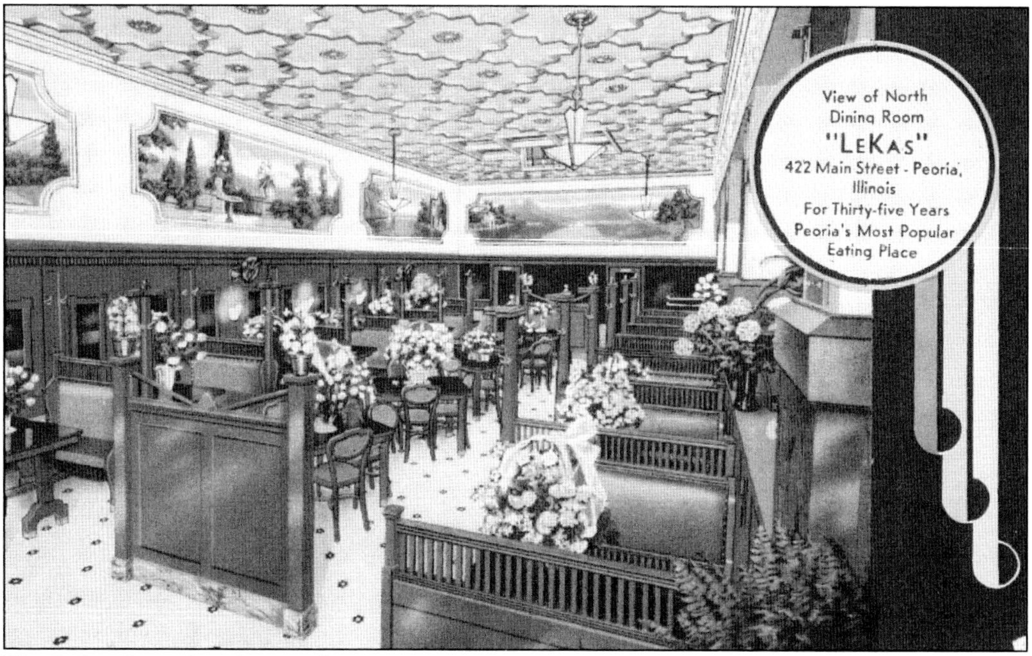

The Lekas Sugar Bowl opened in 1907 at 510 Main Street. A larger restaurant at 422 Main was opened in 1917. Lekas was remodeled in 1924, adding mahogany woodwork, a 19-foot marble soda fountain, hand-painted murals, and marble stairways. In 1940, the owner, Christ S. Lekas, moved the business to 1705 Knoxville, where it remained until closing in 1944 when Lekas retired. He died in 1955.

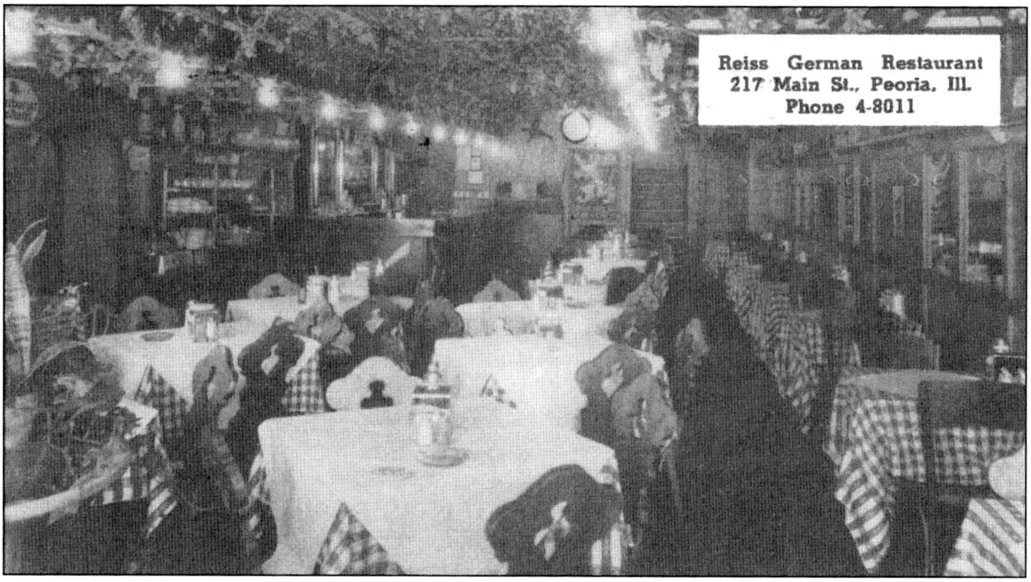

The Lud Hotel opened in 1904 at 217 Main Street, the former location of the Franklin House. The name was derived from the dog of Thomas Webb (the owner)—"King Lud." A stained-glass window of the dog was built into the building. The hotel's name changed in 1920 to Columbia. At this time, the hotel was leased to Karl Reiss. He then changed the name to the Bismarck.

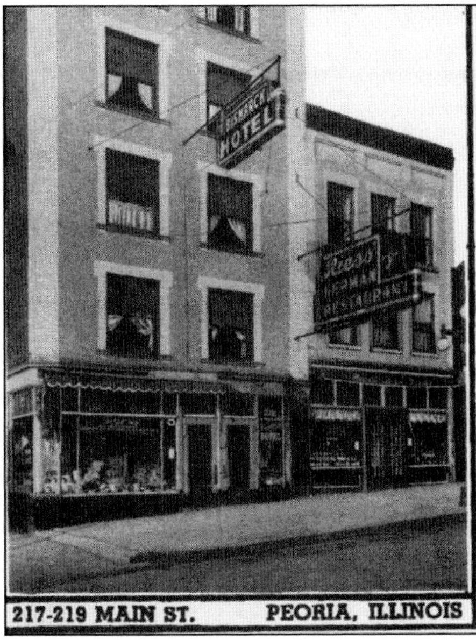

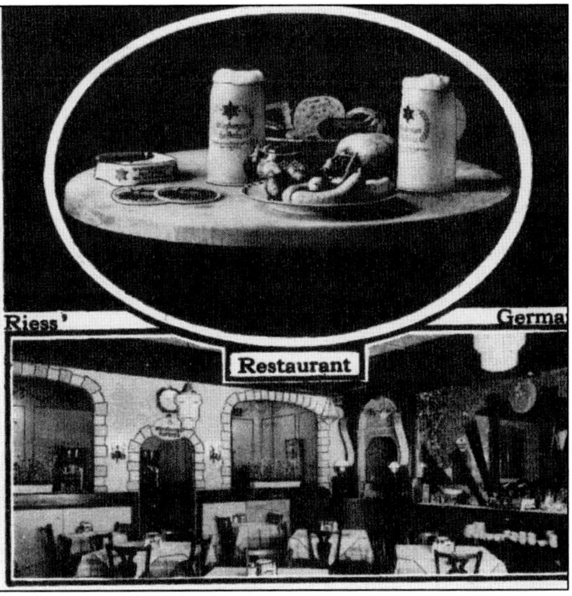

In the 1930s, Reiss obtained a lease for the adjoining building. Thus, 19 rooms were added to the complex of 42 rooms, with nearly 50 percent of the occupants being resident guests. Part of this addition was remodeled into a German garden. The Reiss regime ended in 1947, and the name was changed back to the Lud Hotel. In 1950, the hotel closed and remodeled in a new location in order to make room for the Clark Department Store. The entire complex was removed in the 1970s, and today the site is a parking lot.

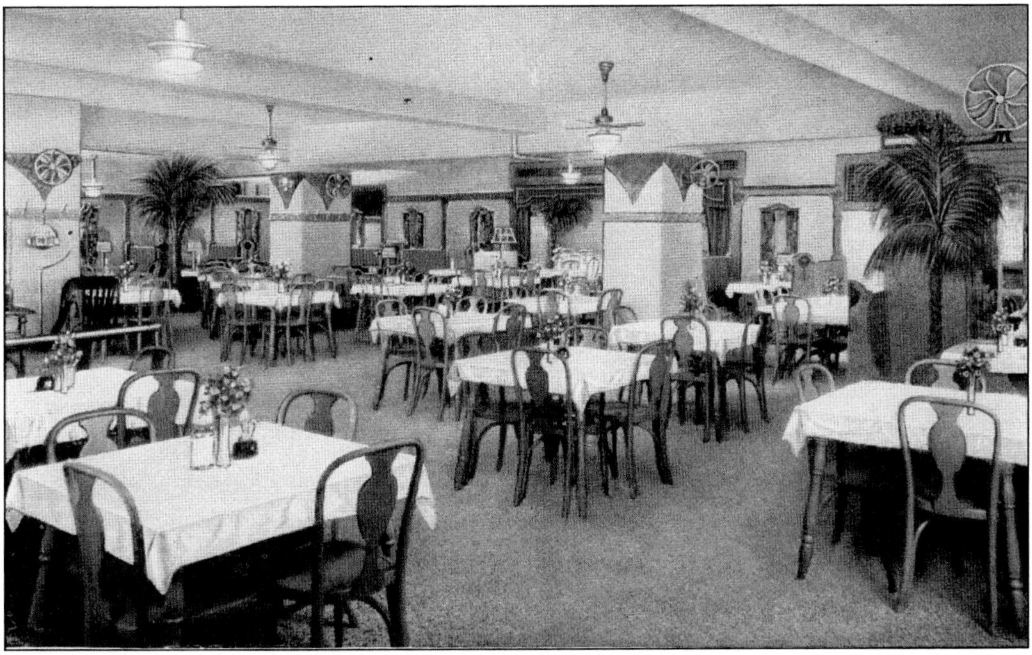

Built in 1920 by Congressman William E. Hull, the Palace Theater Complex, located at Main and Madison, consisted of an auditorium, arcade of shops, and 28 small apartments. The large cafeteria, as shown in the postcard, was located in the basement. In 1973 and 1974 the eatery closed. It reopened just before the building was destroyed in 1980.

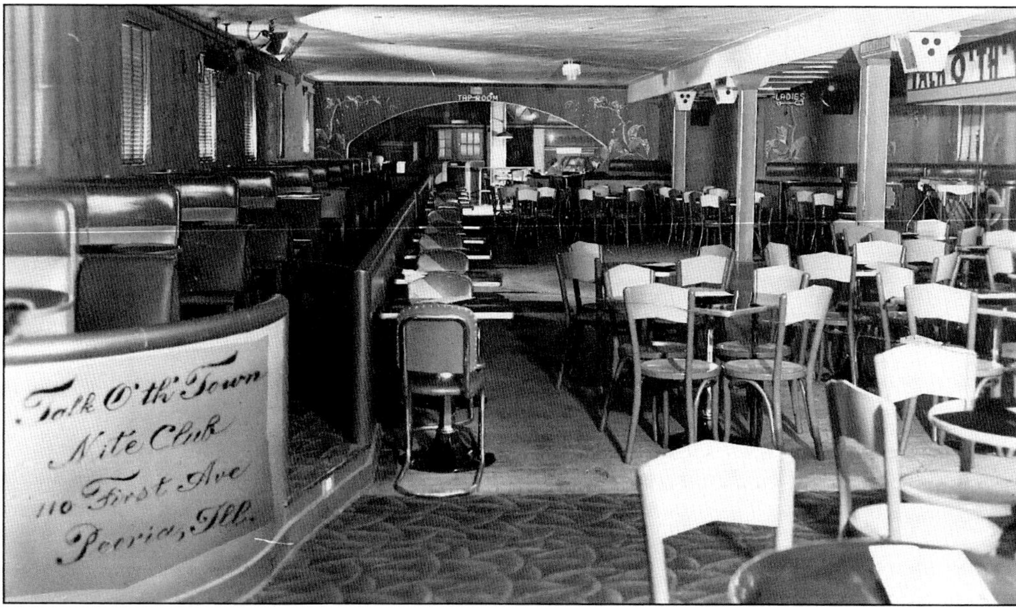

The Arion Hotel opened in 1897 at 110–112 First Street. In 1903, the name was changed to the Bentor Hotel. In 1922, the name changed again to the Colonial Hotel. The Arion name was eventually re-established. Jane McDonald purchased the hotel in 1934, and remodeled and rearranged the main floor into a nightclub called the "Talk of the Town." The postcard above shows another remodeling by Roy Brydon in 1944. The Talk would relocate to Main Street, and today the site is a parking lot.

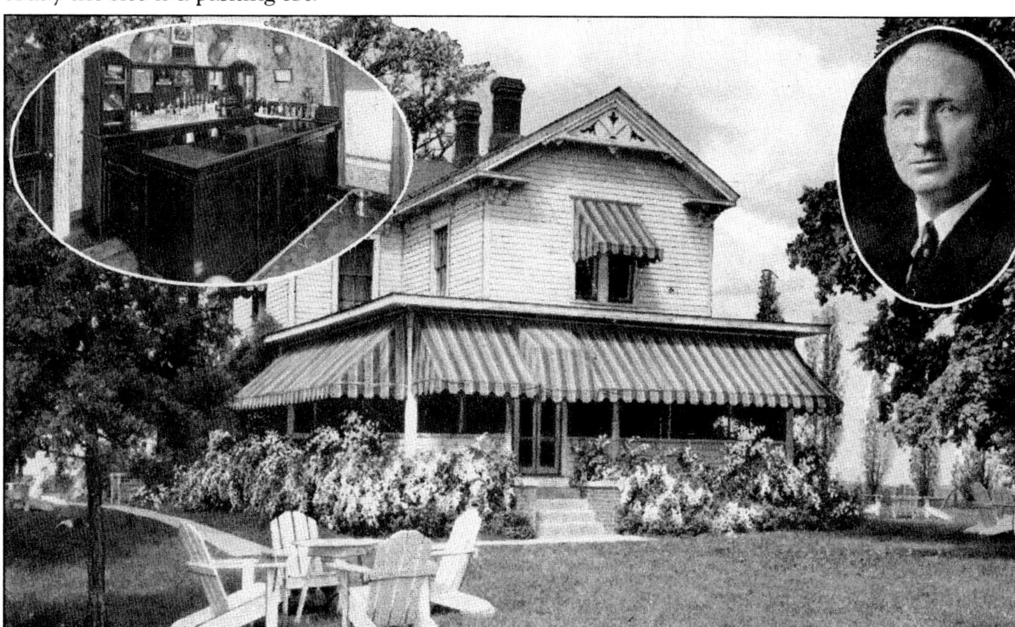

The postcard above was a way of enticing people to travel to the community of Dunlap (10 miles from downtown Peoria) to enjoy real fried chicken with enjoyable surroundings. This restaurant, known as Maple Shade, was complete with a tap room. Lunch and dinner were served year-round. The building closed in the early 1980s, and today has been remodeled into dentist offices.

Five

SCHOOLS

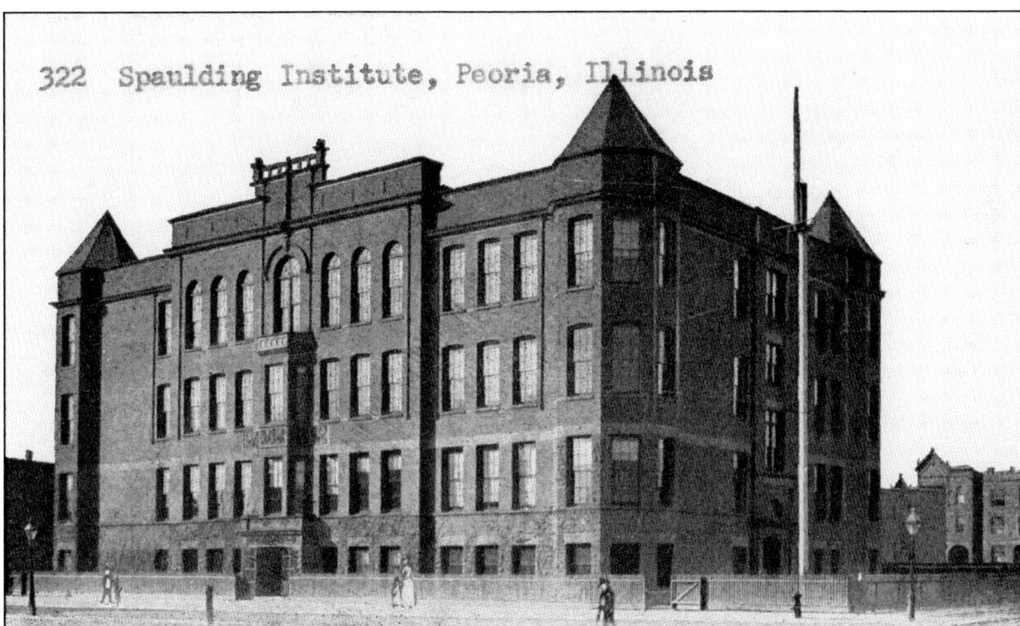

The rare postcard pictured above shows the original Spaulding Institute (note the misspelling with a "u"). Archbishop J.L. Spalding, who arrived in Peoria in 1877, was instrumental in the establishment of this parish high school, which opened in 1899 and was located at the corner of Madison and Jackson Streets.

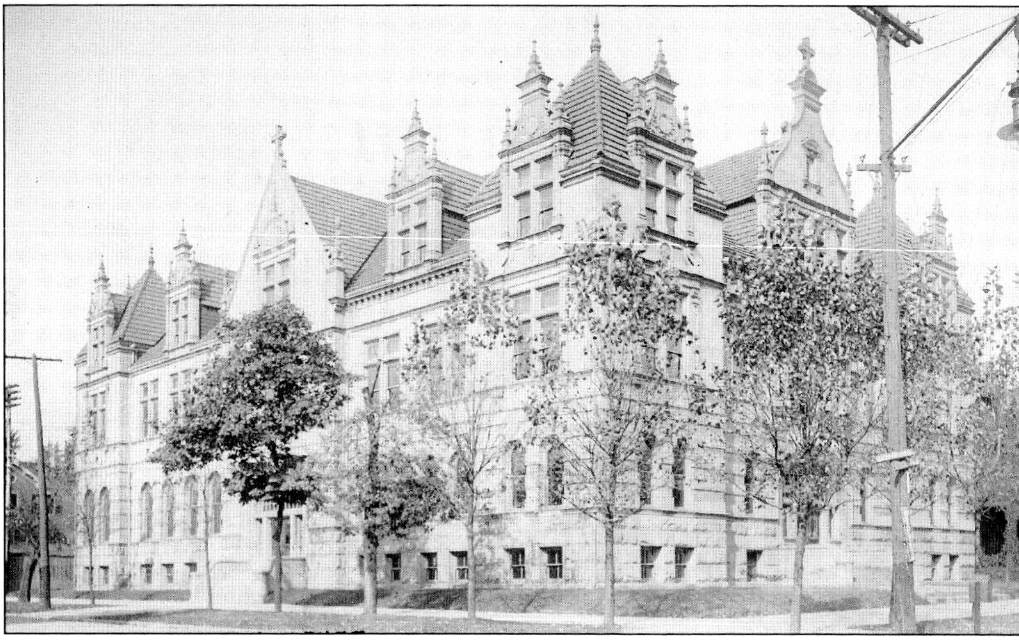

The above card represents the next stage of growth for the Spaulding Institute. The building above opened in 1901. This building was itself one of the architectural triumphs for the city of Peoria, both then and now. Named in honor of Bishop Spalding, the institution offered a high school course of study plus available college work. The above view was taken in 1907. The high school became a co-educational institution, and it later merged with Bergen High School to form Notre Dame High School.

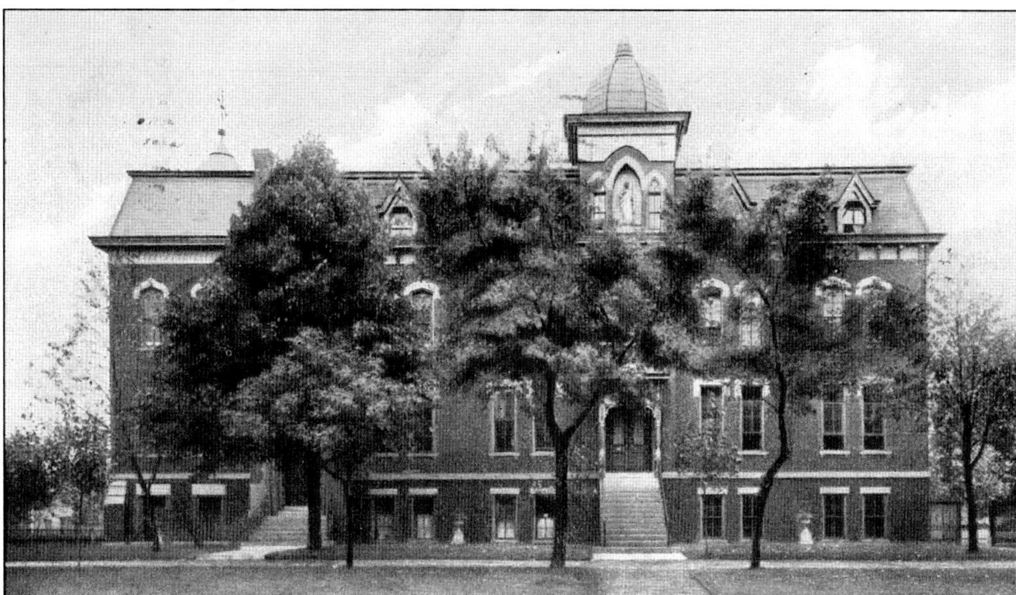

The Academy of Our Lady, pictured above as it appeared in 1908, was founded in 1863 by the Sisters of St. Joseph. At that time, each parish had its own grammar school. This institute for higher learning met the needs of the ladies of Peoria. The school later became Bergen High School.

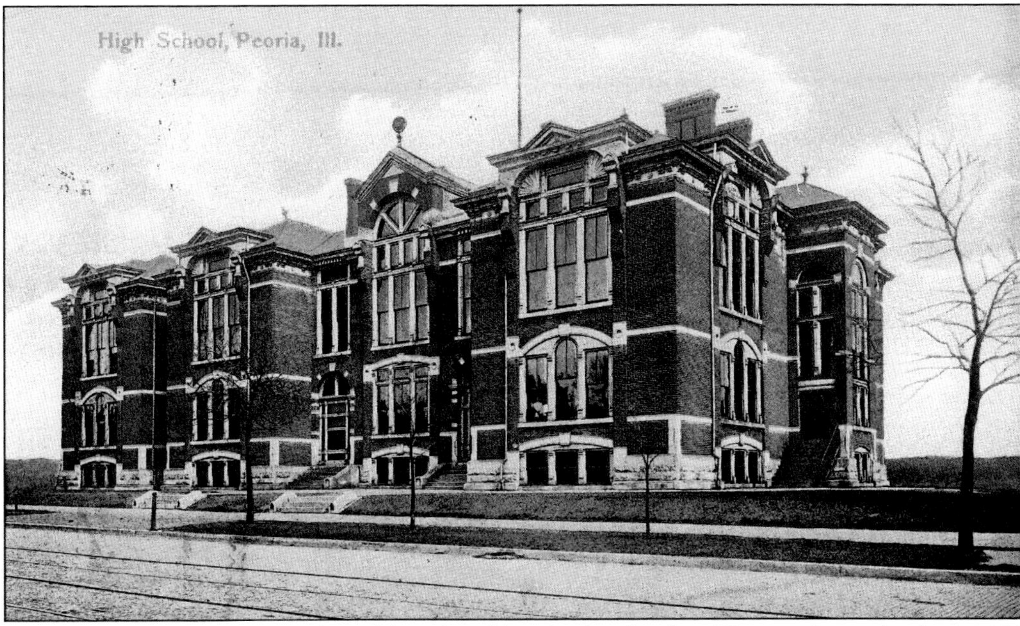

Peoria's high school (Central High) is the oldest high school in Illinois, dating back to 1856. Classes were held at several places, until the above school was erected at Monroe and Fayette Streets. This building was occupied beginning in September of 1885. The original cost was documented at $28,921. The present Central High School, located at North and Richmond Streets, opened in 1916.

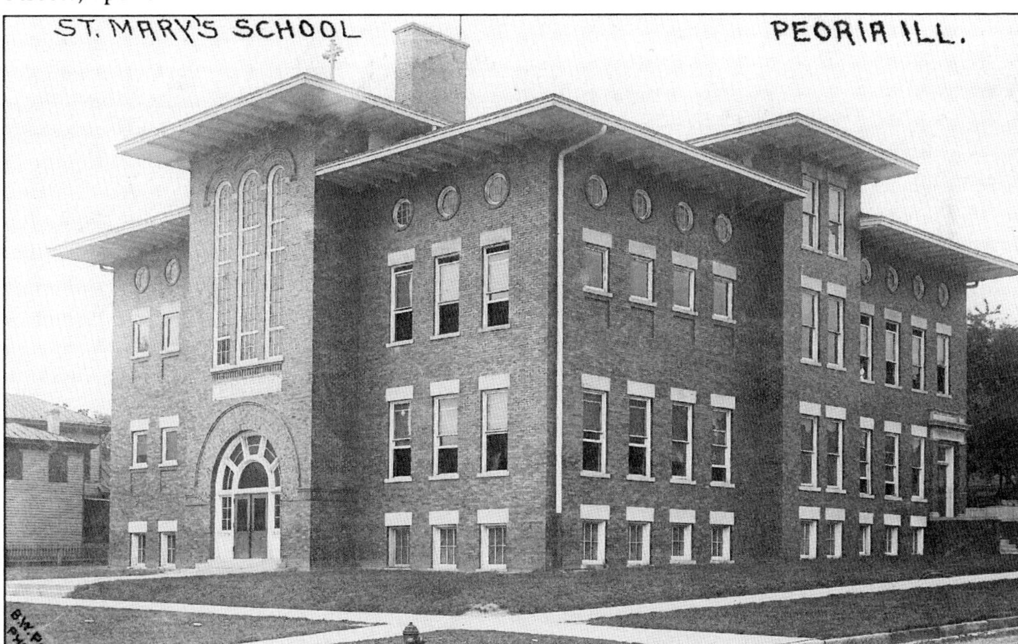

This American Prairie-style school was called St. Mary's and was completed in 1903, near the site of Peoria's first Catholic school, which was destroyed in 1899. This building was located at the corner of Jefferson and Bryan Streets. Unfortunately, the building was razed in the early 1980s.

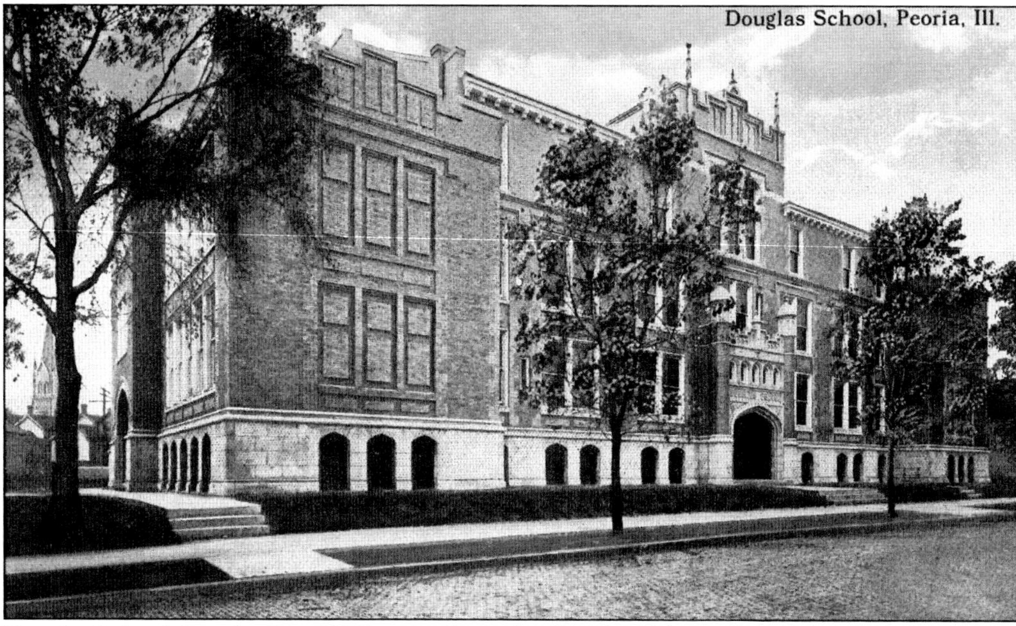

Douglas School dates back to 1855 as the first school in the old Fourth Ward District #1. Several locations were used within the district until 1878, when Douglas School was erected. The board of education adopted the name Douglas in 1882. In 1900 the building was enlarged, and by 1912 a new Douglas (shown here) was dedicated. It was remodeled in 1958. The school was closed in 1969 and the building was destroyed. It stood at 225 Southwest Reed.

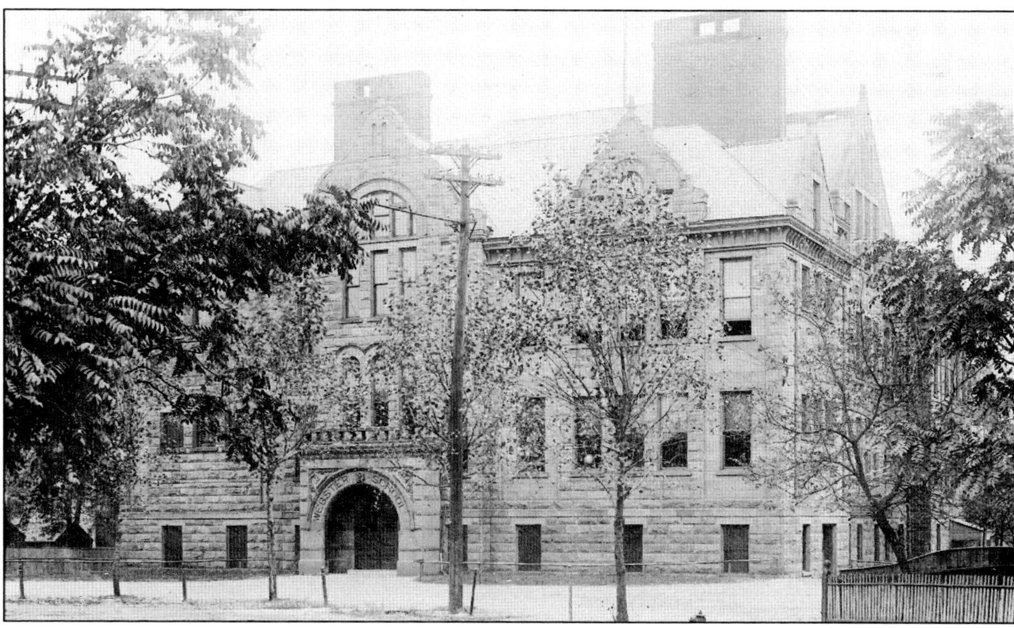

Webster School, then located at 923 West Millman Street, was dedicated in 1898. The above stone building would serve the community for 85 years as a grammar school. The roof was remodeled in the late 1960s, and the building would have a flat roof until its closing in 1983. The Community Action Agency purchased the building in 1987, and today operates a center for the Head Start Program for economically disadvantaged pre-school children.

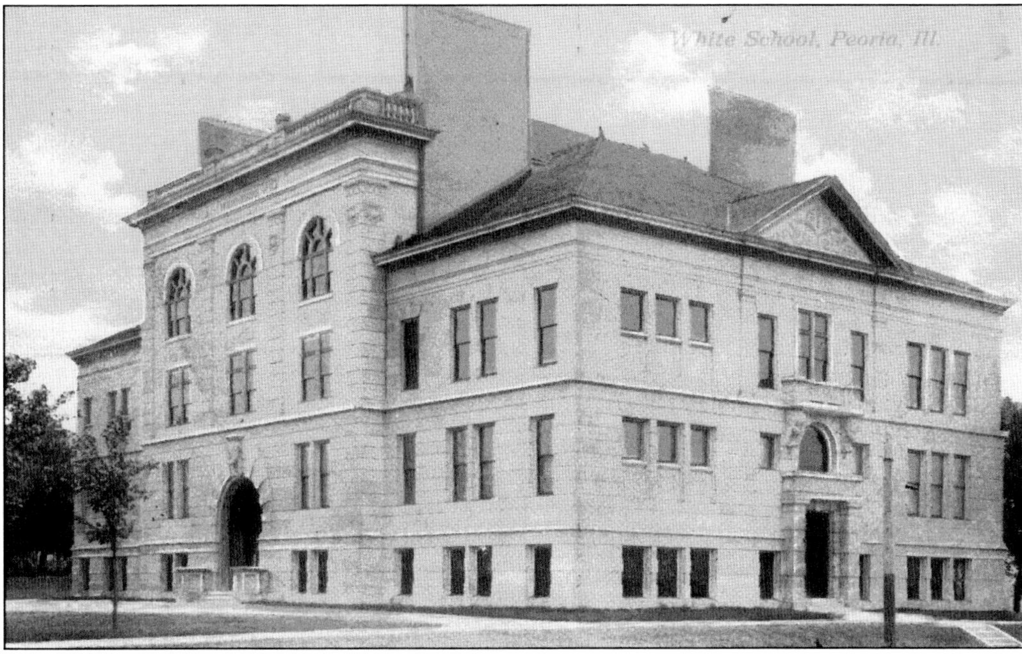

Pictured above is the second and present school, located at 304 East Illinois Avenue. The first school, which carried the same name of White School, opened in 1868 and was named for Professor S.H. White. The present building was dedicated in 1903. Today the building has a commanding view of the city from the East Bluff.

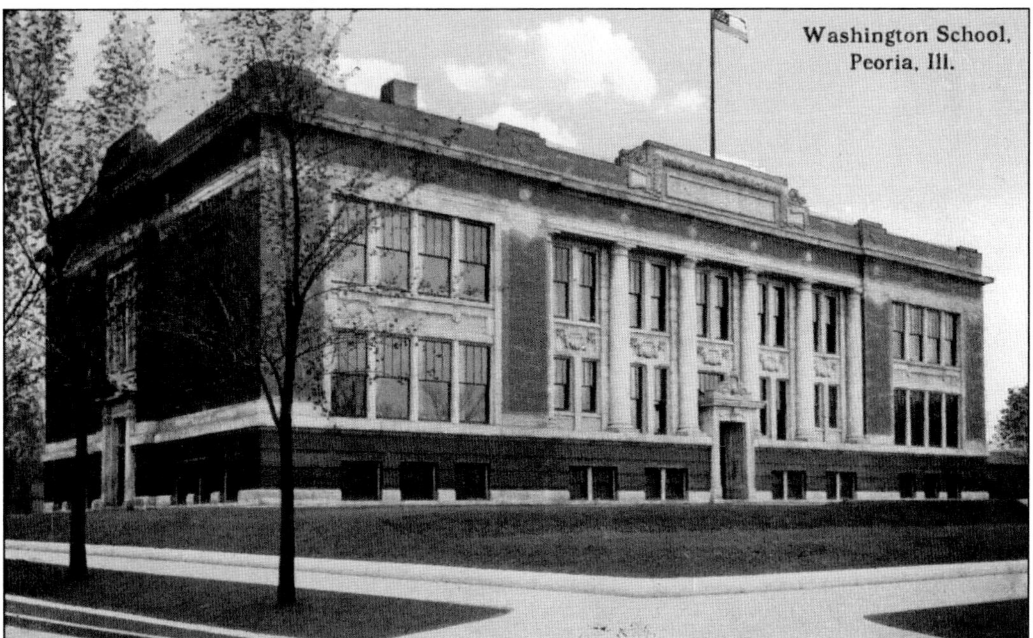

The above building was dedicated in 1911 as Peoria's newest and best-equipped building in the system. The building would close in 1979, and would be reopened as the Adult Education Building. The Adult Education School is still operational, and the building and grounds are well maintained.

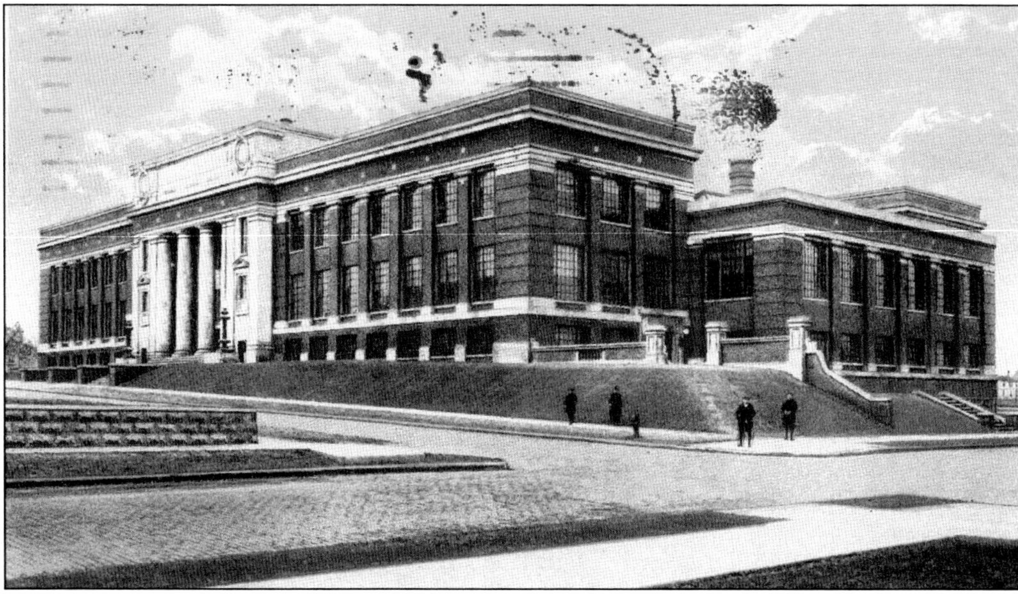

By 1912, it became evident that Peoria High School could no longer accommodate the crowded conditions at the Monroe and Fayette facility. To meet the need, property was secured at 1615 North Street. Plans were laid, and by September 1916, the new $400,000 school opened. Peoria Central High School dates back to 1856 and is the oldest high school in Illinois, and the 17th oldest in the nation.

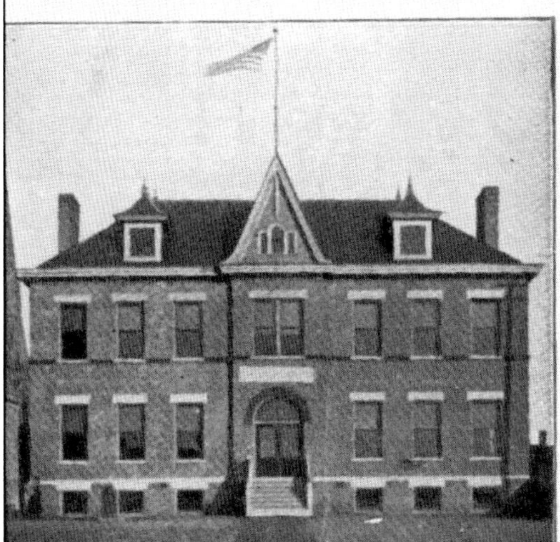

Ev. luth. St. Pauls-Schule, Peoria, Ill.

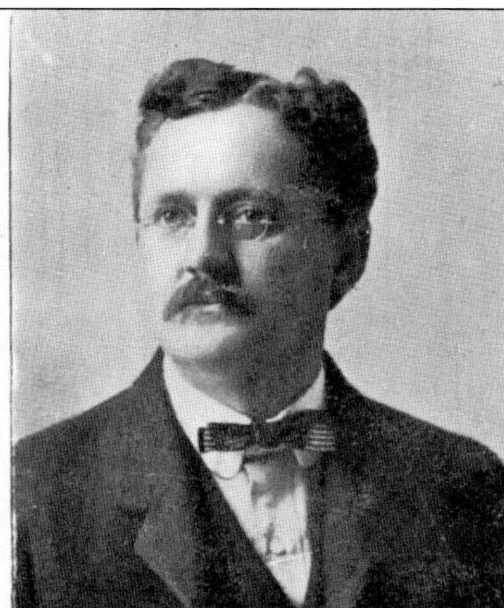

Lehrer W. Semmelmann.

St. Paul's Evangelical Lutheran Church was founded in 1853. In 1854, the congregation erected a church on Fifth and Sanford Streets. A school was located in the building pictured above. The principal was Professor Lehrer W. Semmelman, and his wife was a teacher for the kindergarten. The school was discontinued in the 1930s.

Six

Fires, Wrecks, and Floods

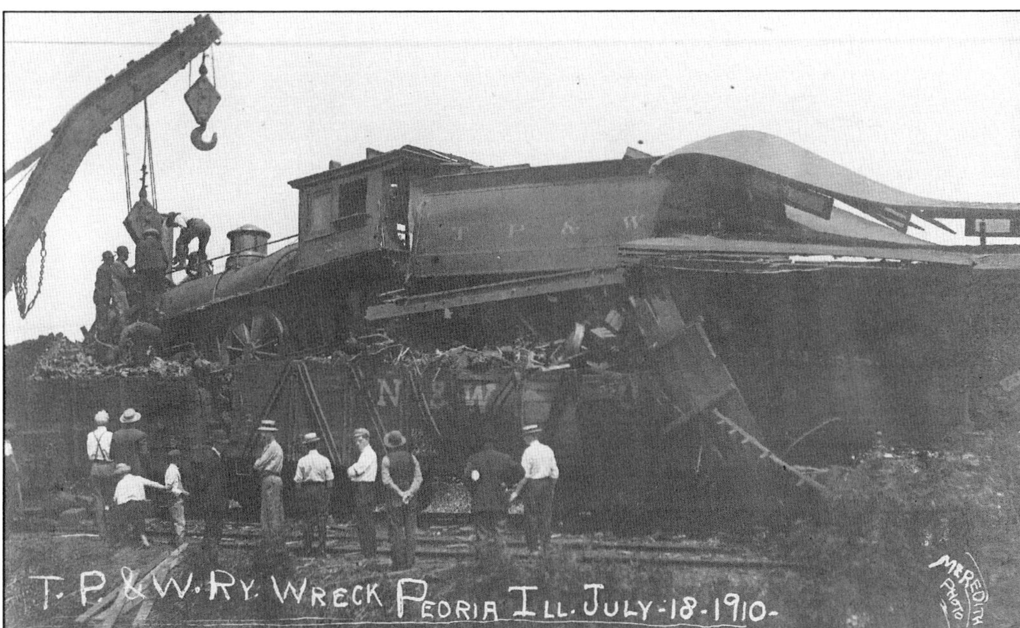

It was estimated that over a hundred trains a day entered the Peoria area, and wrecks were a fact of life. The Toledo, Peoria, and Western Railway endured the above wreck on July 18, 1910. The wreck occurred within the city limits. The TPW president, George P. McNear Jr., would be killed by an unknown assassin in 1947 at High and Sheridan Streets.

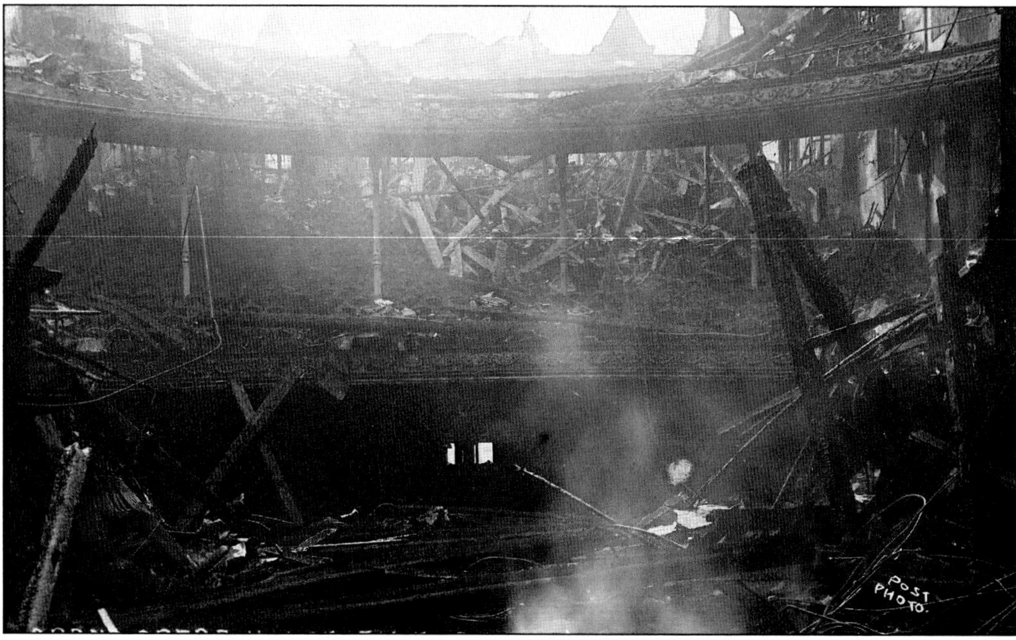

"Will It Play in Peoria" was believed to have originated in the 1850s, when live arts succeeded or failed on Peoria stages. Steps were taken to improve the act or else it was dropped. The Grand Opera House, built in 1882, became the test site for live arts. The building stood across from the courthouse until December 14, 1909, when it burned. The above postcard displays the remains from the stage where so many famous acts played.

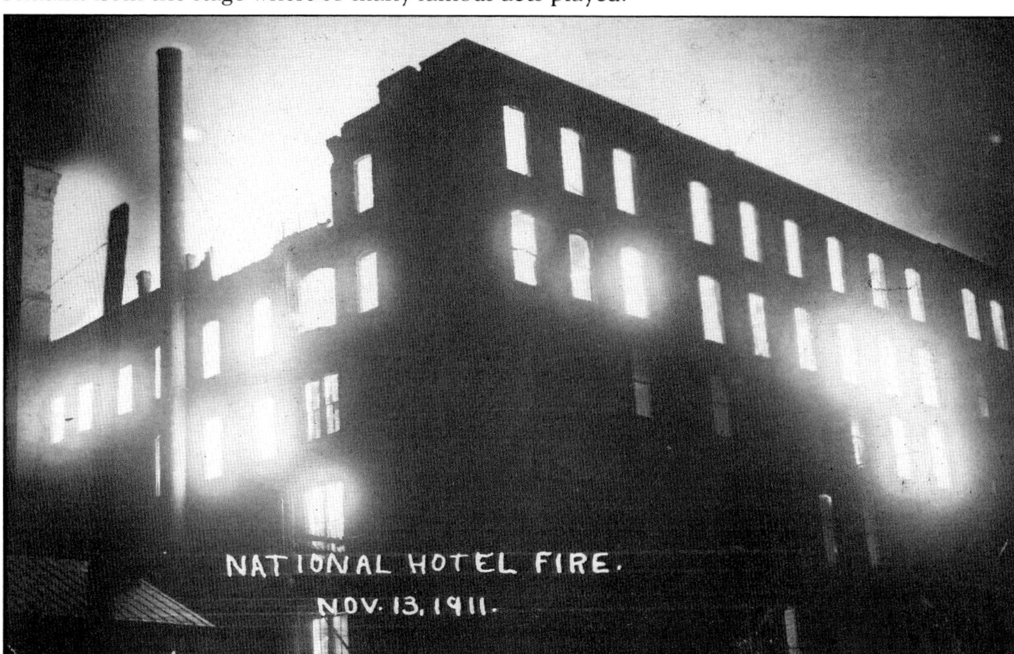

The fire demon seemed to haunt many hotels. A fire causing $110,000 damage destroyed the National Hotel, which was where some of the nation's most famous people stayed when visiting Peoria. The building was six stories high, with this sixth story used by the Elks.

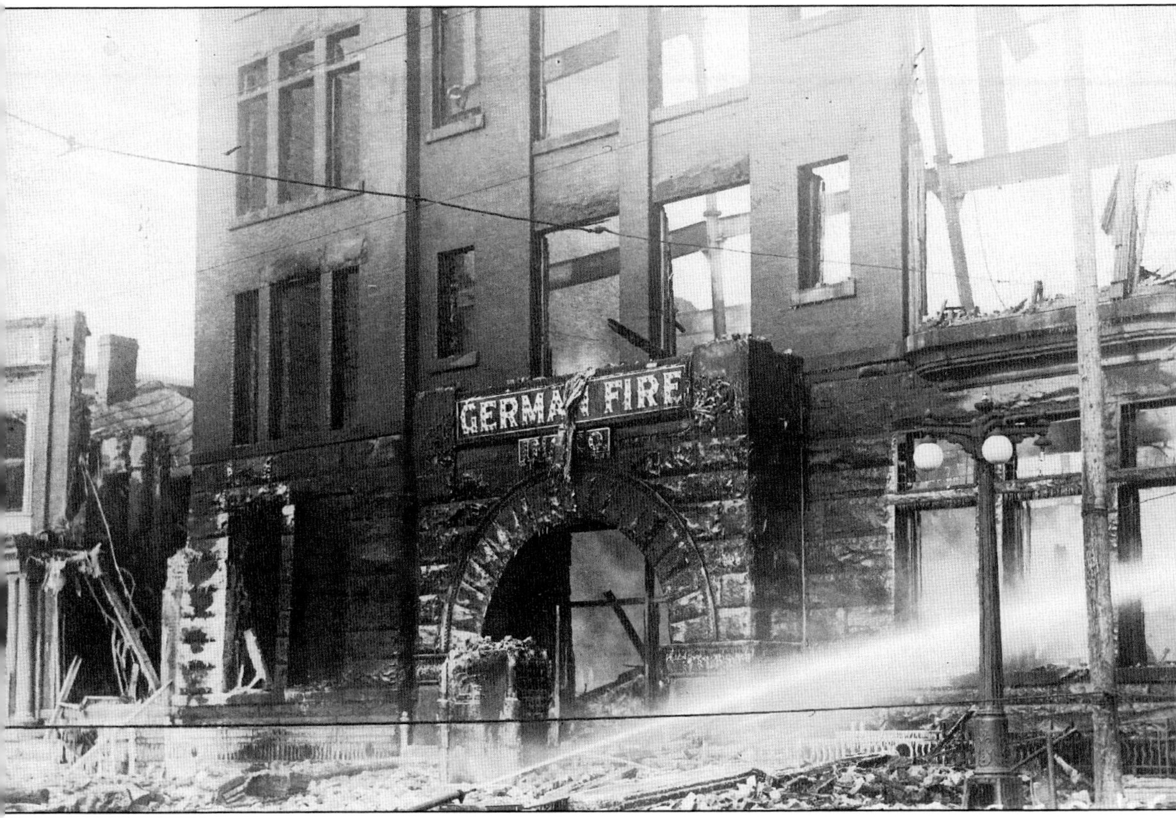

The German Fire Insurance Company, as shown in the picture above, acquired 115 North Jefferson in 1909. The YMCA had erected this building in 1890. The financial burden for the obligations associated with this YMCA necessitated the building's sale to the German Fire Insurance Company. The company occupied the building for less than six years before a devastating fire occurred. The building stood in the middle of the block across from the courthouse. Attorney E.J. Abersoi jumped from the burning building.

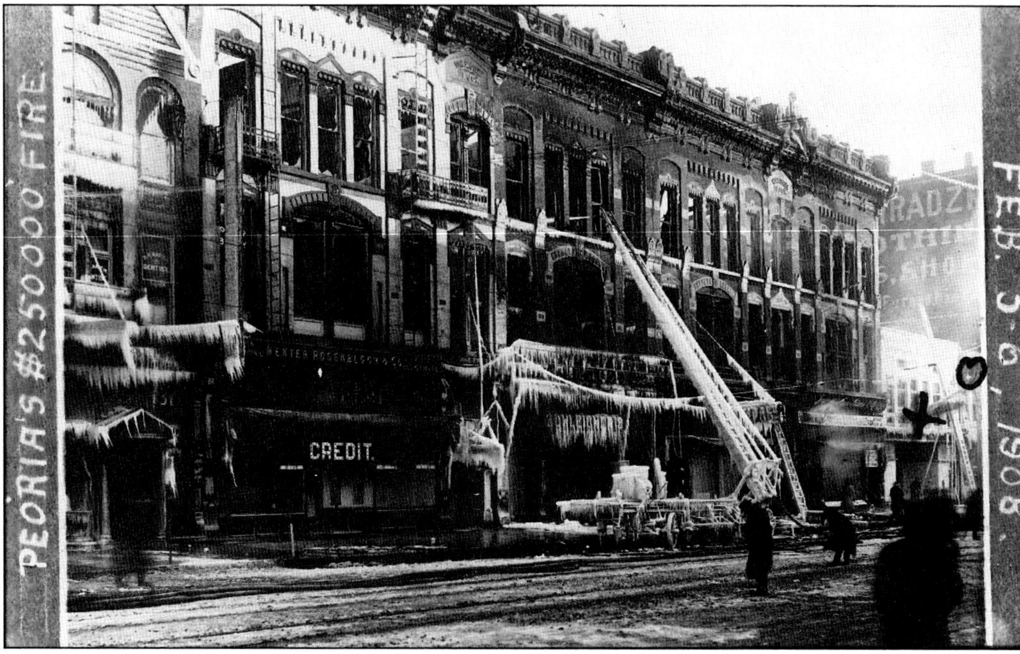

Winter fires are always difficult to fight, as shown by the water freezing on February 5 and 6, 1908. The fire began at Schleicher and Sons auditorium and swept through four three-story buildings in this 300 block of South Adams Street, with a loss of $250,000. Unfortunately, four more fires would occur with over $100,000 damage that same year.

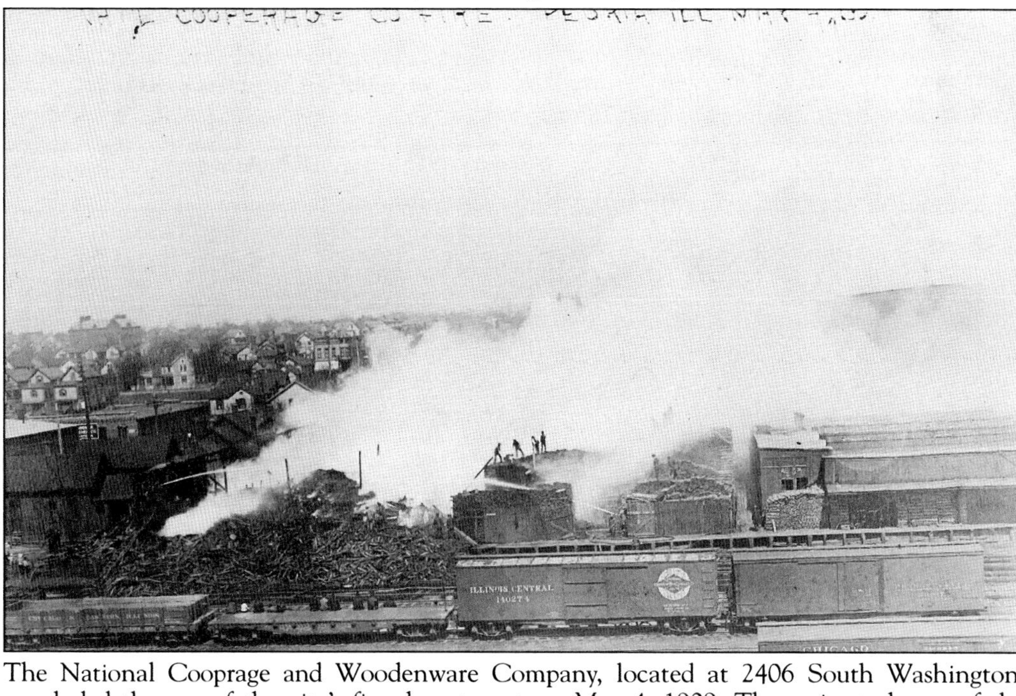

The National Cooprage and Woodenware Company, located at 2406 South Washington, marshaled the use of the city's fire department on May 4, 1909. The estimated cost of the damage from the fire was $200,000. The fire was in progress when the postcard picture was taken. The company rebuilt after the blaze.

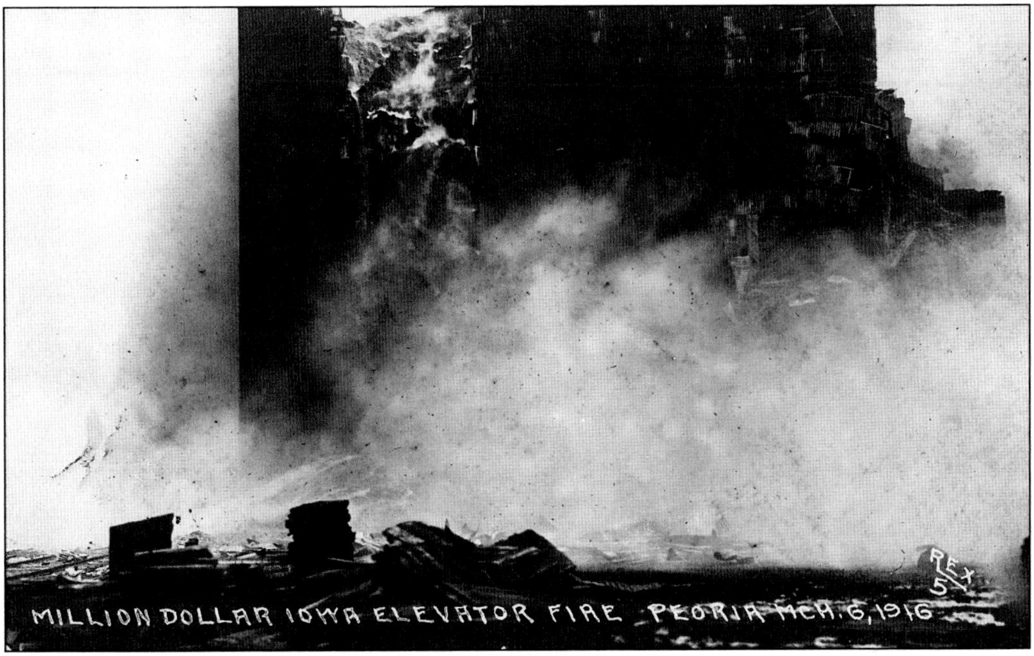

Peoria's first million dollar fire occurred March 6, 1916, after a fire started from a dust explosion. It was the second fire one to occur at the Iowa Elevator site. The rise of the distillers in Peoria created a demand for the huge elevators. This postcard reveals the extent and magnitude of the destruction of the Iowa elevator. Firefighters throughout the tri-county area were requested, but the fire still lasted the entire day.

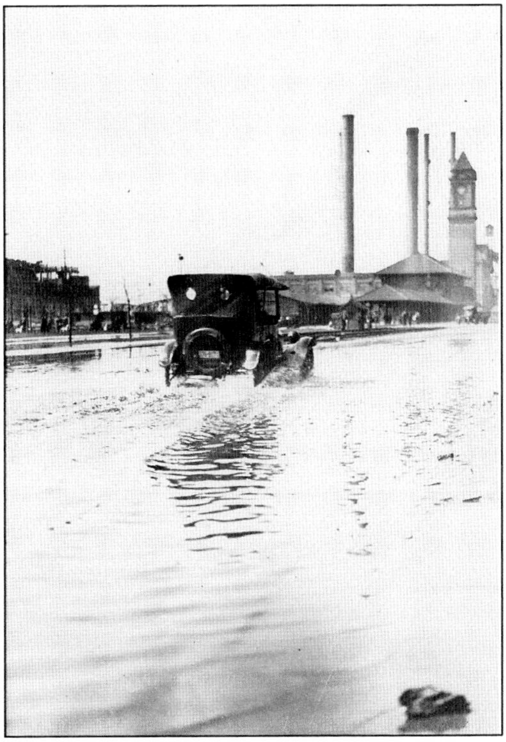

Floods have and always will be a threat to downtown Peoria. This 1930 postcard demonstrates the extent of the flooding, which covered the railroad tracks at Water Street. Note the Chicago and Rock Island Depot in the background.

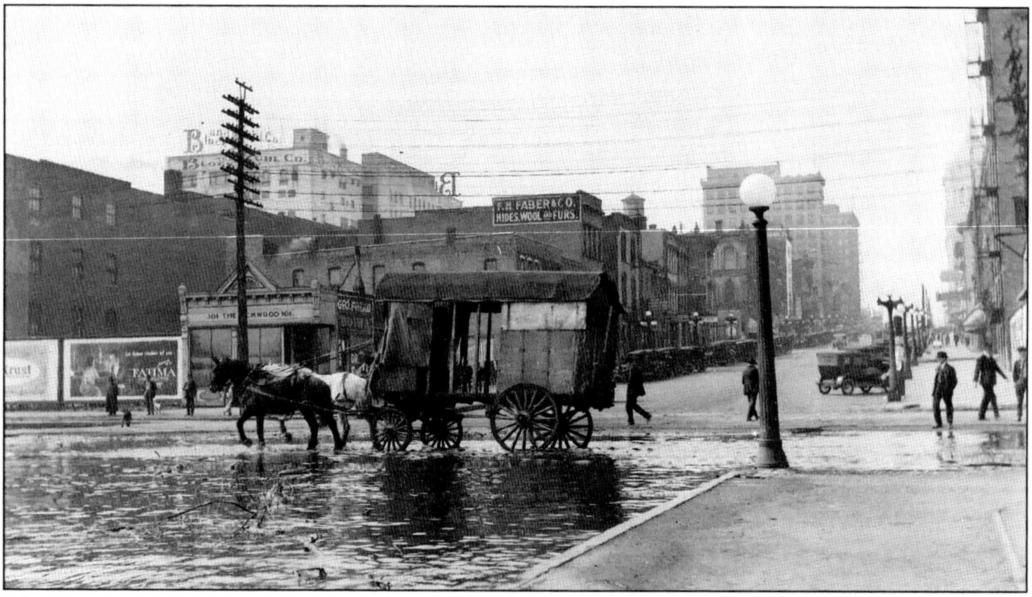

The flood of 1930 reached Main and Water Streets. The Clarke Building, at the top of Main Street (to the left) and Block and Kuhl, can be seen in the upper left portion of the card.

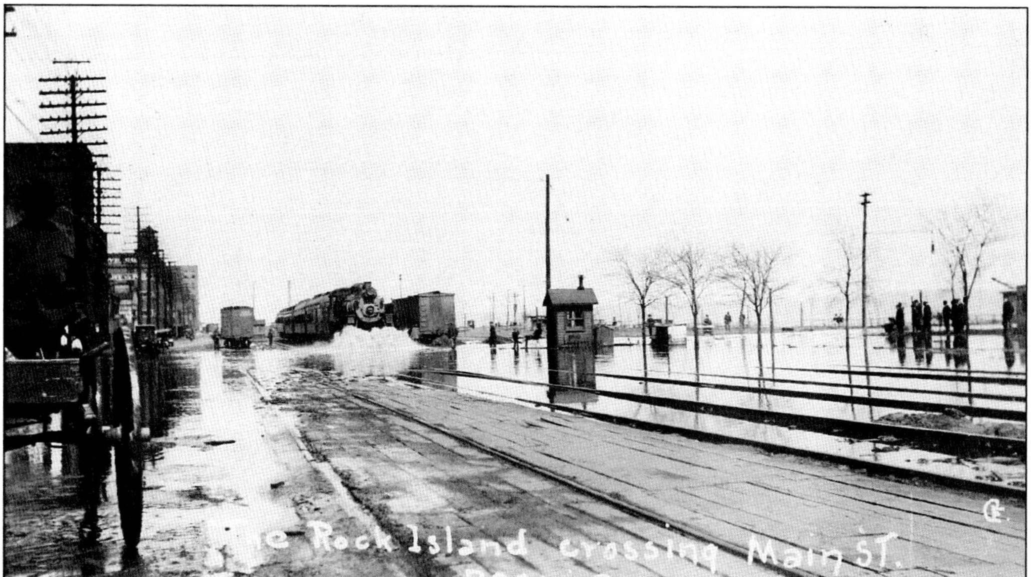

The flood of 1930 did not stop the trains from entering and exiting Peoria. Flooding would again occur in 1933 and 1943. This scene is facing the Illinois River to the northeast with the train station out of view to the right.

Seven

ADVERTISING

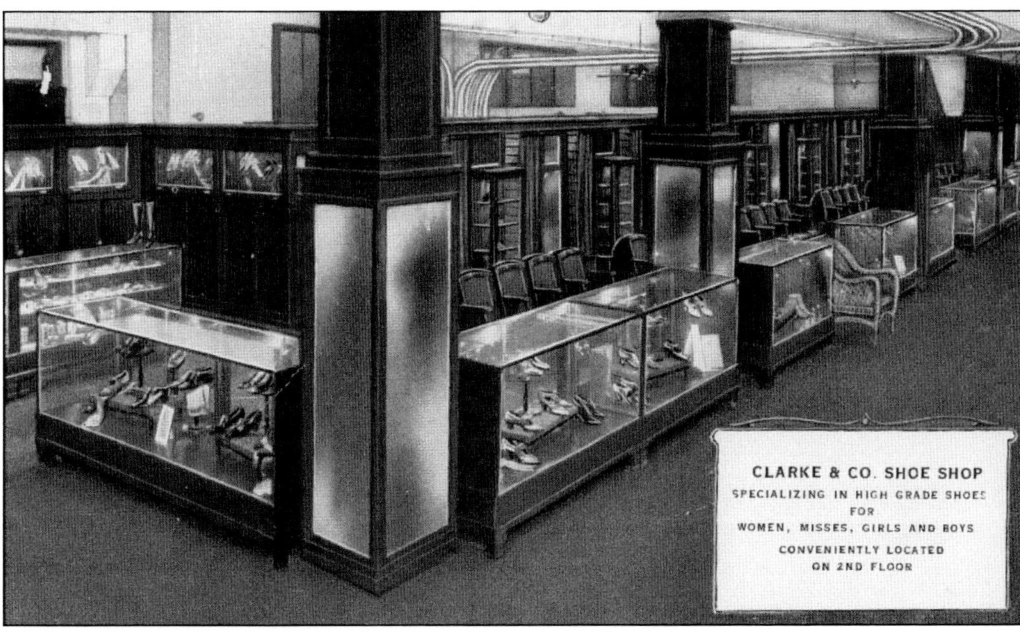

This rare postcard is headed "Clarke and Company Shoe Shop." Clarke and Company was founded in 1863 and was one of the leading dry goods shops in Peoria. The concern was sold in 1944 to Ely Worker of St. Louis, along with the building, which was constructed in 1927. The building later sold to S.S. Kresge, who did not renew Clarke and Company's lease. The move to the Lud Hotel failed, and the building was destroyed in 1980.

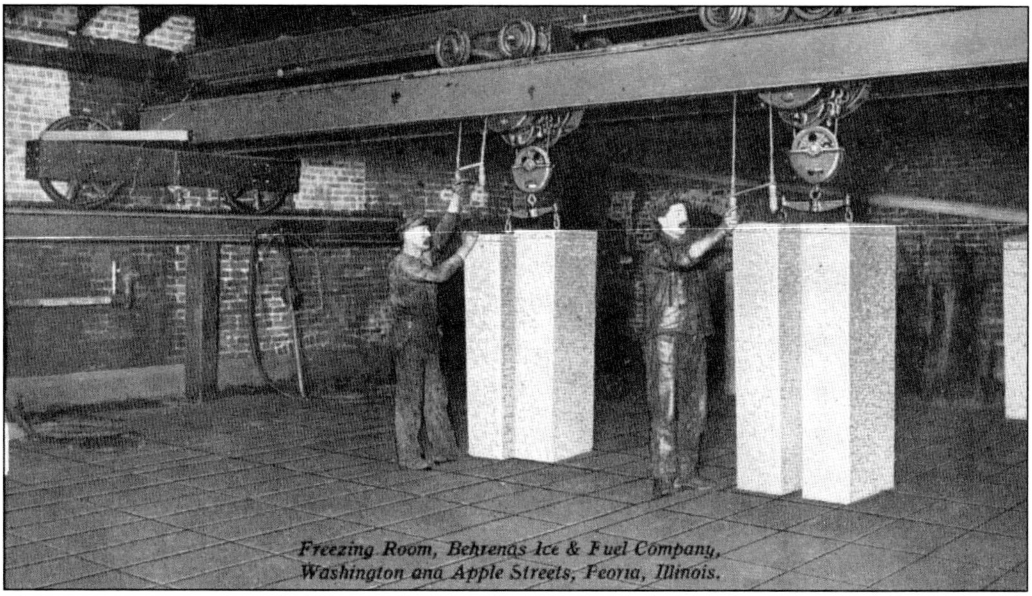

The above card was mailed in 1913 when the Behrends, Inc. Company was just four years old. The company was incorporated in 1909 with offices, factory, and a warehouse located at Apple and Washington. Eighteen ice wagons and ten cool wagons serviced both Peoria and Springfield. The need for artificial ice faded when electric refrigerators began to be used in many households.

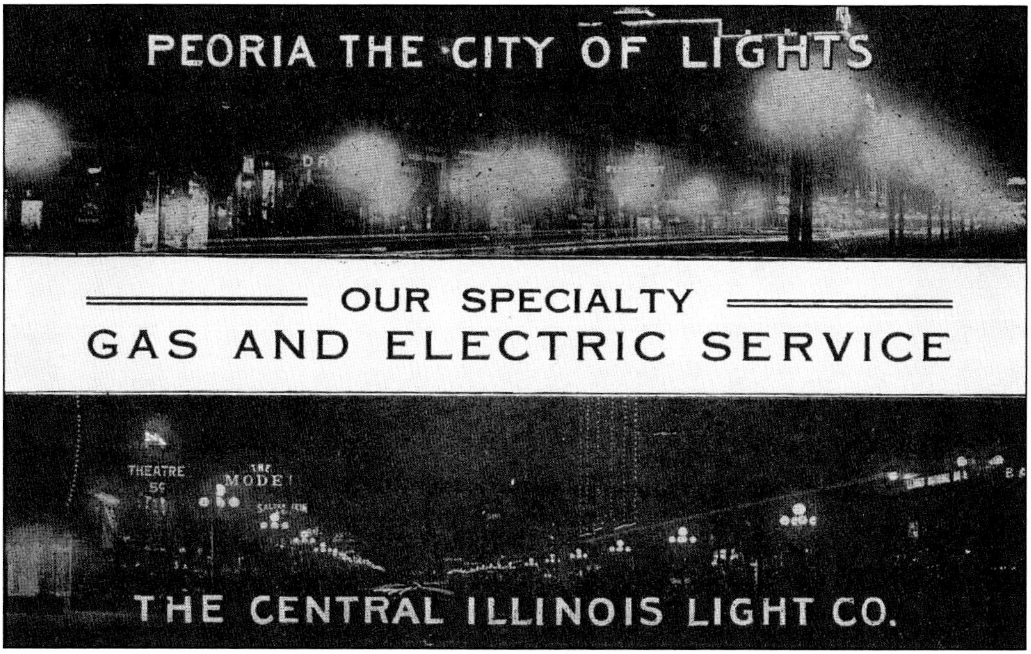

On September 15, 1853, natural gas was introduced into the city of Peoria via a contract with the Peoria Gas and Coke Company. Jenny Electric Light and Power introduced electricity in 1885 from their plant at Hamilton and Water Streets. The two consolidated in 1904. With the purchase of other nearby utilities, it became the Central Illinois Light Company in 1913. The company has since extended electric service to a score of nearby cities and villages.

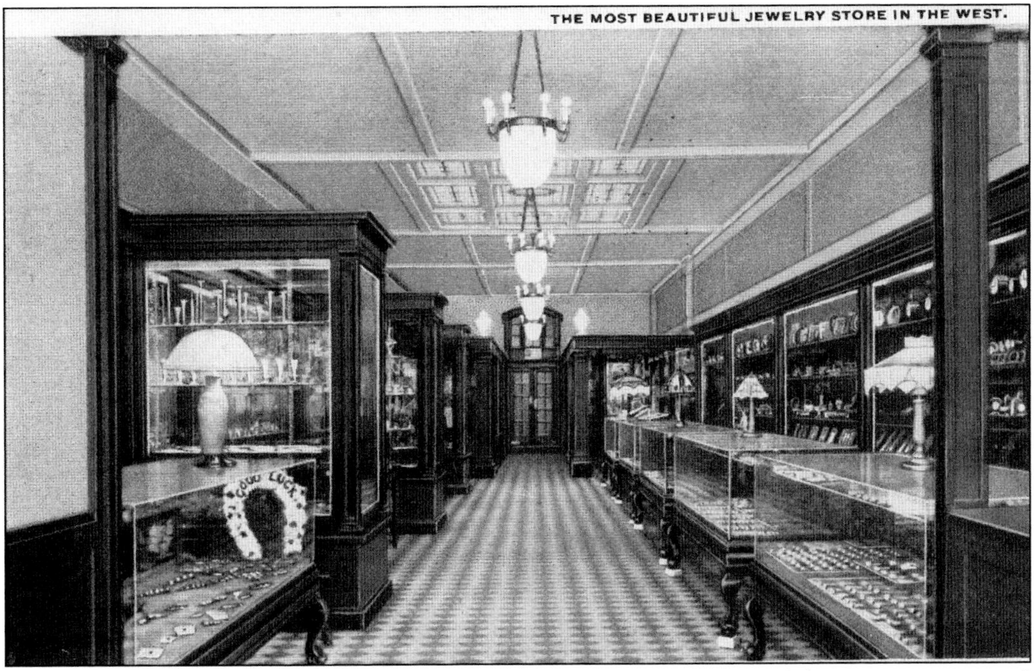

The oldest jewelry store in Peoria, Goldstein's, began operating in 1896. After occupying several different sitcs, it relocated to 211 South Adams, where it remained for 37 years, prior to closing in 1953.

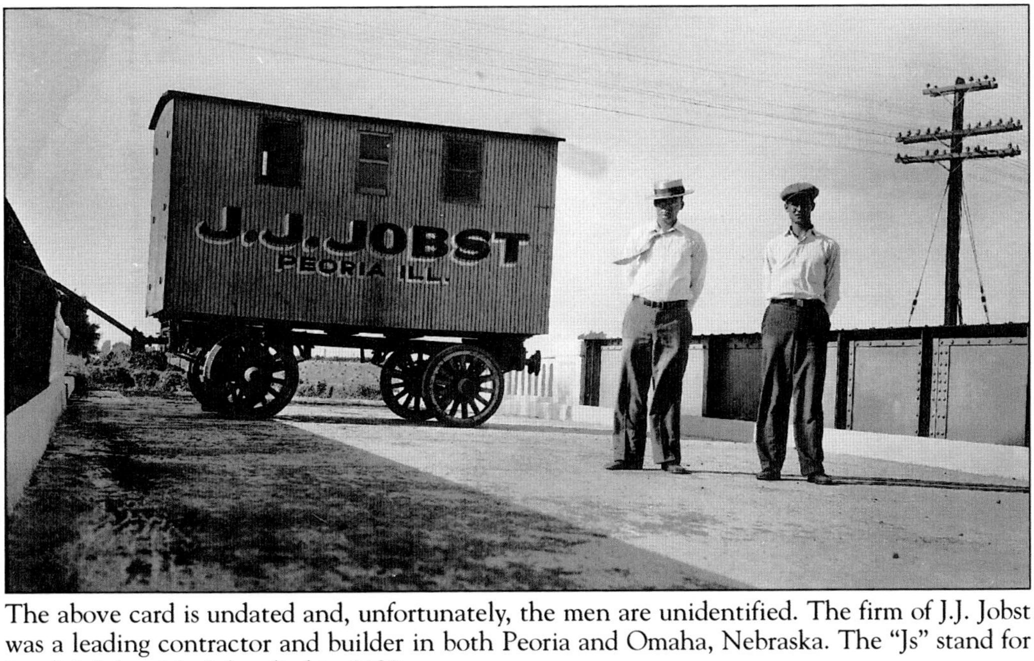

The above card is undated and, unfortunately, the men are unidentified. The firm of J.J. Jobst was a leading contractor and builder in both Peoria and Omaha, Nebraska. The "Js" stand for Jacob J. Jobst. Mr. Jobst died in 1939.

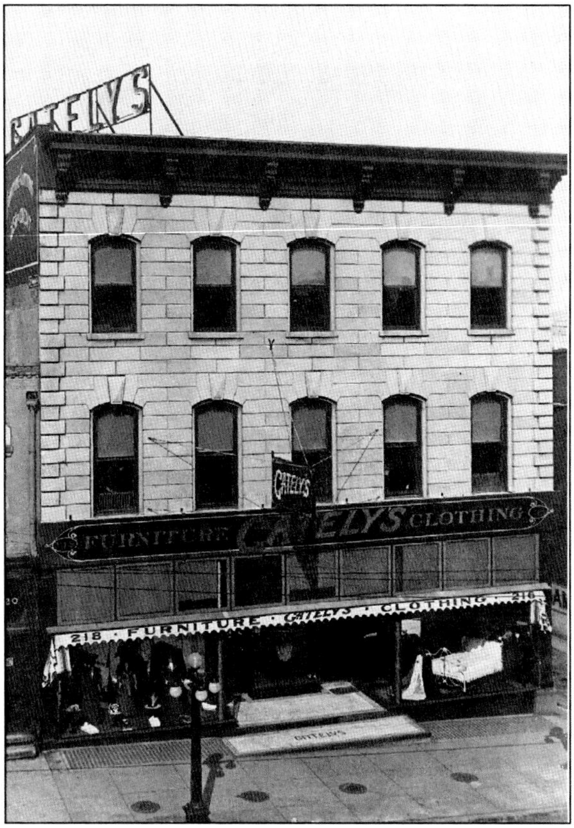

The Gately Furniture and Clothing Store stood on Main Street where the world headquarters of Caterpillar is today. The business opened at this location around 1918 and closed during the early 1930s.

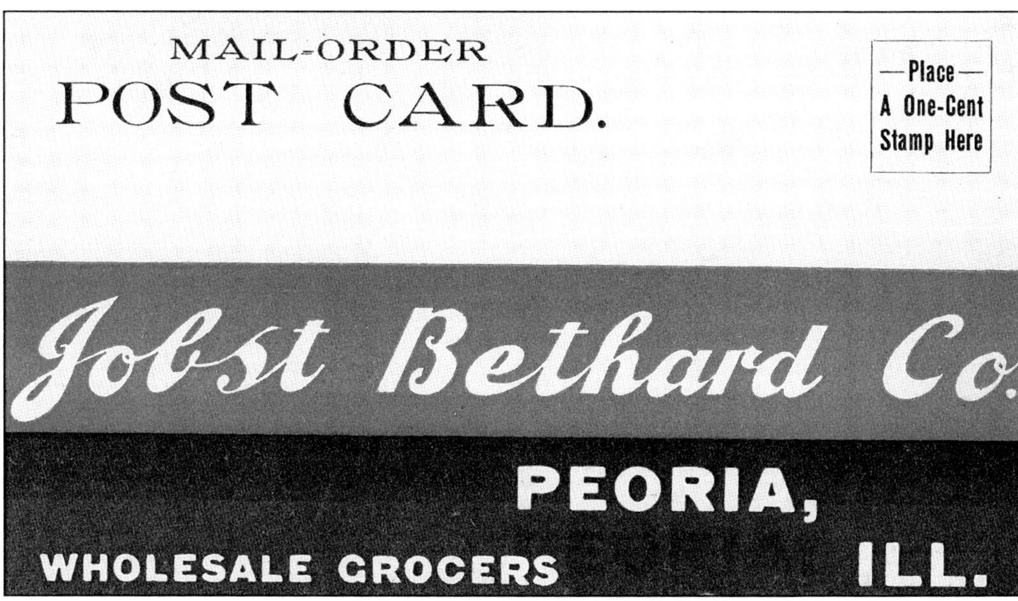

The firm of Jobst-Bethard began as Gauss, Jobst, and Bethard in 1890 on Main Street. In 1911, Jobst-Bethard and Company built a fire-proof warehouse at 801 Southwest Washington. By 1935, small grocery stores were being replaced by the new chains, and this firm discontinued business. The building is still standing today and in the warehouse district of Peoria.

The *Journal Star* newspaper, beginning in the 1920s, formed a birthday club referred to as the Peter Rabbitt Club. The above card was mailed on October 29, 1926. There were several different colors, and this card is actually blue. The club was discontinued and has never been reinstated.

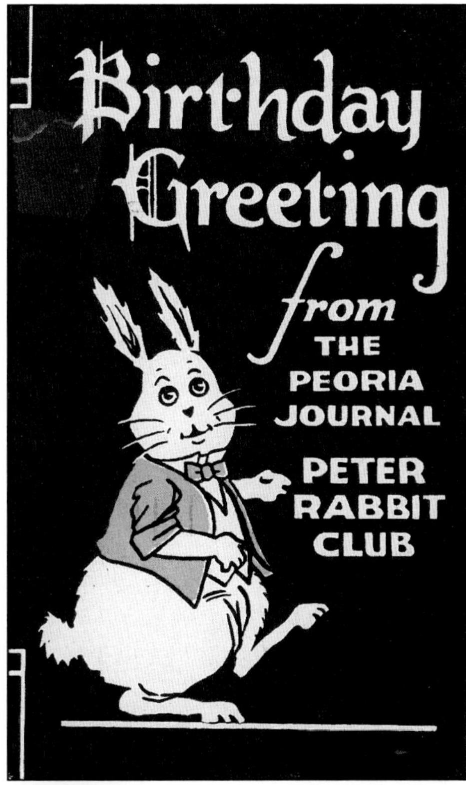

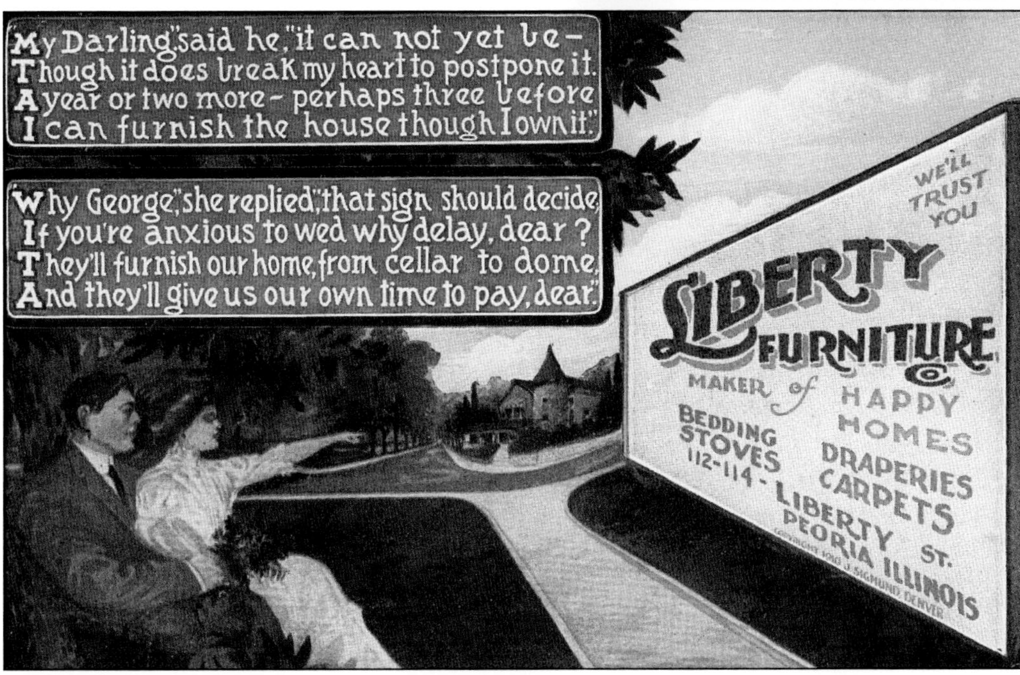

The Liberty Furniture Company stood where the present parking lot of Sears Company is located downtown. The store opened after 1900, and would continue to operate until 1950. The business eventually closed and the Block and Kuhl Warehouse was established.

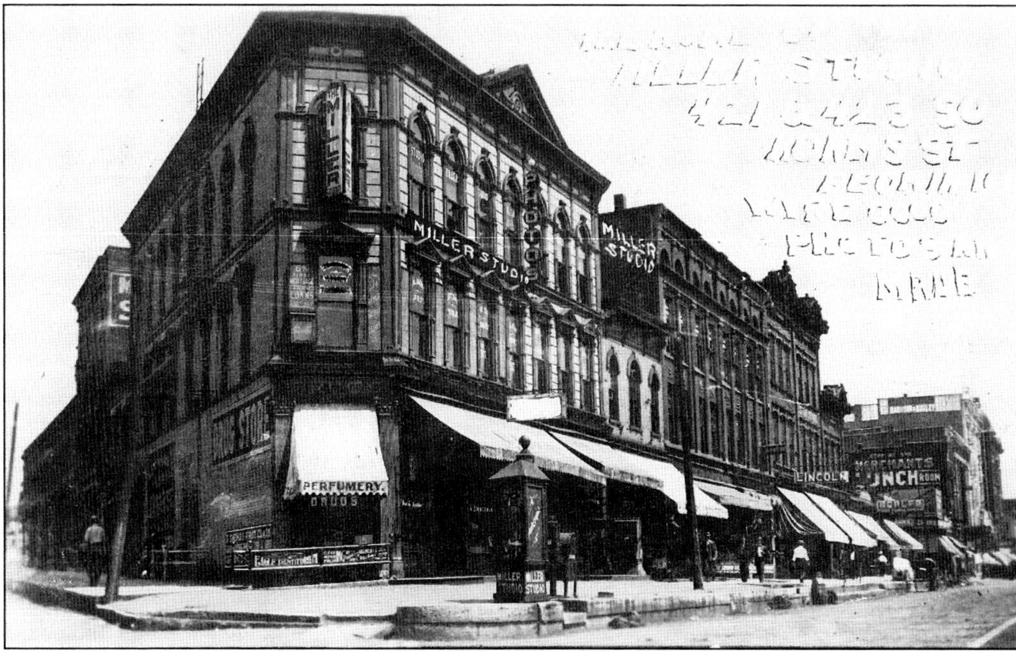

The Miller Studio, which opened around 1905, would operate at this location until 1931. The above card was obviously used for advertising purposes. Twelve high-grade photos, each for $4, were offered in 1910, which is when this card was mailed.

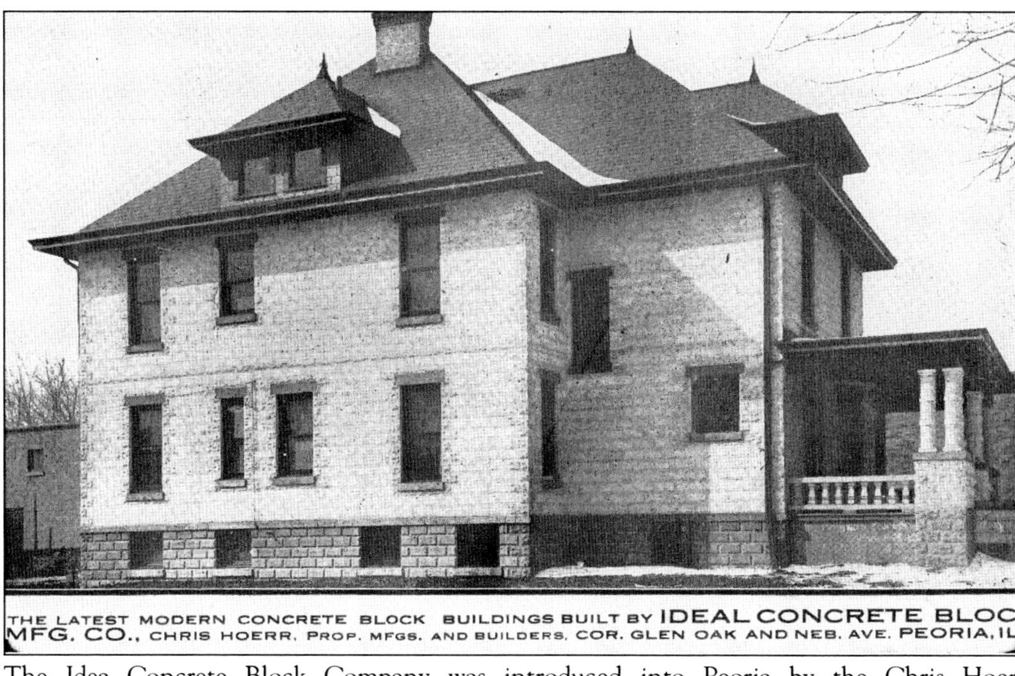

The Idea Concrete Block Company was introduced into Peoria by the Chris Hoerr Company—at that time the company was property manufactures and builders. It was located at Nebraska and Glen Oak. This building material was reasonably successful in Peoria.

Merkle and Sons Monuments, located at 408–410 South Adams Street, is pictured here in 1905. The company was 51 years old at that time and had relocated from Bridge Street, where it had been located since 1854. The building was specially designed to handle the heavy weight of the many monuments and markers made and stored here. It burned in 1983 and never reopened.

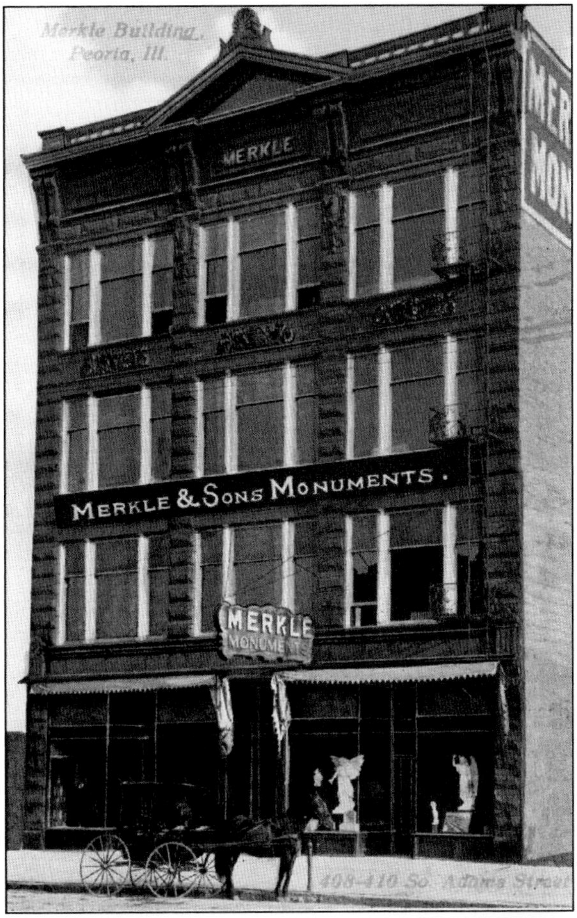

This is a rare view into the interior of the Schradzki Children's Department near the turn of the century, when the store was located at Adams and Liberty Streets. The company began in 1854. Schradzkis was Illinois's first air-conditioned store. The decision to close this and all remaining stores occurred in 1986. This closing was the end of the nation's oldest store still owned and managed by the same founding family.

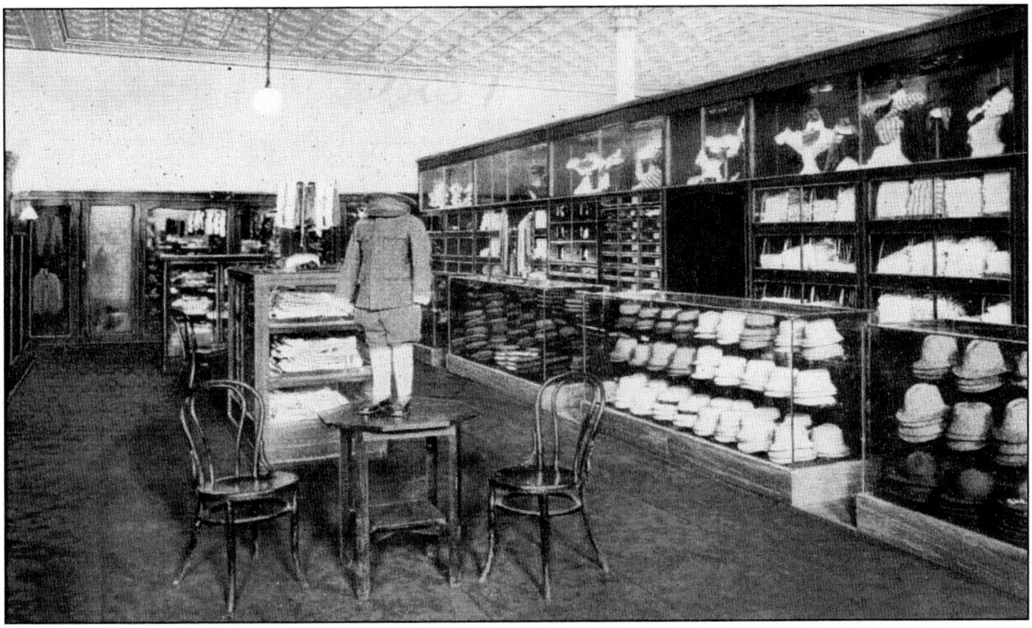

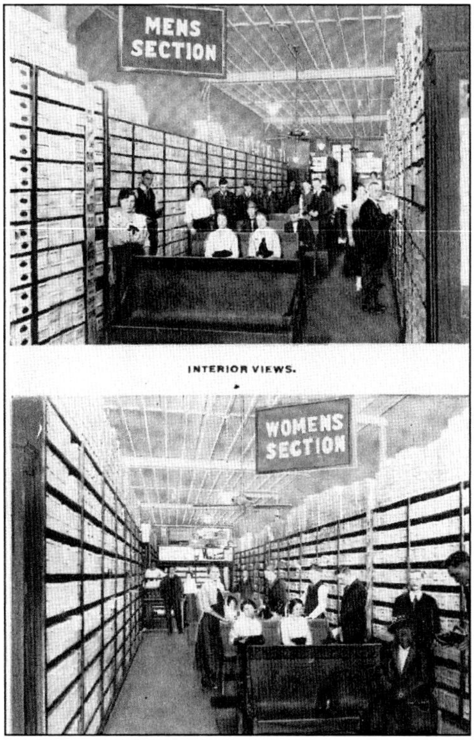

The G.R. Kinney and Company Shoe Store used this postcard for the new chain store in Peoria. At the time the card was mailed there were 64 stores in the chain. This store was located at 413 South Adams. Opening at that location in 1913, the store eventually moved to 315 Southwest Adams. By 1958, a store had opened at 4125 North Sheridan Road in Sheridan Village. In 1971, a store also opened in the Northwoods Mall, where it operates today.

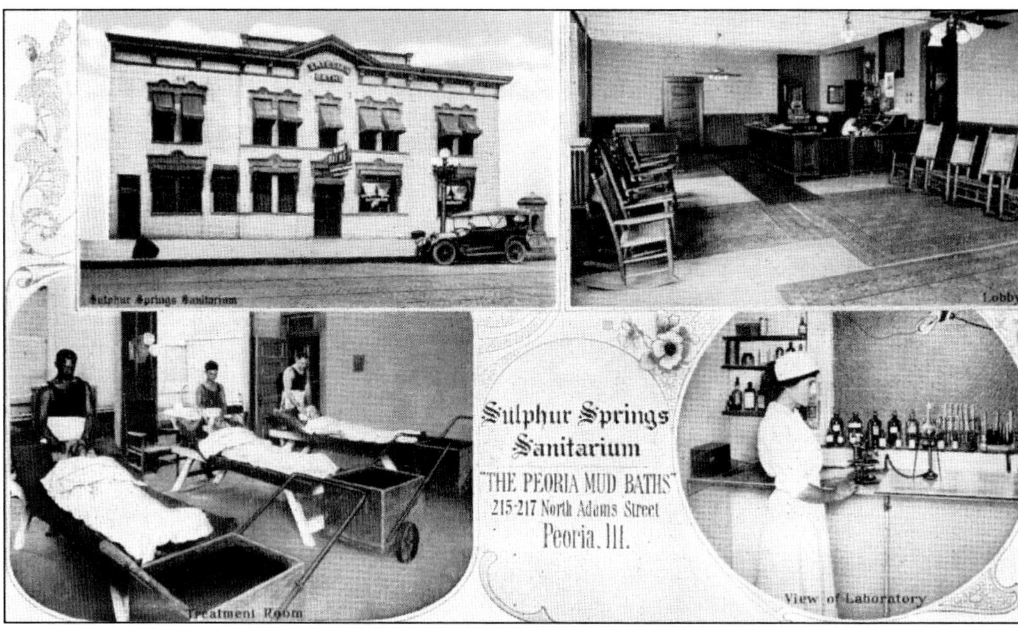

Erected before 1885, the Sulphur Springs Sanitarium stood at 211 Northeast Adams. Their specialty was "mud bath" treatments "paraexcellence" for the elimination of poison from the system. Thousands of cases of rheumatism, neuralgia, neuritis, gout, lumbago sciatic, and certain kidney diseases were treated. Interested parties would write for details and pricing. The building was razed for the construction of the National Building in 1926. Today Peorians know the structure as the Packard Building.

The main office of the Peerless Cleaning and Dying Company was located at 614 Main Street. However, the processing plant was at another location. The company would function at this location until 1937, when the business closed. The Commercial Travelers Building and Loan would occupy the site until razed in 1966, when it became a part of the public library side area.

MAIN OFFICE AND FINISHING DEPARTMENT, PEERLESS CLEANING AND DYEING CO., 614 MAIN ST., PEORIA, ILL.

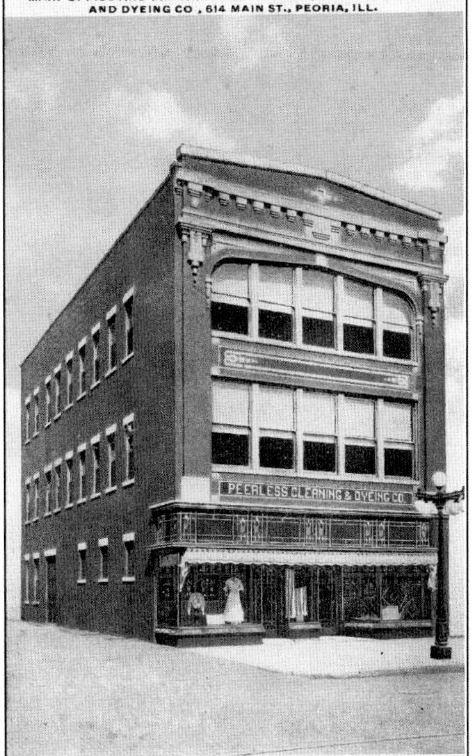

"THE PLANT THAT QUALITY BUILT."

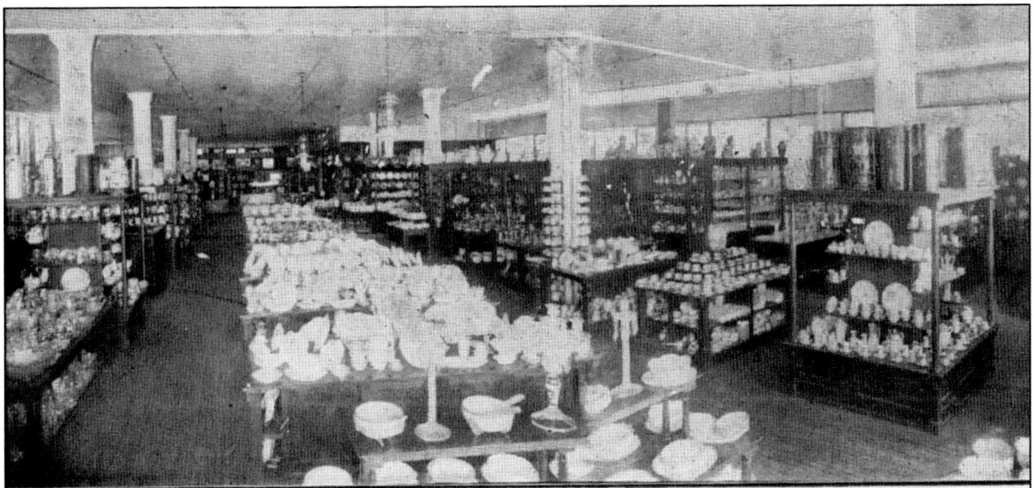

CHINA STORE, SEVENTH FLOOR, SCHIPPER & BLOCK'S, PEORIA, ILL.

The Schipper and Block Company was founded in 1860 in Pekin, Illinois. Moving to Peoria in 1879, the company moved several times before a home was built at the southeast corner of Adams and Fulton Streets in 1905. The name changed to Block and Kuhl in 1914. Carson Pirie and Scott acquired the store building in 1959. Another move occurred in 1974, to Northwoods Mall. Jefferson Bank acquired the building in 1978. Today it is the Bank One building.

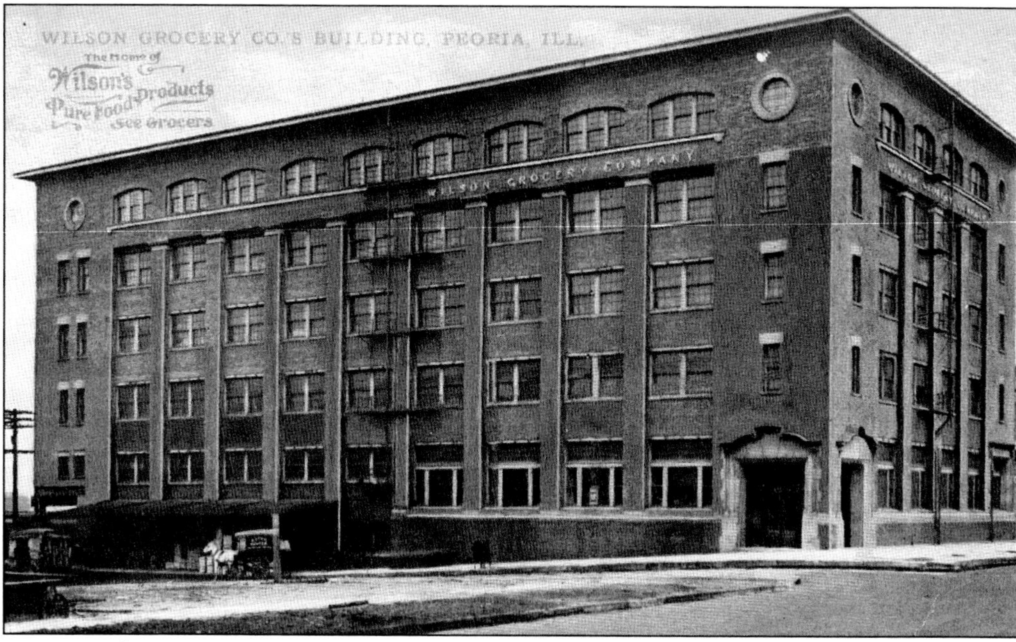

Hewitt and Emerson built the above building in 1904, at a cost of $75,000, for the Wilson Grocery Company. John Wilson founded the business and controlled several others. The company continued until the Depression, when it was forced to close. Later, Cohen's Furniture Company used it as a warehouse. The building still stands, awaiting another use.

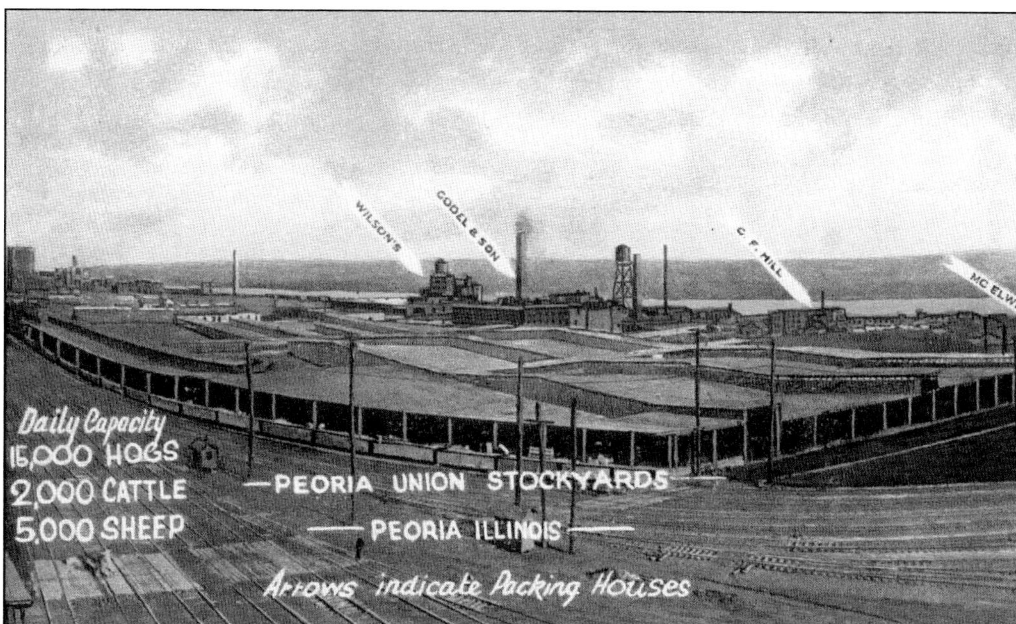

Beef and pork-related businesses have had roots in Peoria as far back as 1837. By the 1870s, herds of livestock were butchered at the Union Stockyards. The above postcard shows four different packers. The Peoria markets serviced Chicago, New York, and Boston markets. Today this industry still flourishes at the Illinois River site.

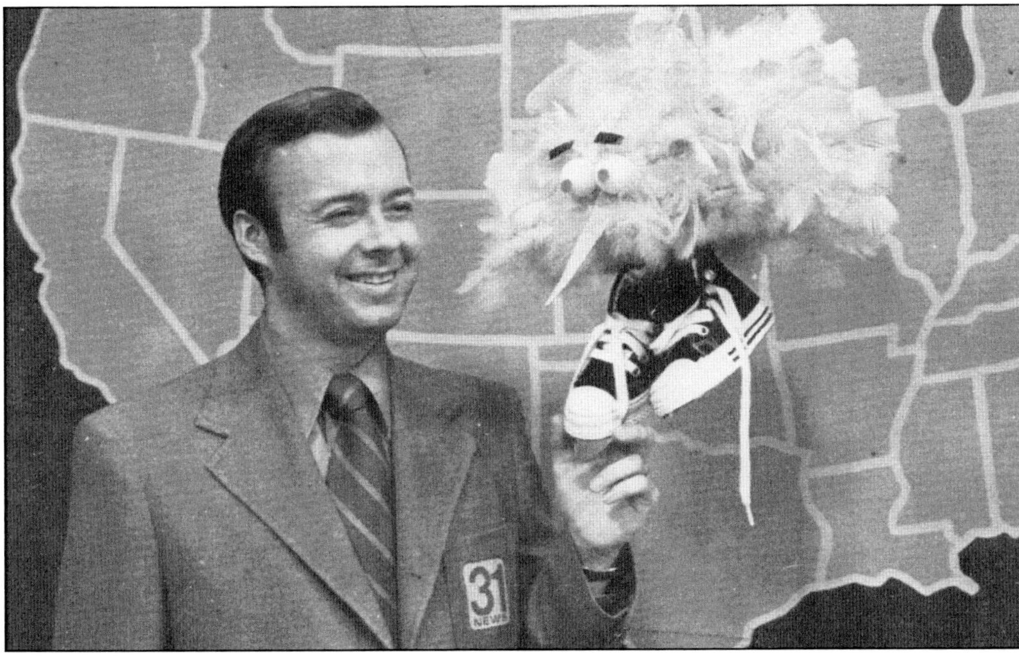

Television station WMBD, Channel 31, mailed out these promotional cards to interested parties during the years 1976–77. The gimmick was a small bird named Simon Degree, who delivered the weather news of John Day, as pictured. Once, Simon Degree fell and required medical attention.

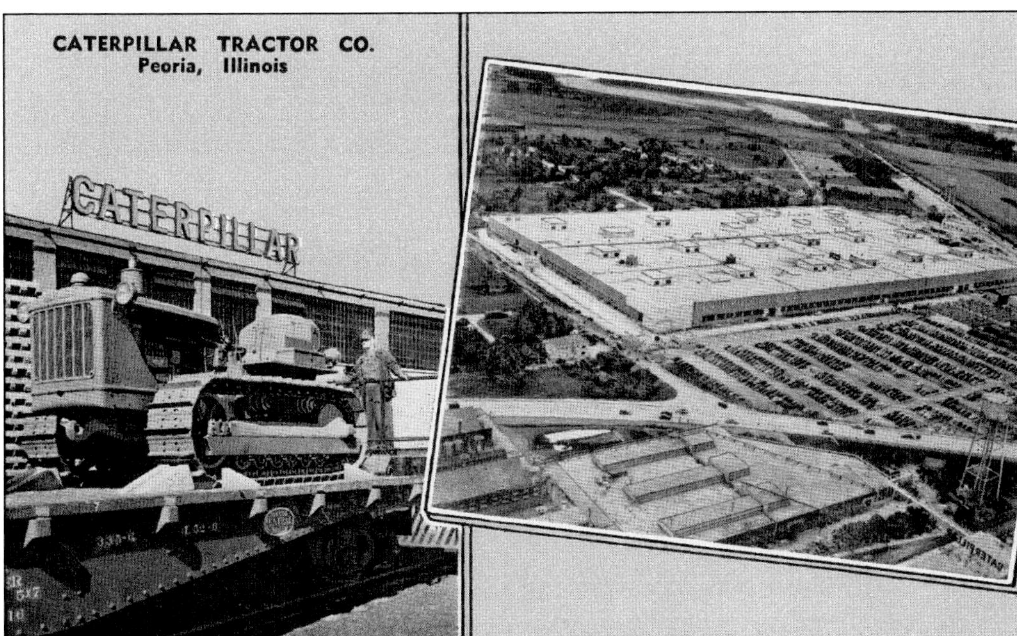

Caterpillar, Inc., came to the Peoria area in 1907 as the Holt Manufacturing Company, through the purchase of the empty Colean Manufacturing Works in East Peoria. The name Caterpillar Tractor Company was adopted in 1925. Pictured above is the Caterpillar Tractor Company East Peoria works, as it appeared in the 1960s.

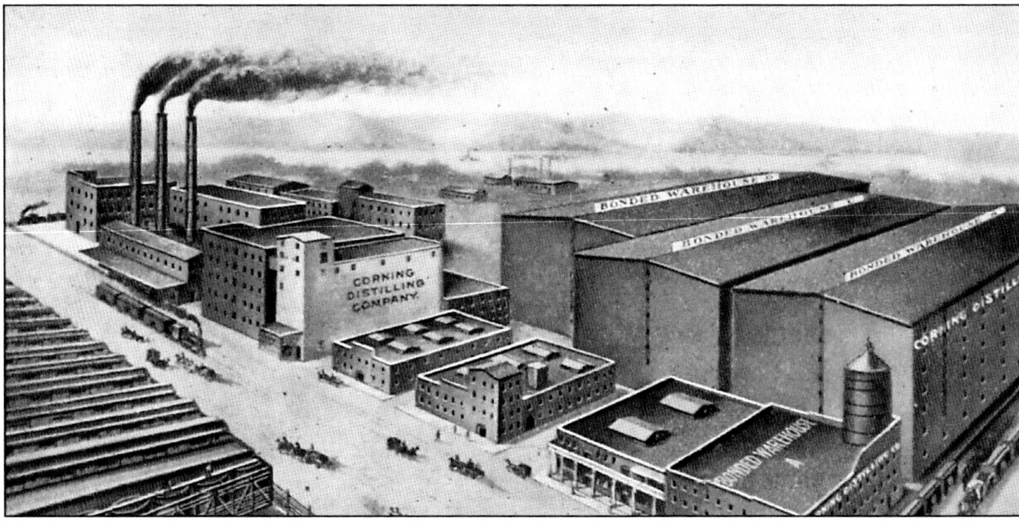

As with the Woolners Brothers, another family, the Cornings Brothers—Franklin, Charles, and Warren—came to Peoria in 1880 and established the Corning and Company Distilleries at the foot of Western Street. The most expensive fire in distillery history occurred on June 4, 1904. Three thousand herd of cattle, 14 lines, and 130,000 gallons of whiskey were destroyed. One source reported the final damage at $4 million. Recovering from this disaster, the distillery would function until 1919, when Prohibition set in. Cornings became Penn-Maryland, and was the first in Illinois to open after Prohibition. In 1935, the Century Distilling Company acquired the Penn-Maryland, and by 1944 both former plants (Corning and Atlas) were merged. Distilling ceased in the 1960s, and today N.E. Finch uses some of the buildings as storage.

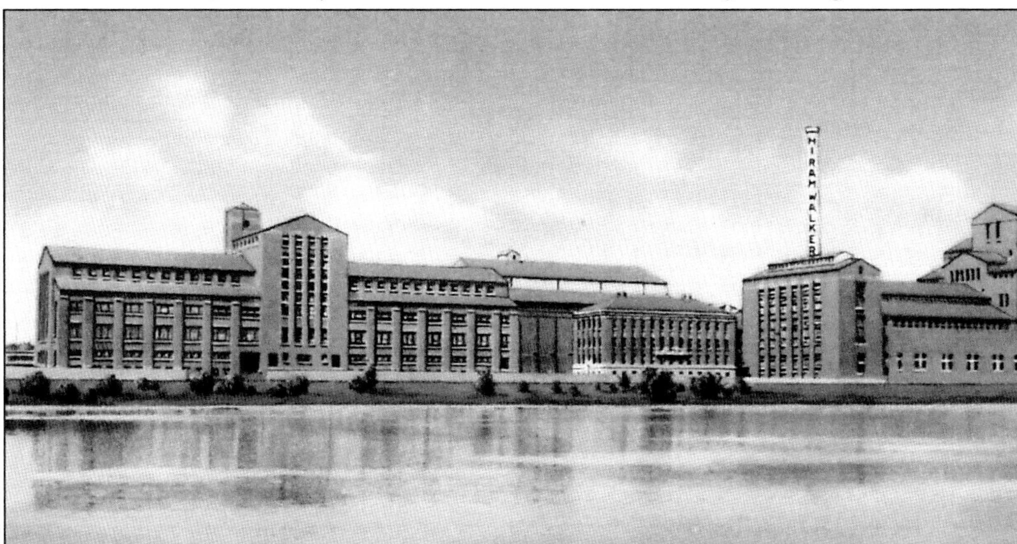

William E. Hull, newly defeated candidate for Congress, approached Hiram Walker and Sons of Canada to return distilling to Peoria. Hull, formally a distiller, lobbied and persuaded this company to locate in Peoria. In 1933, plans were laid out, and on July 4, 1934, at a cost of $12 million, the above plant opened. Hull would remain general manager until his death in 1942. By 1982 the plant closed, and operations were turned over to ADM, which still operates the plant.

Eight

PARKS

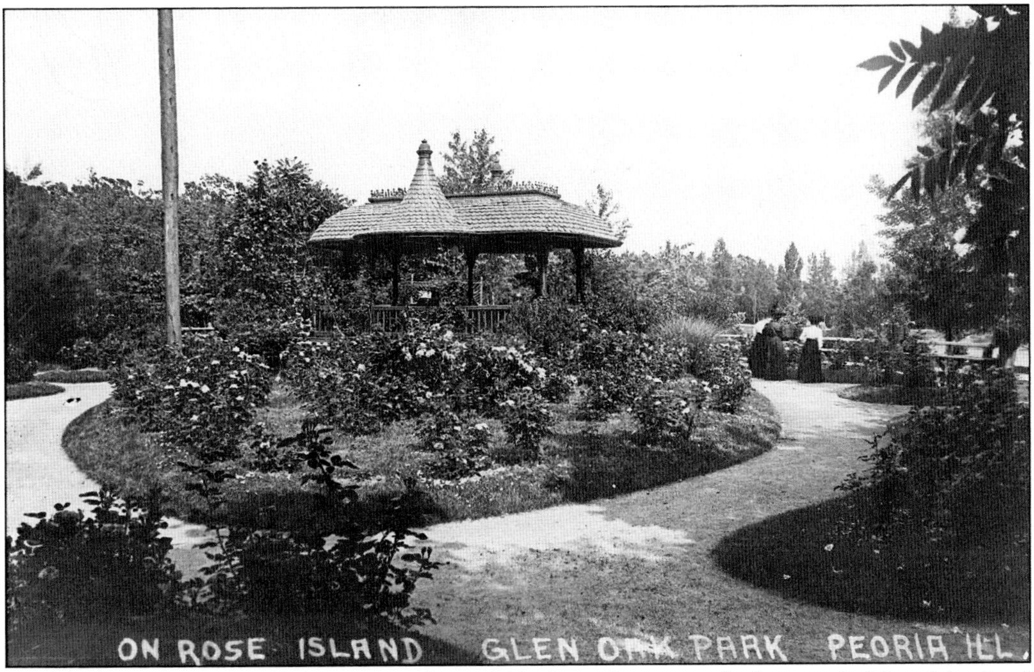

The Peoria park system was organized in 1893 through a special election held in March of that year. As a result, the citizens of Peoria now take great pride in their park system. The first purchase for this new broad acreage was known as Birkett Hollow. Consisting of 72 acres, it cost $60,000 in 1894. Small tracts were later added. Work began immediately, and Rose Island was opened. The above card shows an island in the artificial lake.

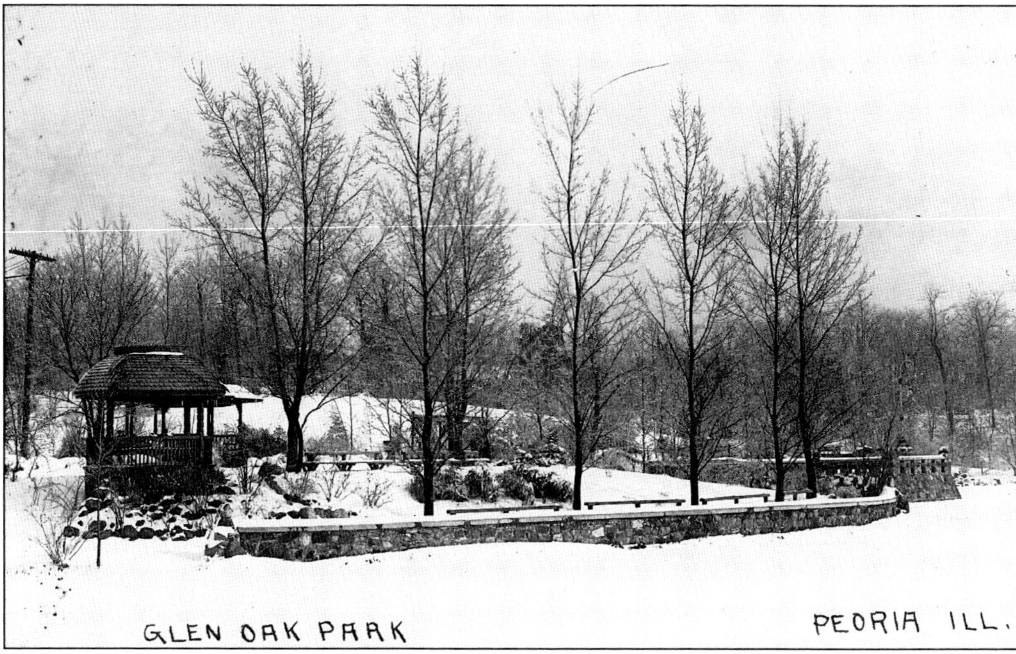

Pictured above is a winter scene in 1912. The park board moved quickly to create the walks and gazebos.

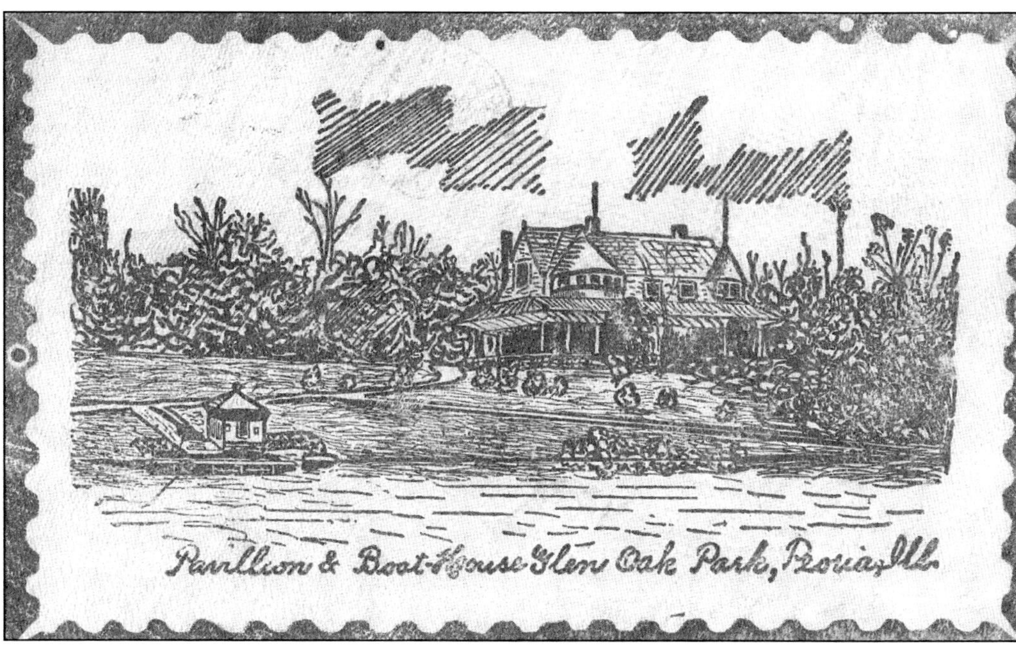

The only leather card used in this book is pictured above. Used many years as the administration offices and a dome pavilion, this building still stands near the center of the park. Recently, the park board administration moved to the Knoxville area.

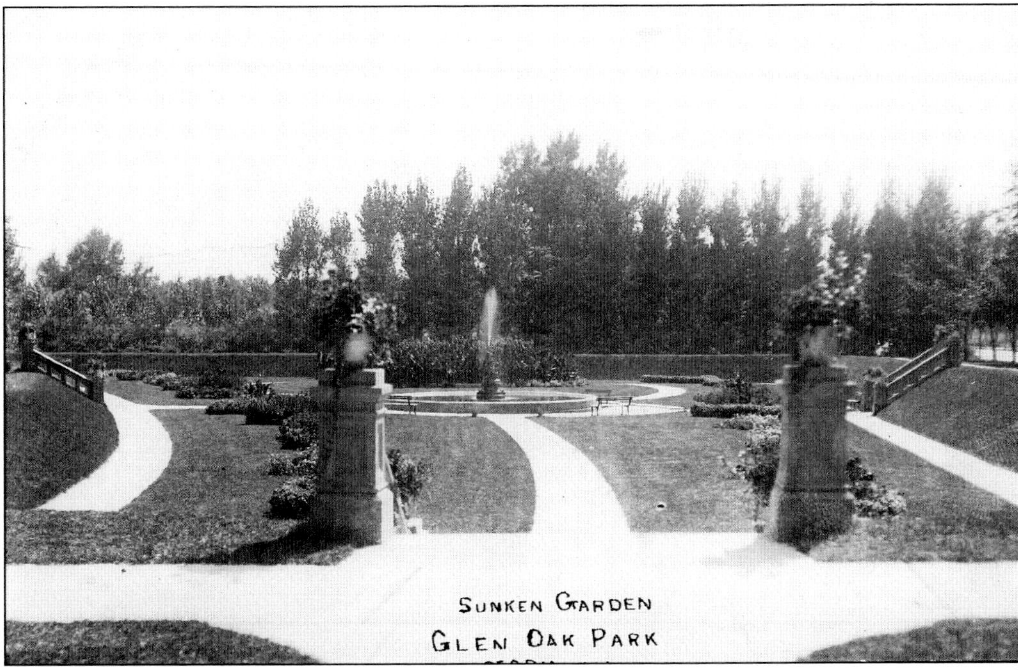

Glen Oak Park is probably the most photographed of all Peoria parks. There are more cards produced with illustrations from Glen Oak than any other park in Peoria. The postcard above illustrates how much progress had been made by 1912, when this card was mailed. This sunken garden was destroyed in 1954.

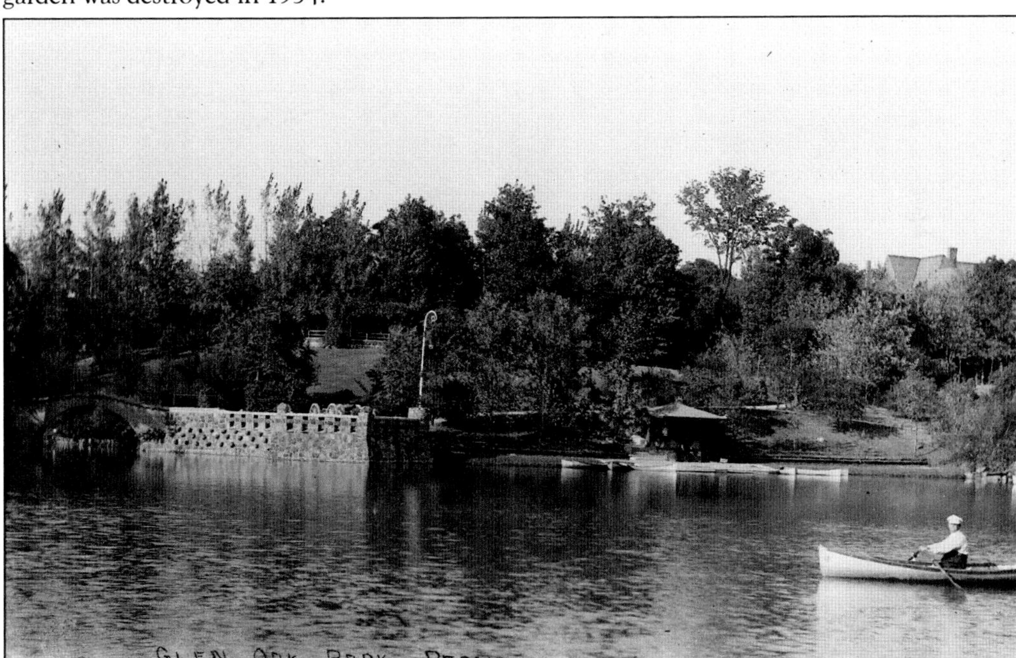

An artificial lake was created at Glen Oak to accommodate the many boaters that enjoyed the sport. This card shows the boathouse, plus several additional rentable boats. In the background, to the right, was the administration office.

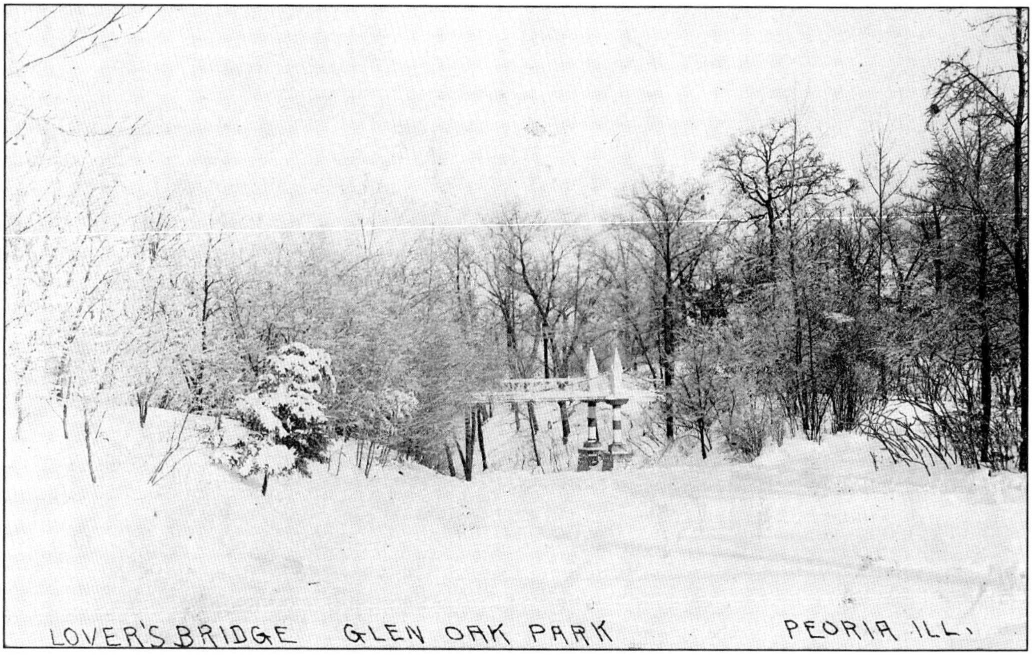

This winter scene was mailed in 1909. The metal bridge, appropriately called "Lover's Bridge" here, was also known as the "suspension bridge." Today, it still exists and is enjoyed by yet another generation.

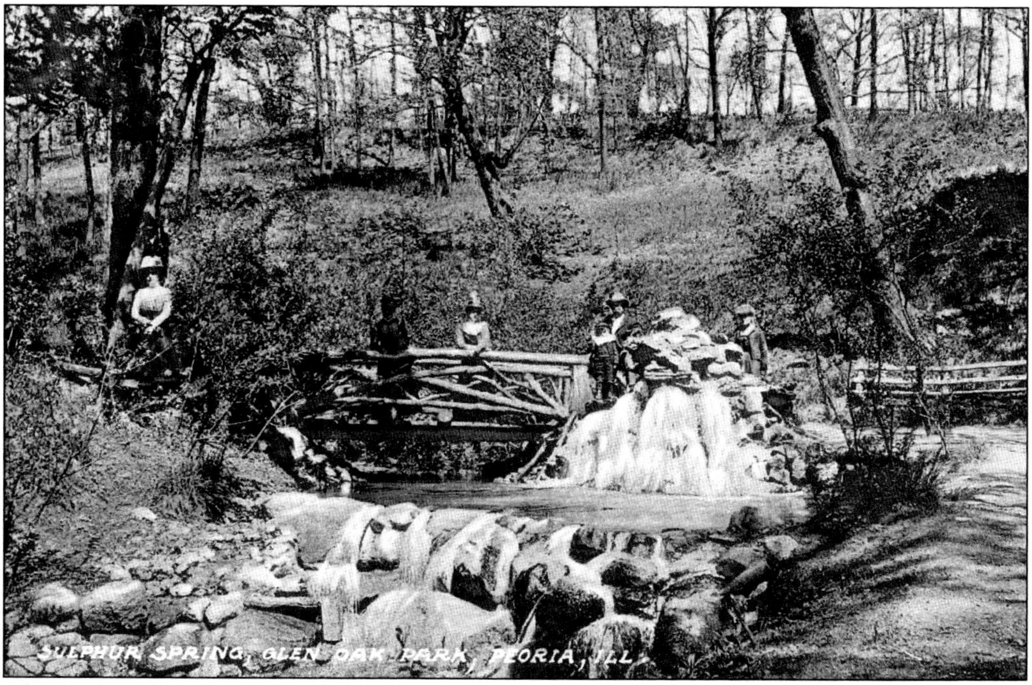

Glen Oak Park was also known for its sulphur spring. This postcard shows the size of the flowing spring, which was a popular place to visit during the summer months.

In the beginning, Bradley Park was the largest park in the Peoria system. It was a gift from Mrs. Lydia Bradley. In her later years, Mrs. Bradley named a portion of the park in her late daughter's honor. This was one plan for her to dispose of her immense fortune. The other was to establish Bradley University near the park. This card was mailed in 1911. Its location in the park is undetermined.

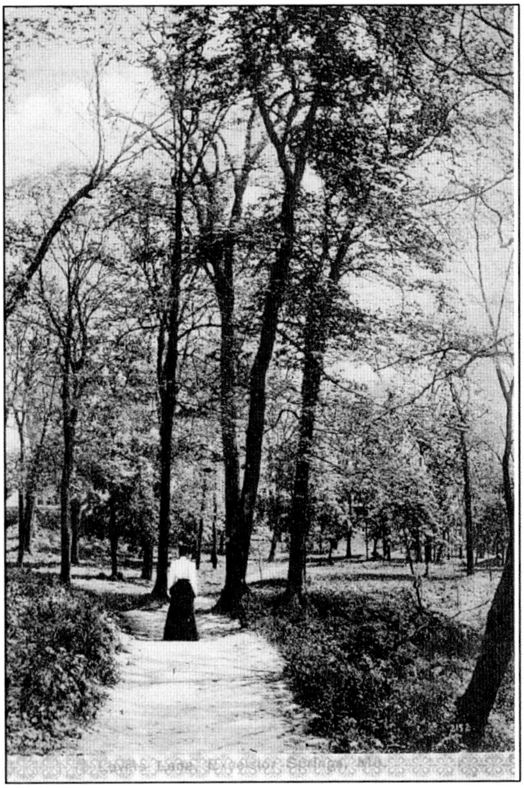

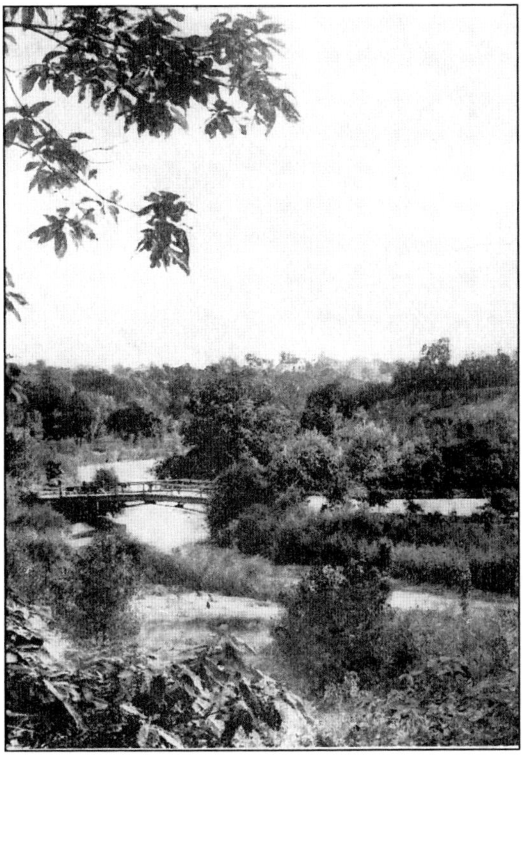

To perpetuate the name of Bradley and give joy to untold thousands, the gift of Bradley Park was made. Thus a park was established with dry run creeks winding through the center. The beautiful hills and hollows were quickly created for citizens' use. The bridge pictured here is still in use today.

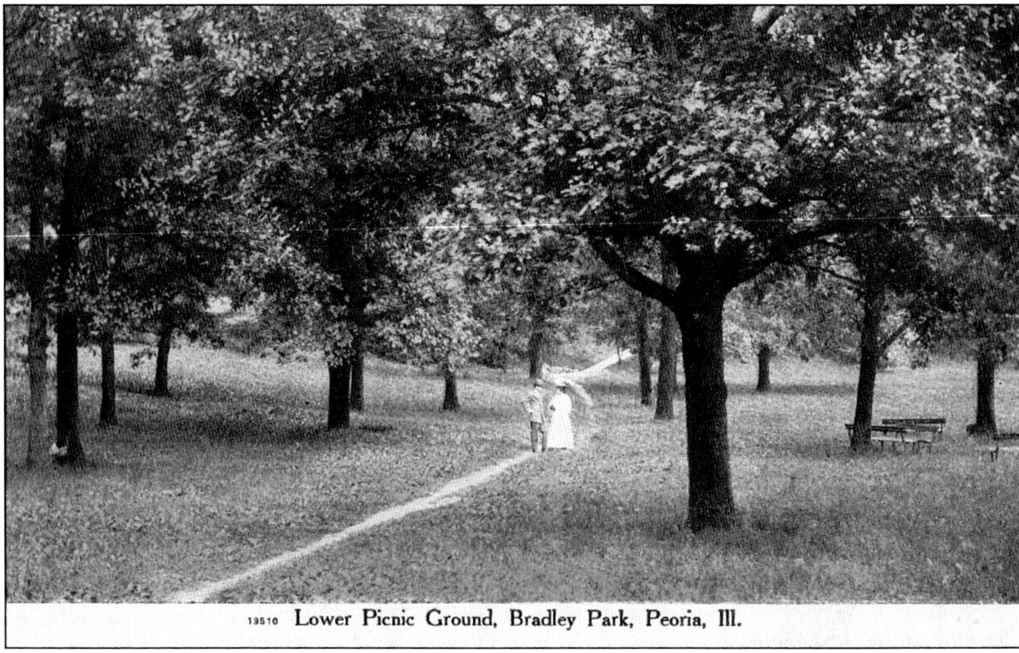

Bradley Park is today commonly divided into upper and lower Bradley Park. This card, mailed in 1909, is the lower area, which now accommodates the baseball diamonds and large picnic area. In winter, the park draws a parade of area residents to sled.

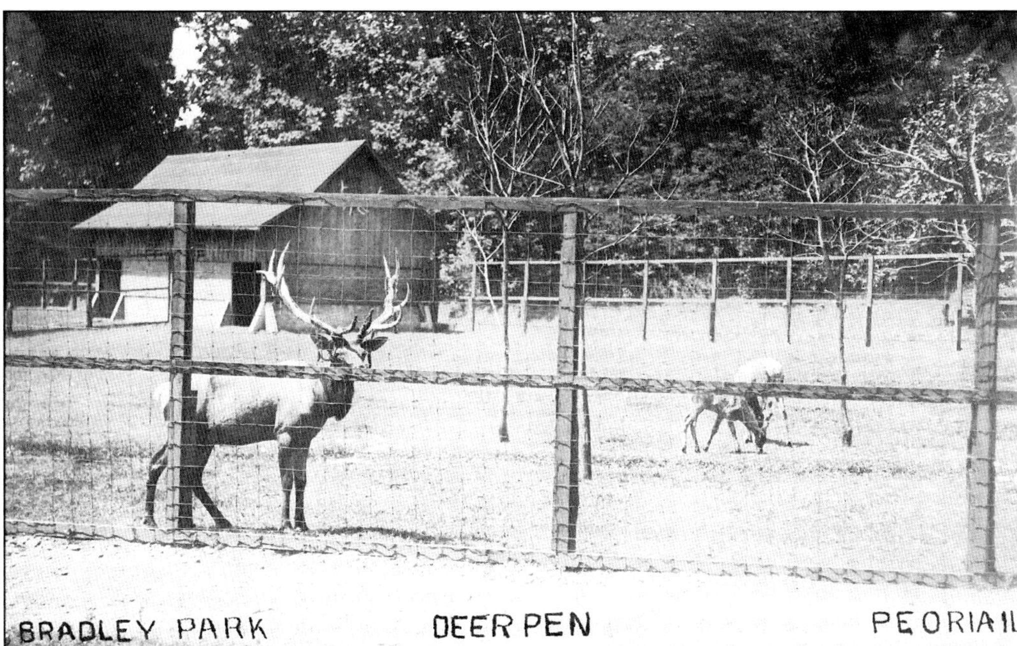

The deer pen was located near upper Bradley Park and was used to house animals and for exhibits. Before the establishment of the Peoria Zoo, animals were housed in several different parks. The deer pen eventually moved to Dettwiller Park.

Dry Run Creek, as evidenced by this wall, wound through Bradley Park long before it was acquired. Pictured here is one side of the creek, which partially divides the lower part. Water flows here spontaneously throughout the year.

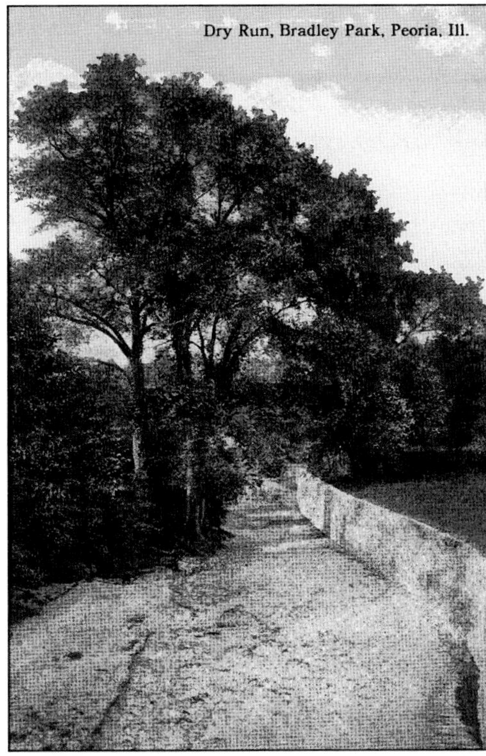

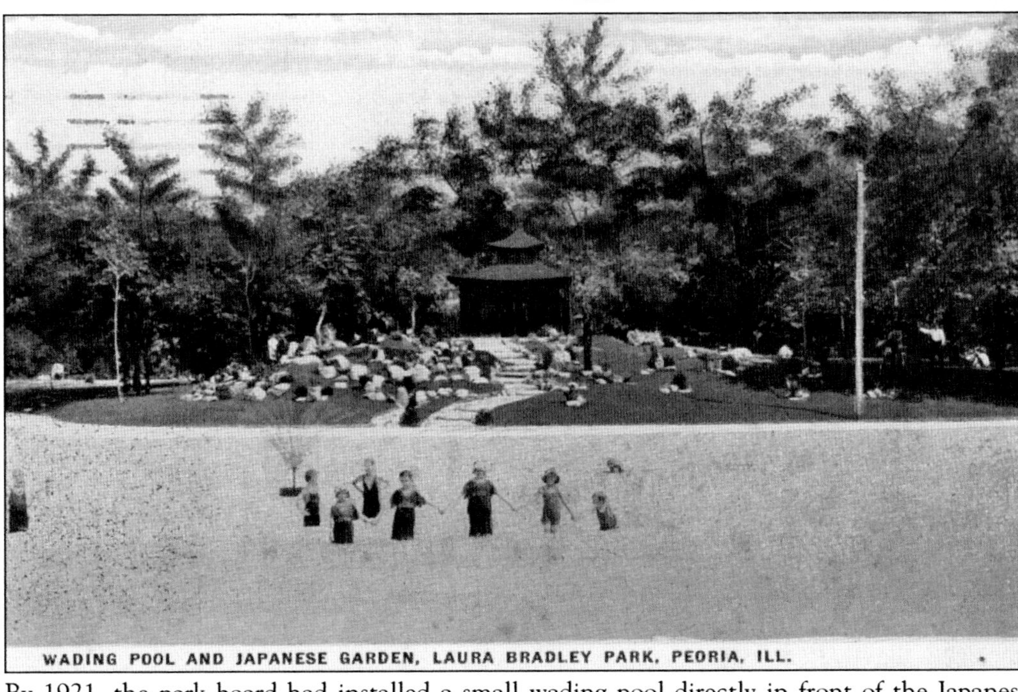

By 1921, the park board had installed a small wading pool directly in front of the Japanese garden. For the approach to the garden from Dry Run Creek, a Japanese bridge was constructed in 1922. The garden was removed during World War II, but has been partially restored in recent years.

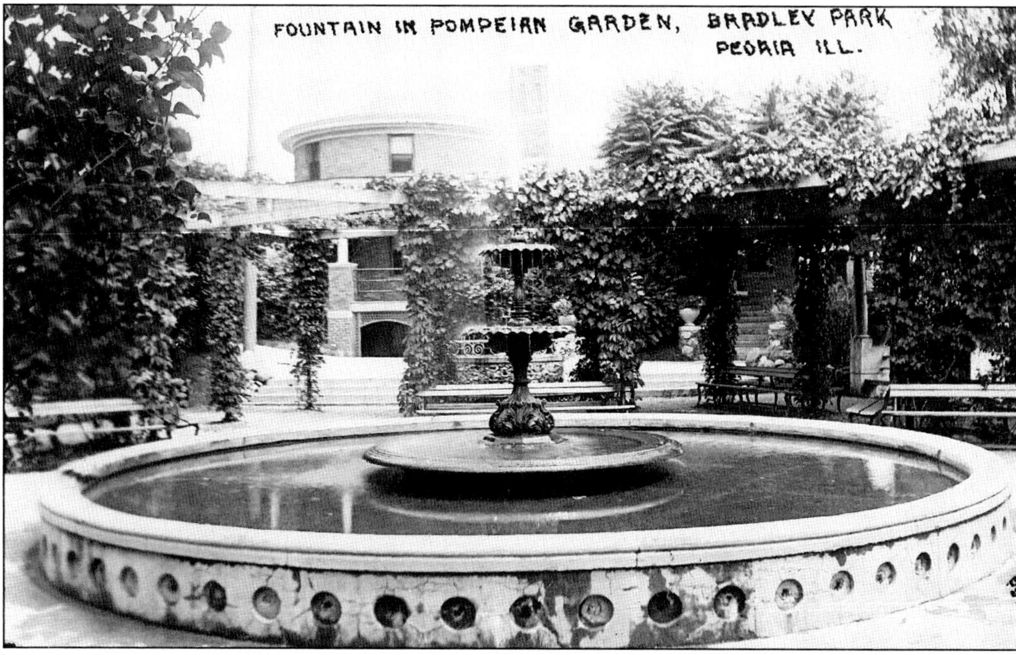

During the summer season, upper Bradley Park is visited by local residents and visitors alike. What a surprise it is for them to see this fountain in the Pompeirn Garden. This card, mailed in 1911, indicates the extent to which the park was established to serve the people of Peoria. Today, the garden is gone and very few signs mark its former location.

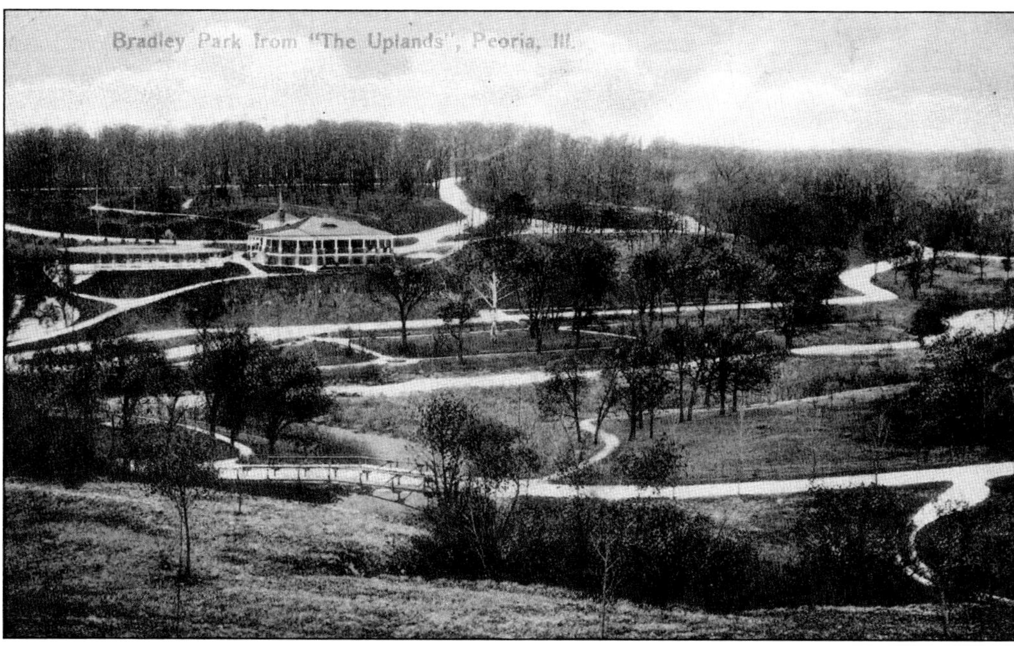

By 1910, Bradley Park was complete, as evidenced by this panoramic view from the nearby subdivision known as the Uplands. Even the woods in the background are untouched today. The center pavilion was removed when the cost of maintenance became too high, probably during World War II.

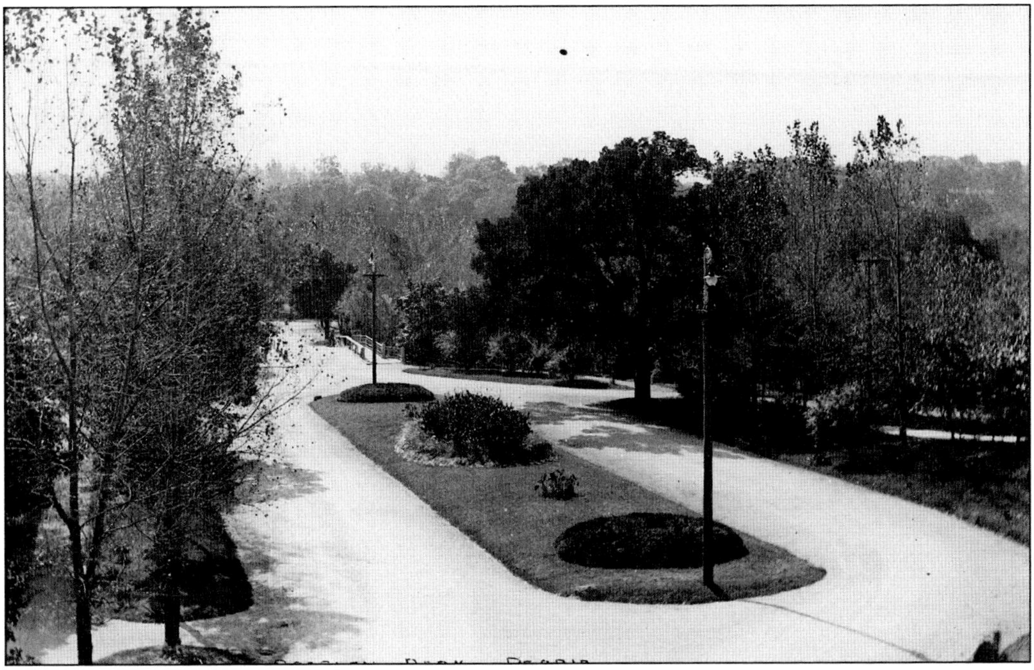

Bradley Park, which now has many drives that accommodate autos, had wide roadways constructed as early as 1912, when this photograph was taken. Flower beds were built and maintained in the center boulevard of the park.

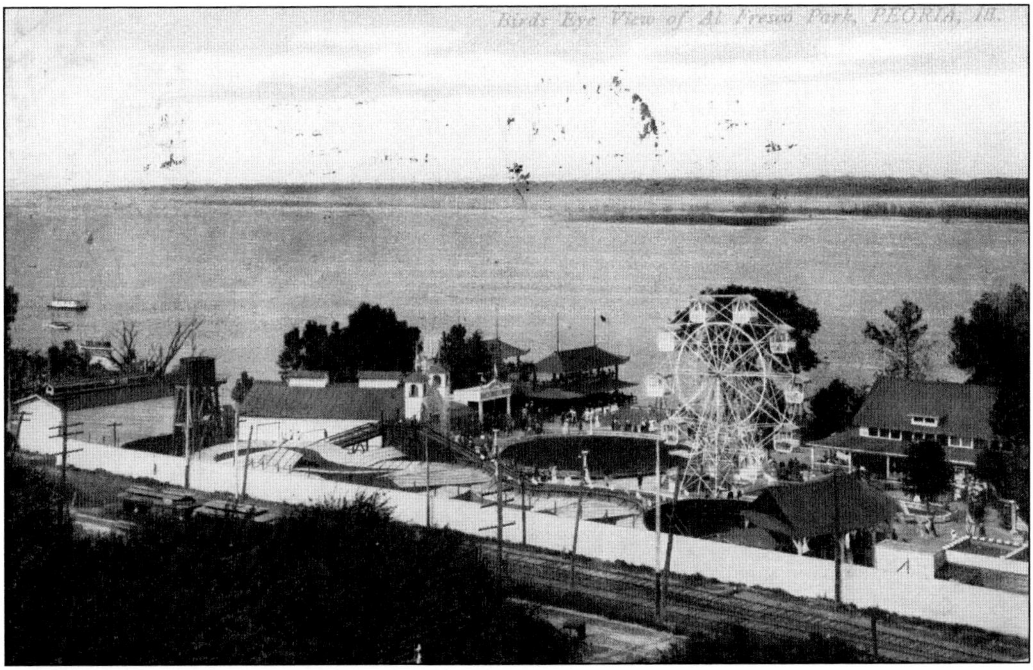

In 1906 the Al Fresco Amusement Park (Spanish for "open air") had its grand opening. Its builder, Vernon Seaver, a Chicago capitalist, patterned the park after the "White City" park in Chicago. The above postcard was mailed on October 16, 1907, one year after the opening. It was located 4.5 miles north of the courthouse in Peoria on the Galena Road.

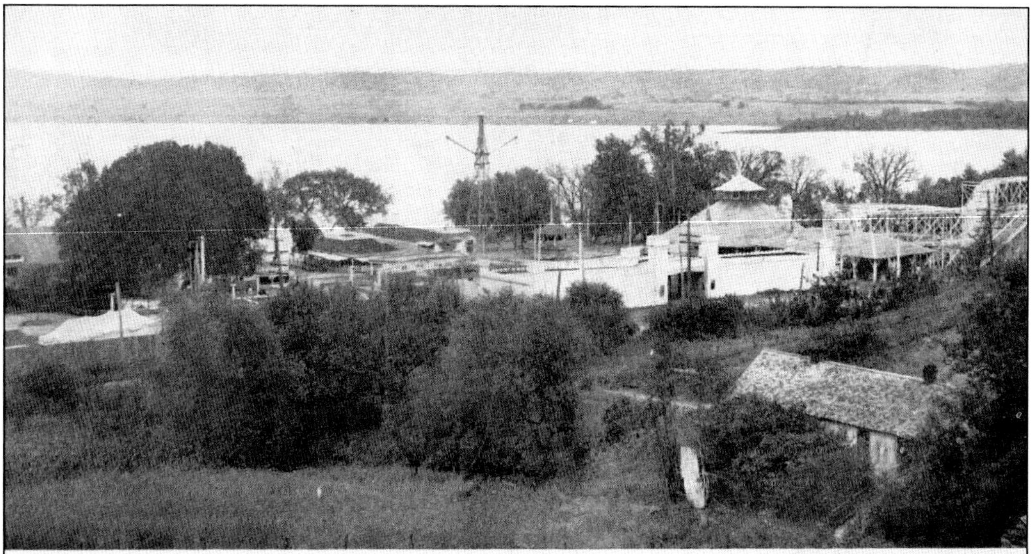

Al Fresco Beach, Peoria, Ill. Peoria Souvenir Co., Box 367

The Al Fresco Park complex consisted of a Ferris wheel, figure-eight roller coaster, giant aerial swing, and a house of mirrors. Located inland were the tunnel of love, a merry-go-round, a North Pole building, and a temple of Palmistry (fortune telling) for 5¢. The beer garden was built overlooking the park, where patrons enjoyed schooners of beer. Most visitors rode the streetcar to the park. An additional streetcar took patrons to Grand View Drive's Gibson Path, where stairs were provided to enhance the view of the Illinois River.

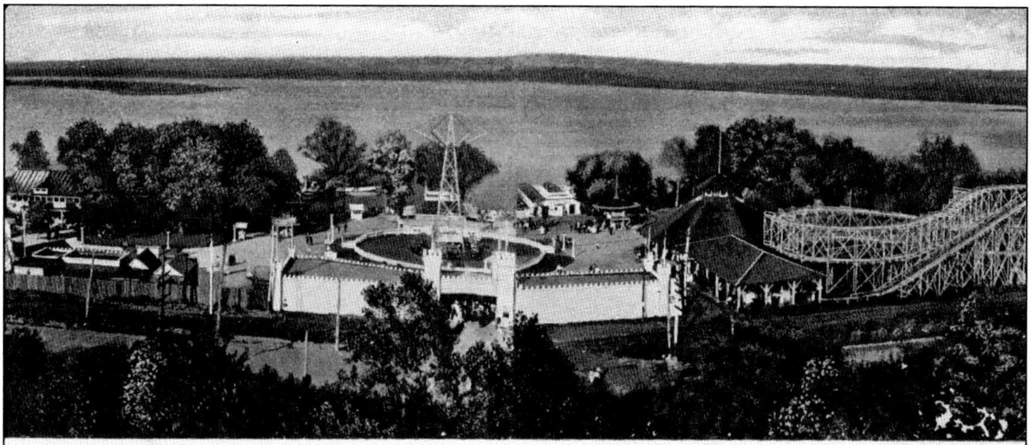

Al Fresco Park, Peoria, Ill.

Free entertainment was provided three times a day. Among the entertainers were John L. Sullivan, Harry Houdini, and Buffalo Bill. Also present were actors Tom Mix and Bill Hart. The park even had a silent screen on the second floor of the pavilion showing silent movies. After World War I, the park was closed and its properties fell into decay. Fred C. Feyler reopened the bathing beach, but in 1944, the shortage of men and material due to the war again caused the park to close. Much later, the site became a mobile home court. Today the land remains undeveloped.

Nine

AROUND TOWN

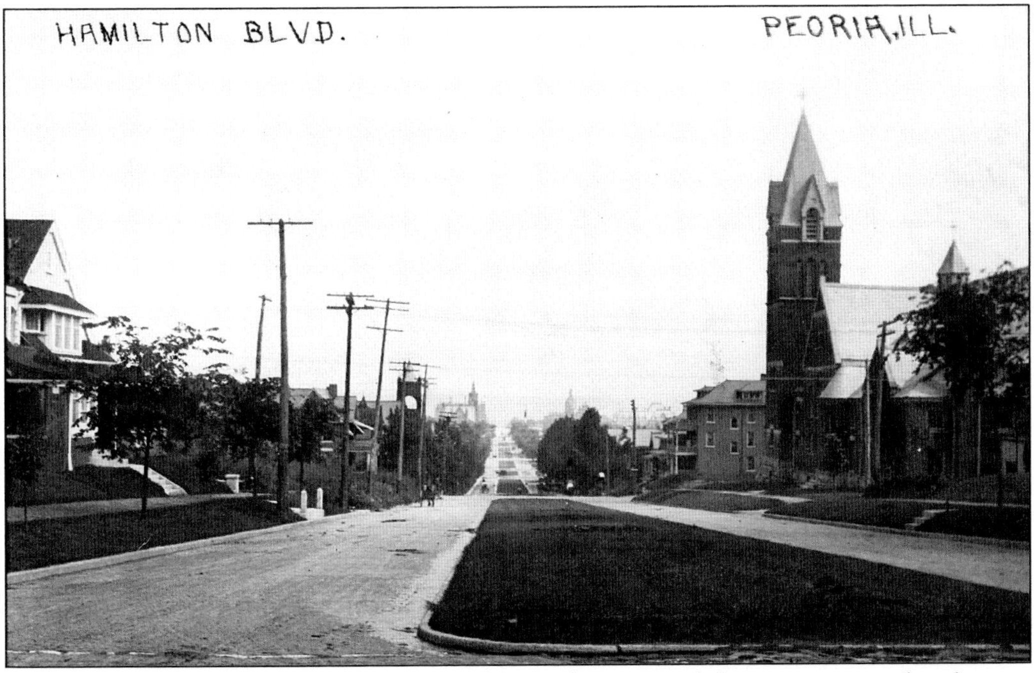

Hamilton Boulevard is pictured here in 1917. Looking toward downtown, two churches are visible. On the left-hand side is the First Baptist Church. On the right is the tower of the First Presbyterian Church.

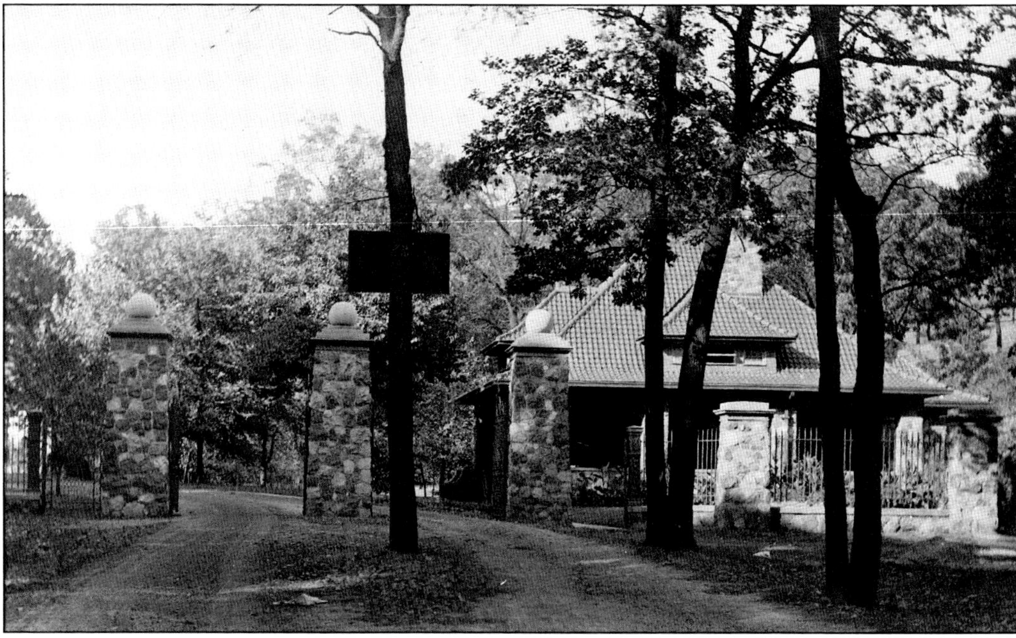

The Springdale Gatehouse was built in 1900 to accommodate the administration and provide lodging for the gatekeeper. The above Japanese-influenced gatehouse is located at the end of Perry Street and was the original entrance to Springdale Cemetery. Both the building and gates were built of natural stone of many colors. The building still stands but suffers from heavy neglect.

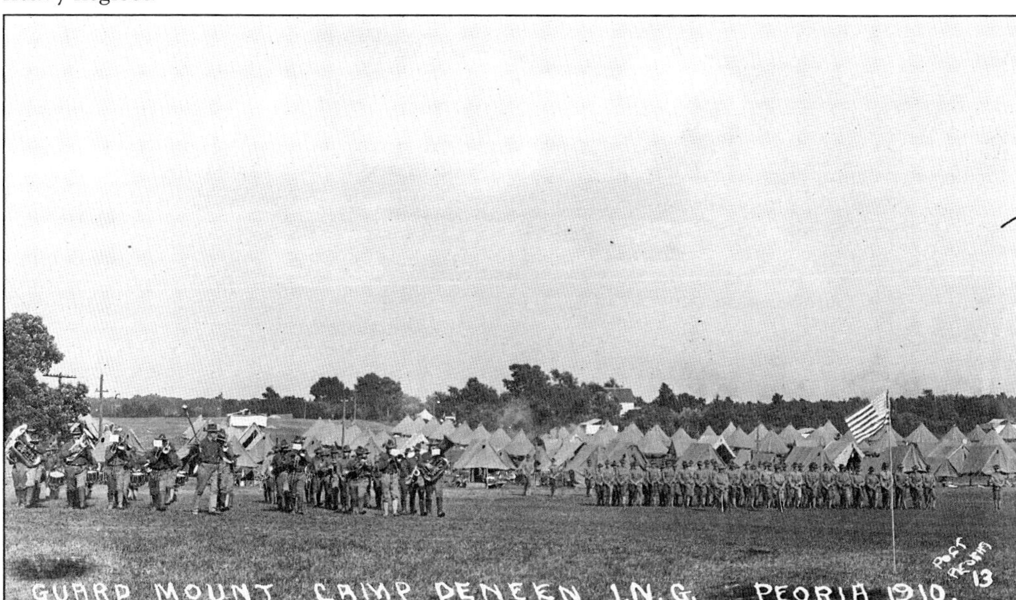

A little-known fact in the military history of Peoria Heights was Camp Deneen. For two weeks in the summer of 1910, the encampment of the Illinois National Guard occupied this site. The camp was so named to honor the governor of Illinois at that time, Charles S. Dineen. It was located on 2 acres of land, north of the railroad tracks to Lake Street, from Monroe to Boulevard. The other boundary was War Memorial Drive to London, from Prospect to Monroe.

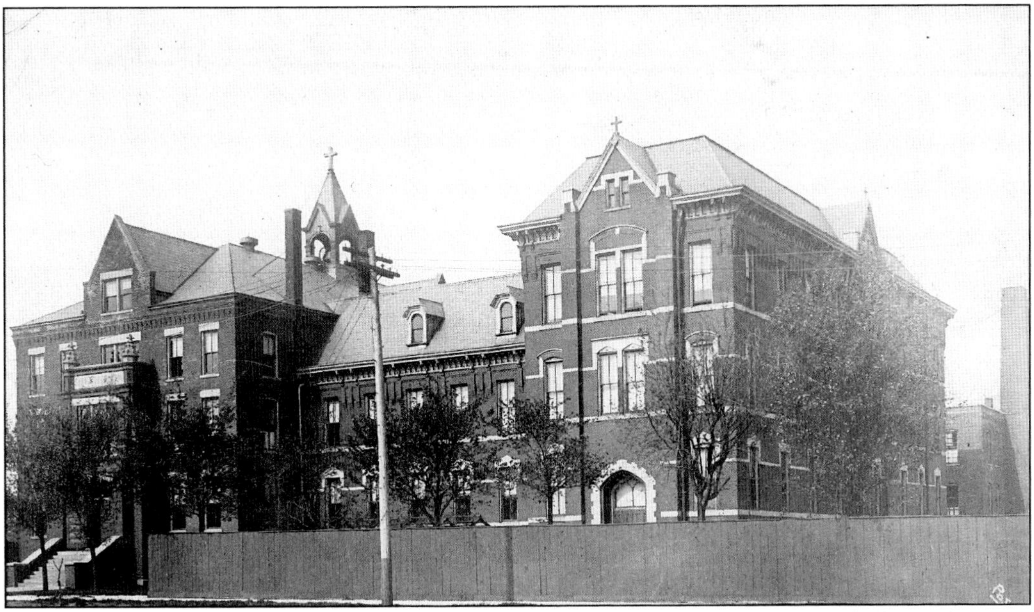

This home, as shown above, was opened in 1891 by John I. Spalding, the first bishop of Peoria. The complex, four-story, brick-and-wood structure was licensed by the state child welfare agency for the care of 70 girls. The convent of the Good Shepherd was located on 4 acres known as 517 Faraday Street and the corner of Starr Street. Finally unable to meet fire requirements, this complex was closed in 1953, and the building was razed in 1956.

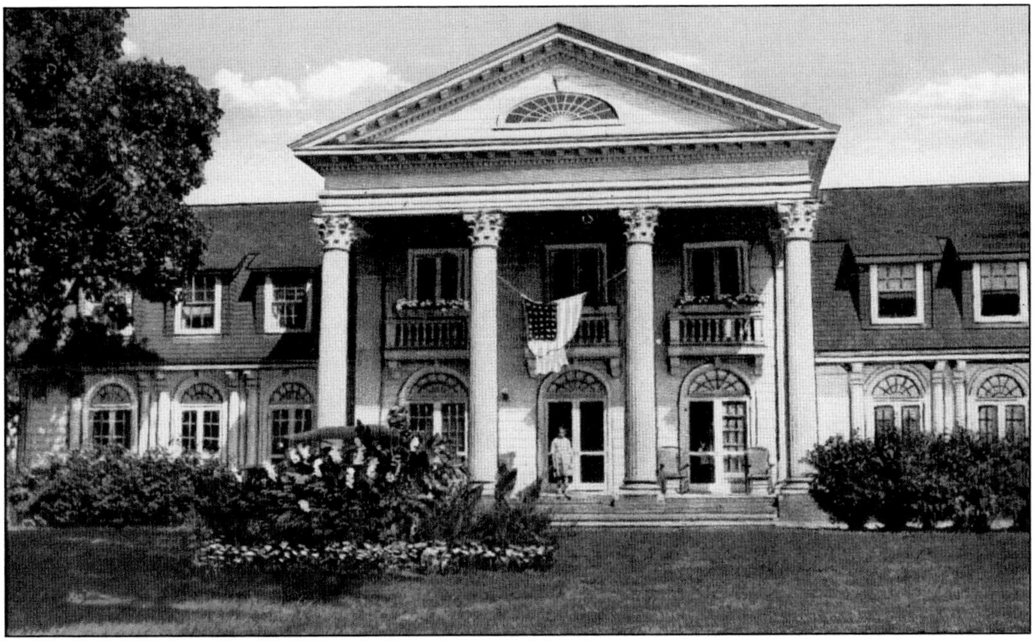

This original "Peoria Automobile Club" was located 17 miles up the Illinois River from Peoria, as shown in this card. The club was incorporated in 1912, and the above building erected. It was a popular social center for ten years but suffered financial difficulties and eventually disbanded. The property was acquired by William Stone, who operated a resort known as Shore Acres for a number of years. Today this property is owned and operated by the Chillicothe Park District.

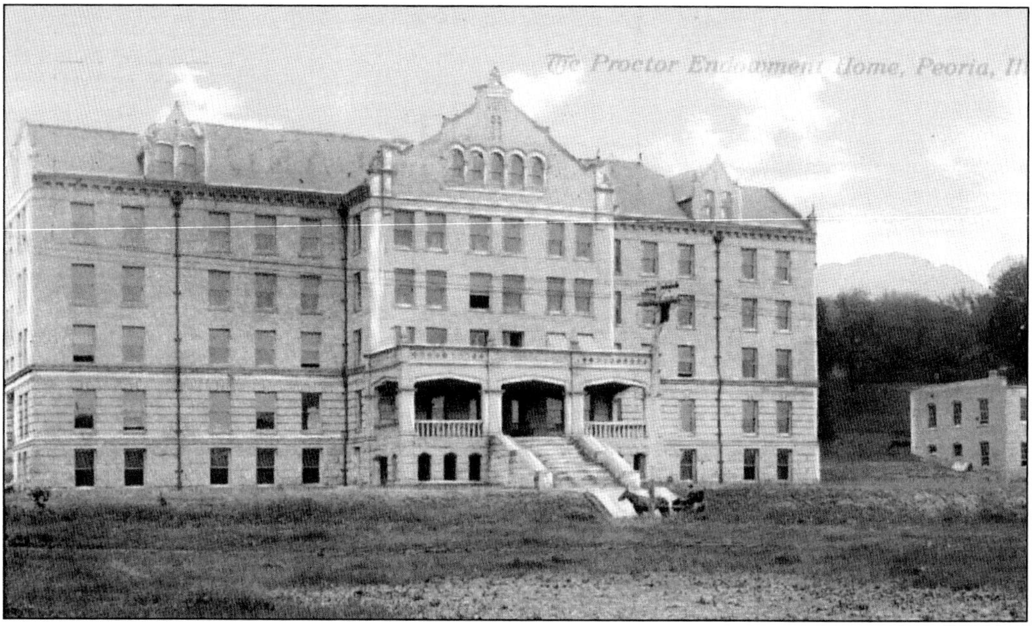

The John C. Proctor Endowment Home was completed in August of 1906. The benefactor, John C. Proctor, was responsible for its creation. The above building is one of the handsomest structures of its kind in the city. It is 160 square feet, four stories in height, and built of grayish Ohio stone. The house is presently located at 1301 Northeast Glen Oak, and the name is now St. Augustine Manor.

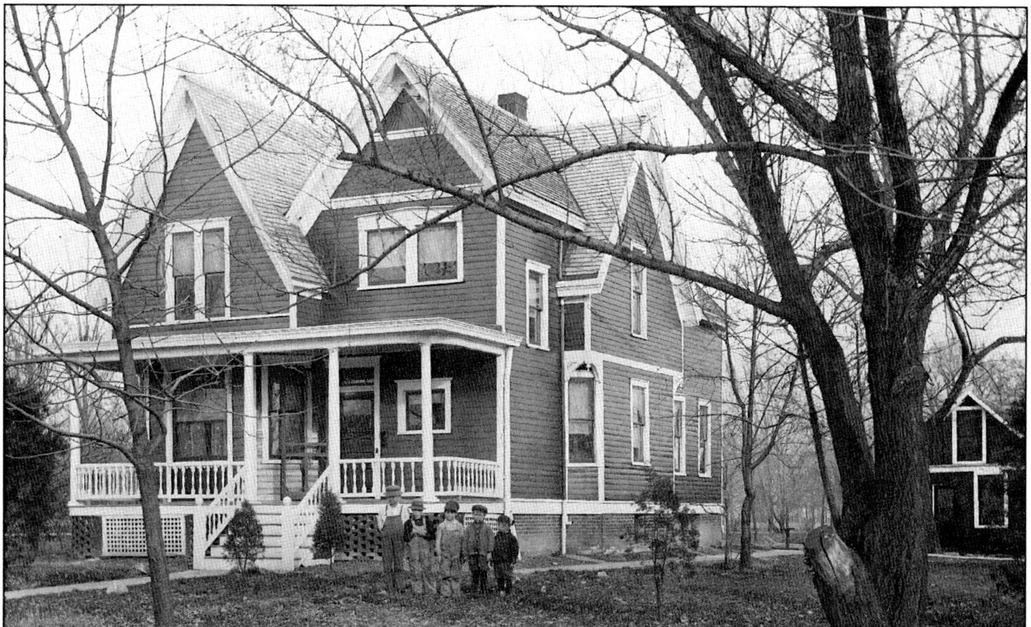

Over the years this house has changed its street number, street name, and out-right appearance, yet it has never moved. It is presently on 2208 Prospect Road, near Republic Street. The children in the card are Louis, Shirley, Walter, Phillip Fredwick, and a neighboring child. The card was mailed February 8, 1910.

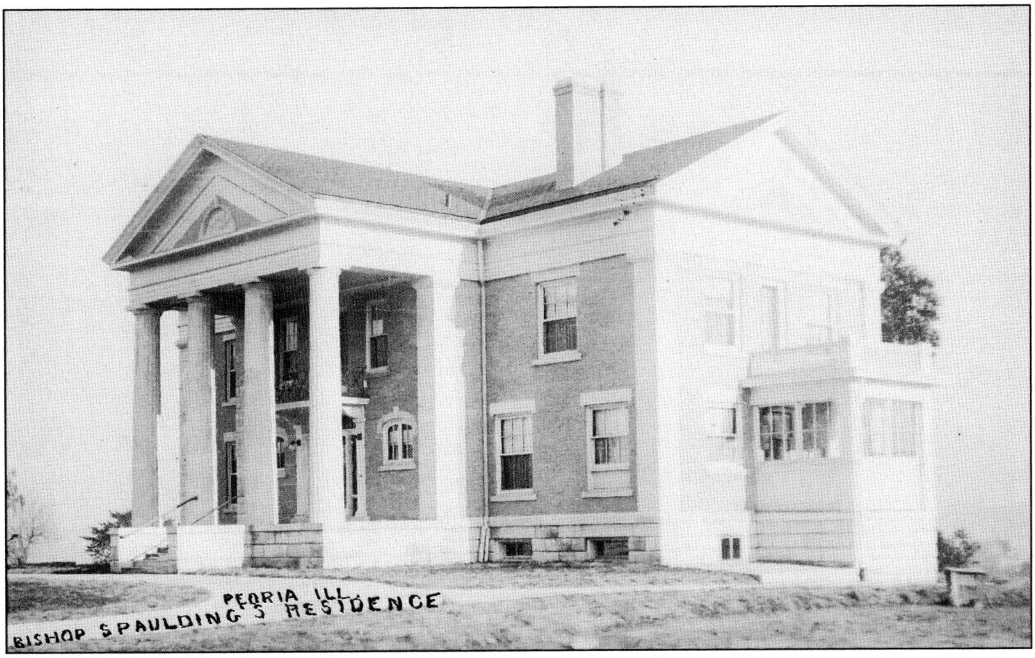

The above Greek Revival house was built in 1909 as the official residence for the arch bishop for the diocese of Peoria. As the postcard notes, the arch bishop at the time was John Lancaster Spalding. The building still stands at 740 Northeast Glen Oak, along with a new addition. It is a part of the St. Frances Complex and is well maintained.

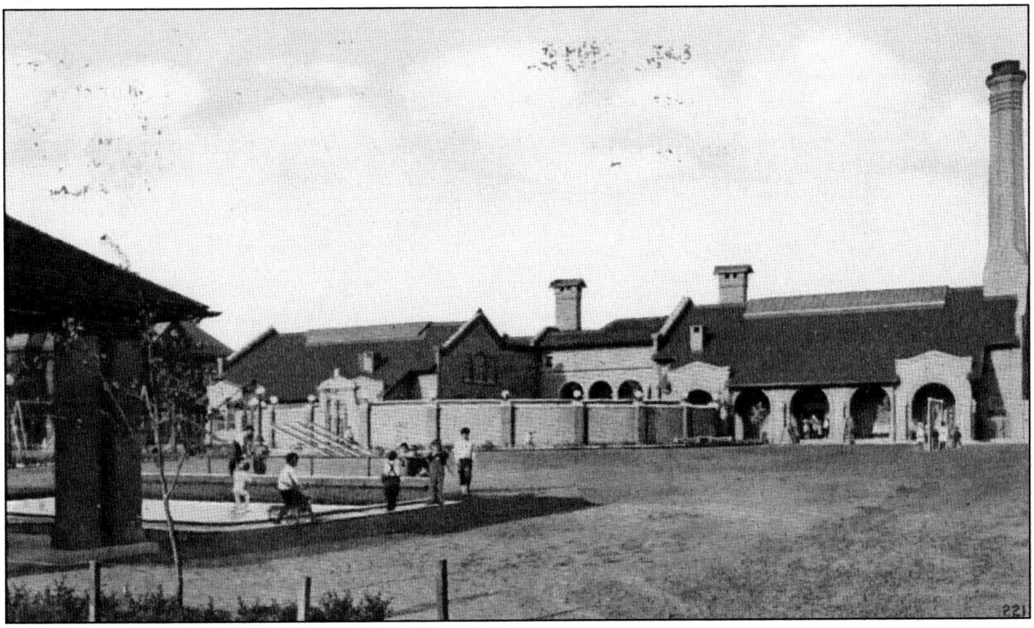

This is a very early view of the Proctor Recreation Center, located at 309 South DuSable Street. It was constructed in 1913 through funds left by John C. Proctor. Organized games, playgrounds, and wading pools were a major part of this south side complex. The bathing facilities were one of the more interesting functions offered in the early days. The center still serves the south side community and has been managed by the Peoria Park Board since 1934.

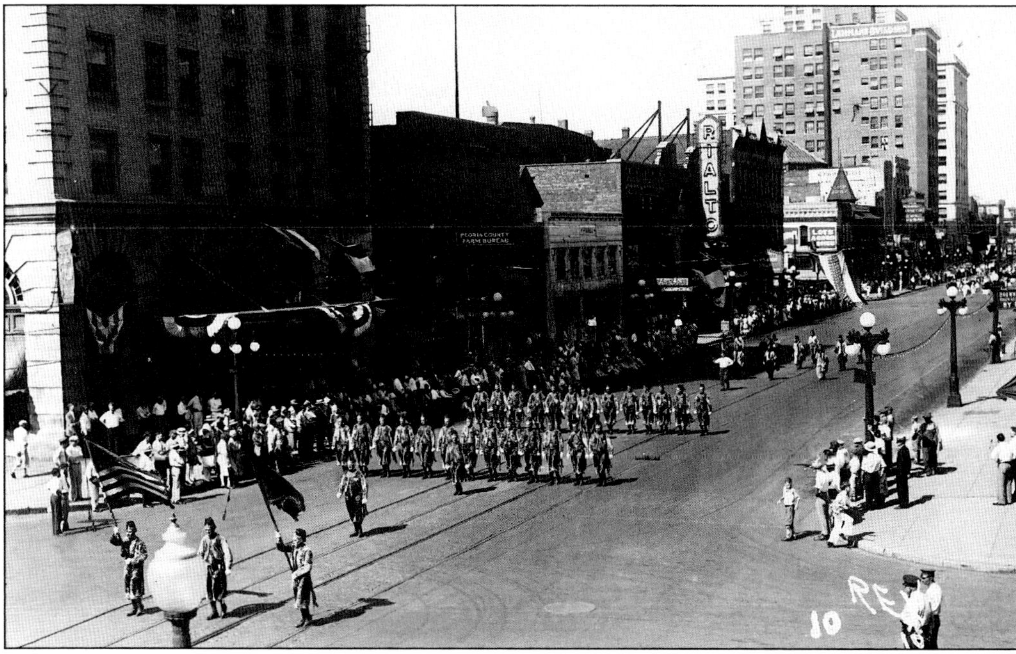

Parades have always been a priority in Peoria, as seen here. The above card is a 1950s Shrine parade in front of the Jefferson Hotel on Jefferson Street. The Rialto can be seen clearly, as well as the First National Bank Building.

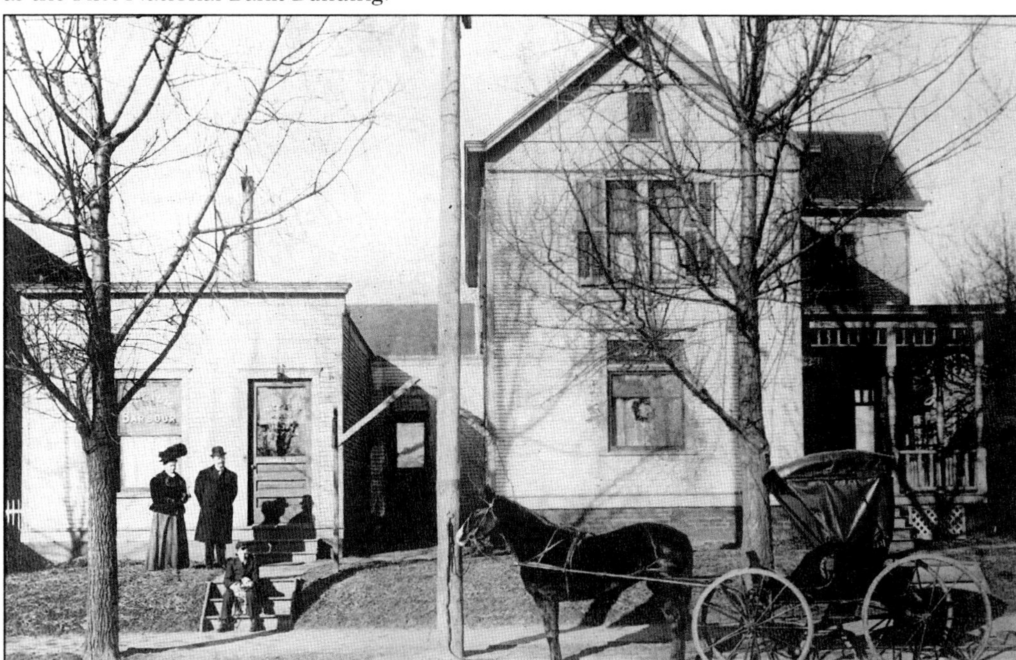

This is an example of an early photograph taken to tell a story or to show how well off the family was doing at the time. It shows 2113 Northeast Adams and was mailed January 1, 1909. The small boy has been identified as Cleo A. Barbour. The small, flat-roof house on the left was later added to the main house. The property is still a residence.

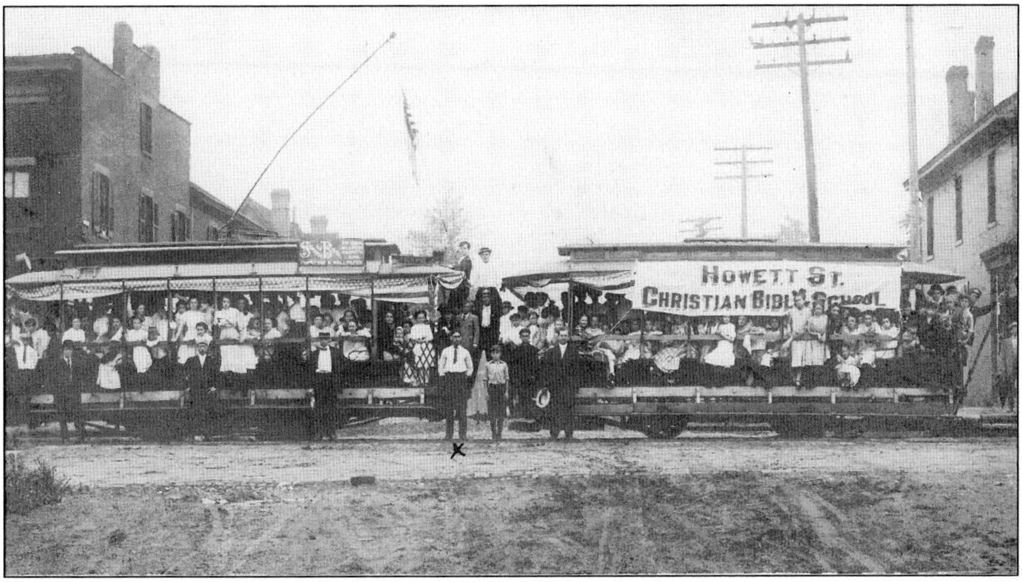

The Howett Street Christian Bible Class poses for a picture at an unknown location. This group was probably on their way to a picnic at Central Park. Note the Schipper and Block sign on the car to the left; the dirt streets would date the ride at around 1900.

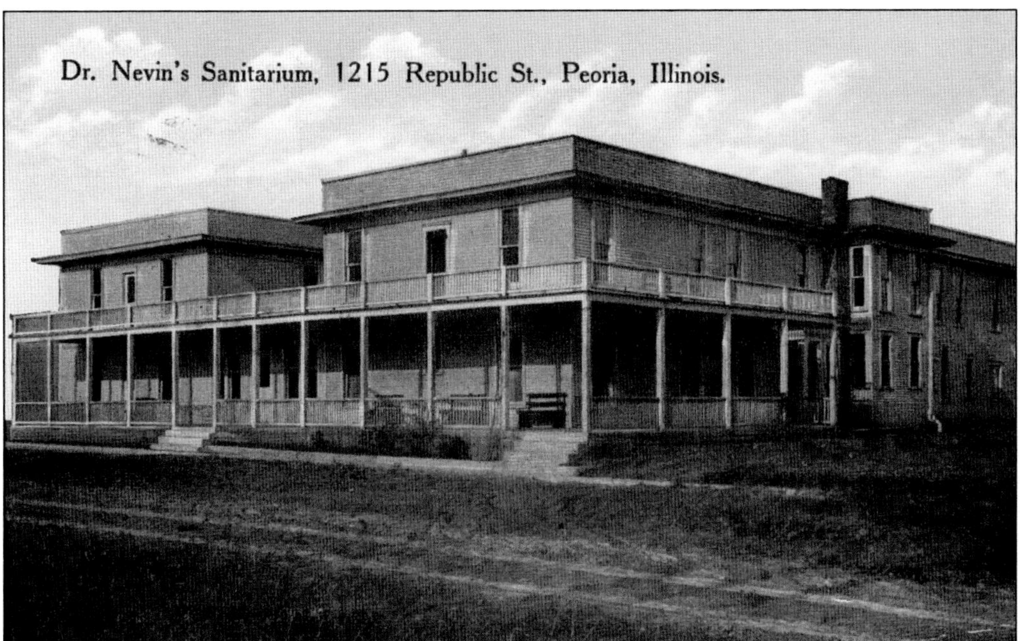

Dr. Herbert Nevins arrived in Peoria in 1909 and established the Nevins Sanitarium in 1912. This location also served as his residence for many years. The institution would remain open until the late 1930s, when Dr. Nevins separated the building, thus creating 1205 and 1215 East Republic. The conversion of both buildings into apartments was undertaken at that time. Today it is hardly recognizable, but the buildings are still apartments.

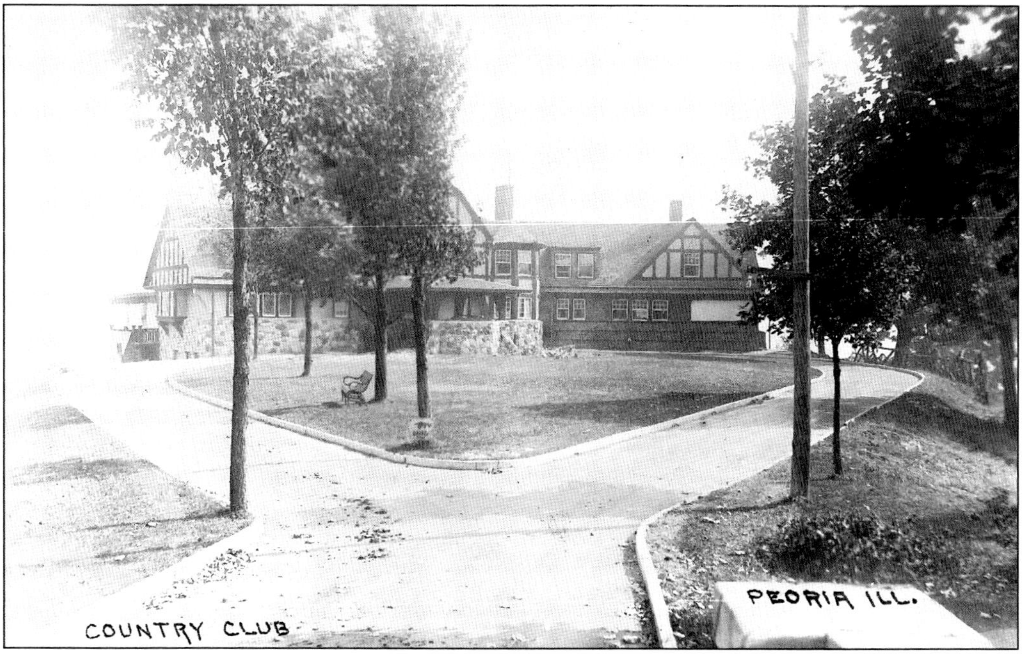

On June 26, 1897, Peoria's socially prominent community organized the Country Club of Peoria. The site chosen was Mrs. Caroline S. Gibson's 20 or so acres on Grand View Drive, overlooking Peoria Lake. A small, white-frame house accommodated the 135 members in the beginning. At a cost of $187,000, the building pictured above was dedicated in July 1922, replacing the earlier clubhouse destroyed by fire in 1921. A golf course, swimming pool, and tennis courts have been added as part of the present complex.

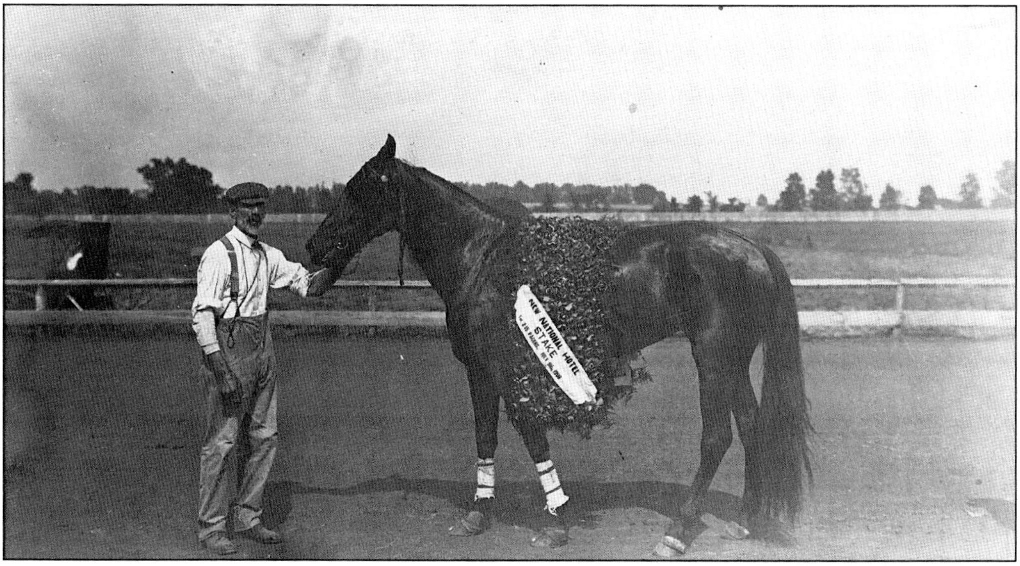

This postcard commemorates the winner of a horse race held at the Peoria Fairgrounds on East War Memorial Drive. The new National Hotel sponsored the winning race, held July 9, 1908. The facility, along with horse barns, exposition buildings, and a mile-long track, was destroyed as a WPA project in 1935. A new Central Athletic Field was then built to serve the city's young athletes.

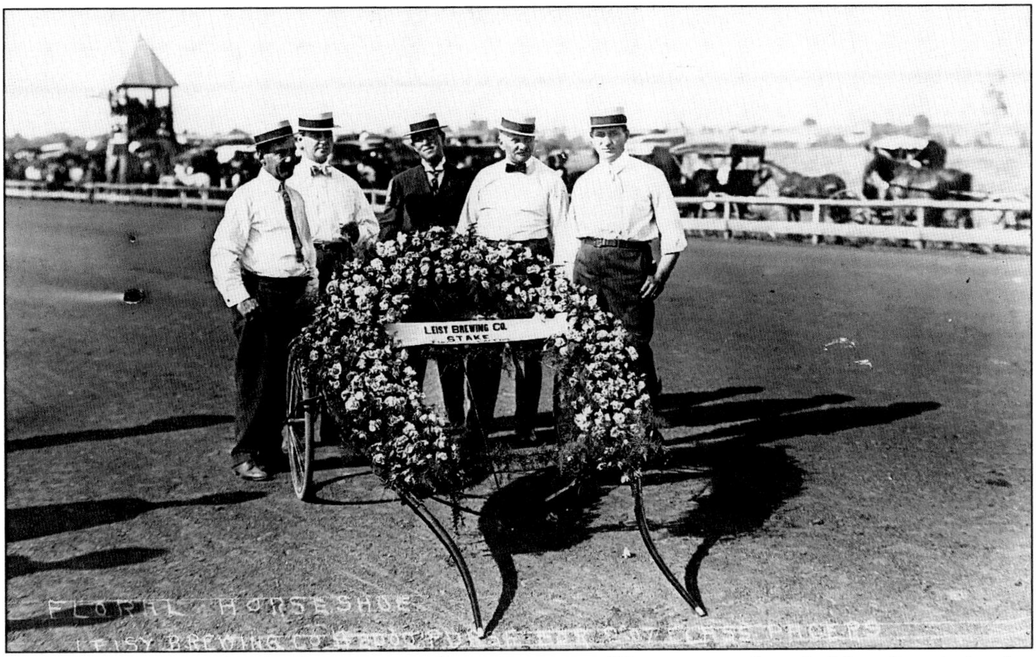

Harness races brought the largest crowds to the many Illinois state fairs held in Peoria in the 1890s. The above floral horseshoe was awarded to the winner of the harness race sponsored by Leisy Brewing Company. The winner received $2,000 in prize money in the 1908 race. Lakeview Park, and later the War Memorial mile track, were the sites of these races. The last race held at the Mile Track was in 1932.

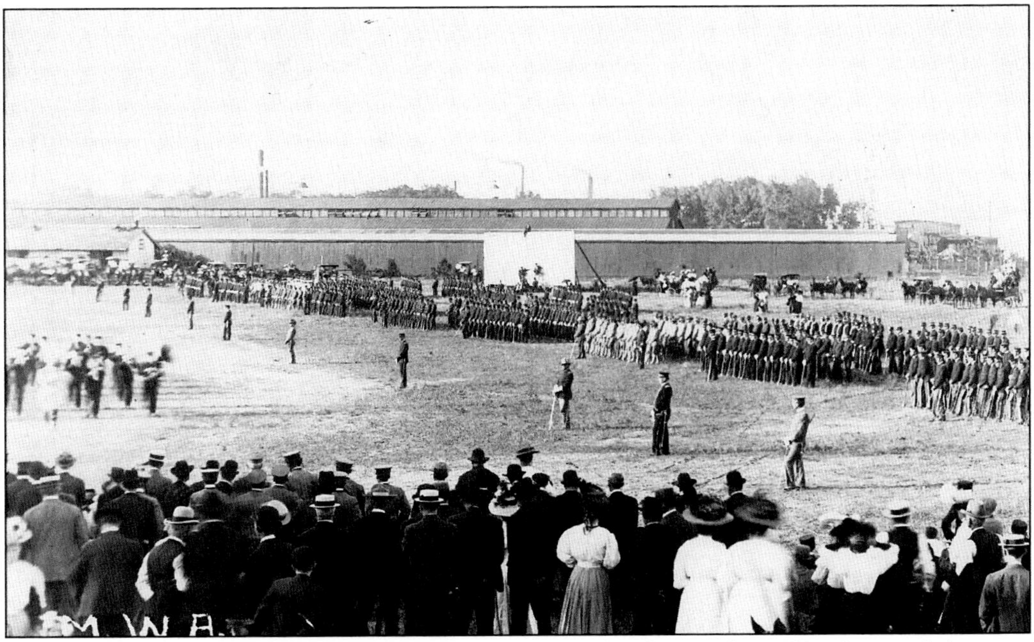

The above postcard indicates the support in Peoria for the Modern Woodmen of America Foresters of Peoria. The event was held in June 1908 in Peoria, probably at the War Memorial grounds, as would be indicated by the large building and open spaces.

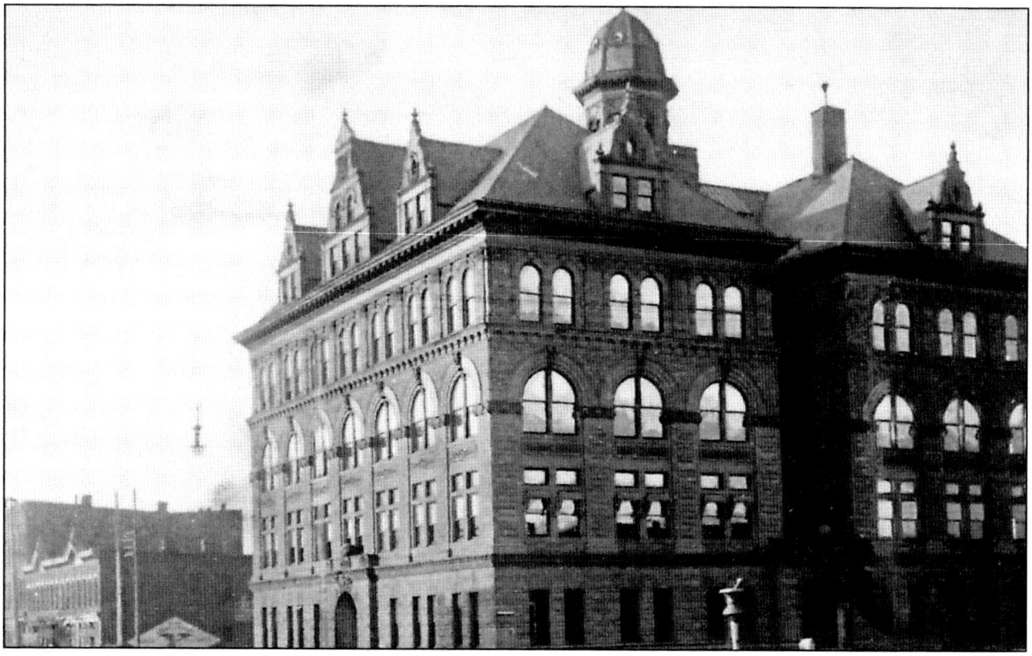

The above 1908 view of the Peoria City Hall seems strange because the building was on a corner. It has not moved—just the street has. Madison no longer crosses Fulton. The building was erected in 1899 and designed by Reeves and Ballie at the cost of $271,500. This Flemish, Renaissance-style building was placed on the National Register of Historic Places in 1978. It is still in use and has been carefully restored, including the Victorian Ball Tower—a remnant from the original city hall.

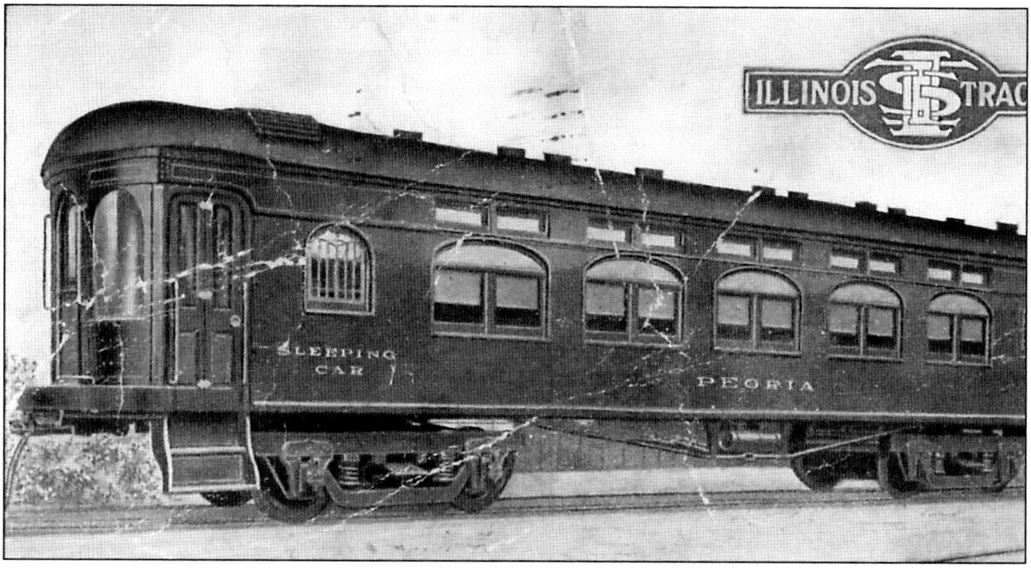

With nearly 35 years of sleeping car operation, the Illinois Traction was one of only three in the county. This electric railway (McKinley Lines) operated in Peoria from Bloomington in 1907. Trains ran from Peoria to St. Louis, Missouri, and to Danville, Illinois, via Bloomington, Illinois, and Champaign, Illinois. By the early 1950s, service was reduced to freight shipments. Eventually, all service was discontinued and the rails were removed by the late 1950s.

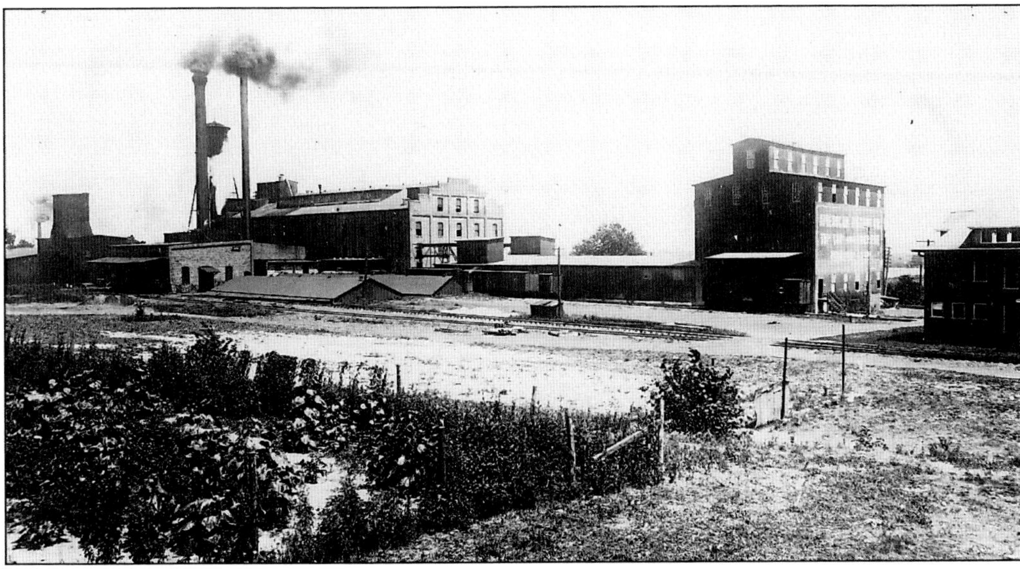

The American Milling Company began business on October 15, 1903, at the above site on the old Peoria-Pekin Road below Bartonville. This then-stock company manufactured dairy feeds under the name of Sucrene Feeds. In a merger effective in 1929, the above plant was taken over and operated as an Allied Mills Inc. plant. This facility would continue until the 1990s, when it was closed.

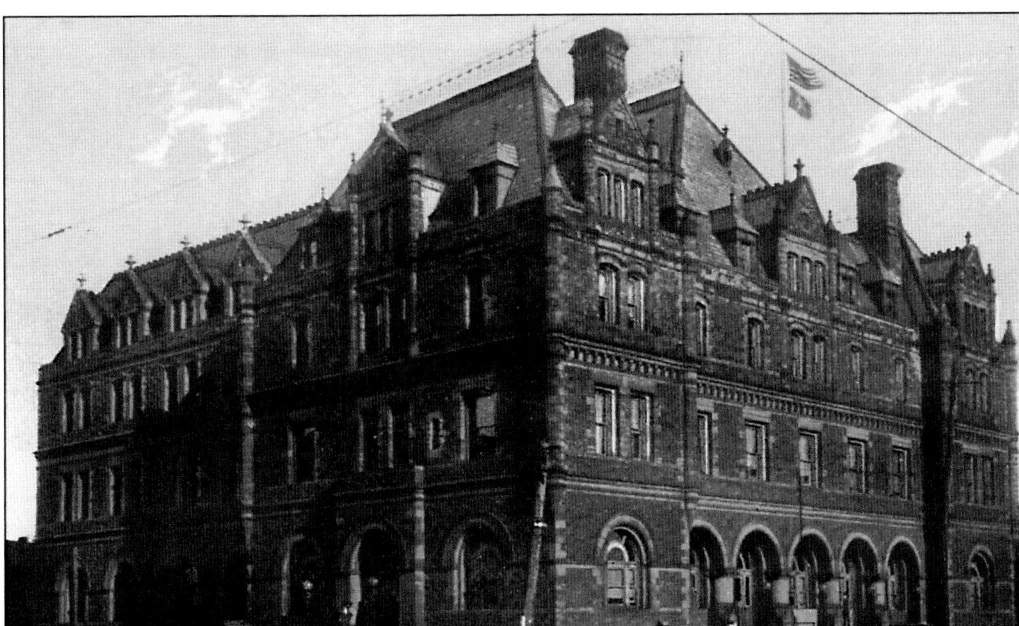

The United States Post Office erected their first building, pictured above, for use between 1885 and 1889. This building also housed the Federal courts and other agencies. The back addition was added in 1910. It was razed in 1937, and a new building erected at the cost of $1,100,000. The more recent building still stands at Main and Monroe Streets.

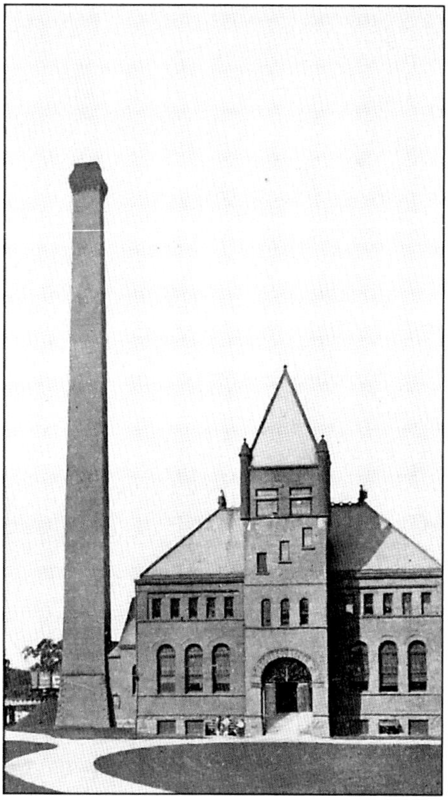

The pumping station shown here was built by Moffett, Hodgkins, and Clark in 1890–91. The former franchise holder failed, and Moffett, Hodgkins, and Clark assumed all debt and built this facility at the foot of Lorentz Street, just north of the McClugage Bridge. Today, the Illinois American Water Company owns and operates the Illinois Water Museum at this main purging station. The building was placed on the National Register of Historic Places in 1980.

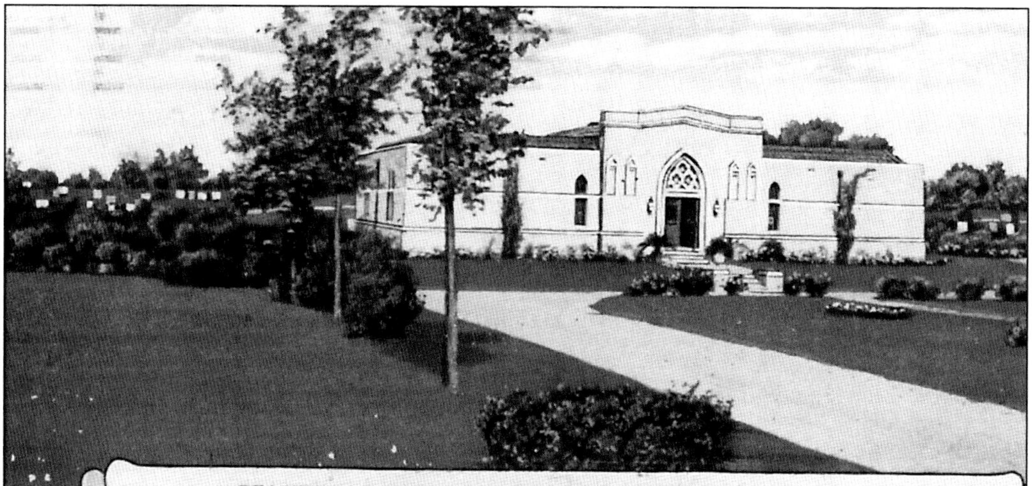

BEAUTIFUL NEW MAUSOLEUM ~ In Parkview Memorial Park
Peoria's Perpetual Care Cemetery

Parkview Cemetery completed the mausoleum, as pictured above, in 1928. Parkview opened in the early 1920s at North University and Nebraska Avenue. When it opened, the cemetery adjoined Bradley Park, until the Interstate 74 construction separated the two. The mausoleum and cemetery are well maintained and visitors are welcome. Prior to being the cemetery, this site was the country home and farm of Judge Jacob Gale, a former mayor of Peoria. His home was carefully dismantled in 1928 and a new caretakers residence (which can still be seen today from University Street) was constructed from the materials.

In October 1879, Bryer Post 67 of the Grand Army of the Republic was organized. It occupied a rental space until moving into its new home, Greenhutt Memorial, at 416 Hamilton Street in 1909. Former Peorian Captain Joseph B. Greenhutt of New York City donated $14,000 toward the whole cost of $22,800. This building was carefully restored and is well maintained today.

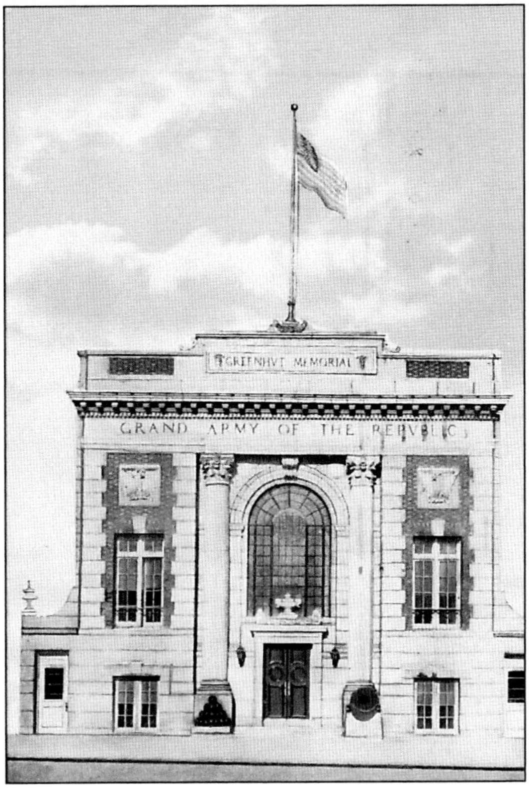

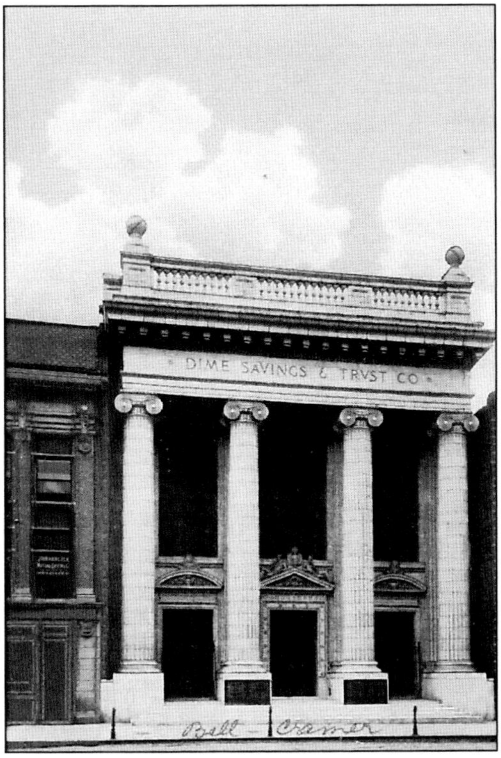

Eliot Callender, Oliver J. Bailey, Frank Meyer, Henry Ayers, and Seth W. Freeman formed a co-partnership to establish the Dime Savings Bank of Peoria at 113 South Jefferson in 1887. The residence of A.P. Barlett on Jefferson was converted for the bank's needs. Incorporated on March 1, 1904, the name became the Dime Savings and Trust Company. In February 1906, the building at left was erected at the original site. This building was the first erected especially for the commerce of banking. Commercial National Bank purchased the Dime Savings and Trust Company in 1926, the same year it opened its new building at 301 South Adams Street. Profitlich Fur Store removed the pillars and remodeled the building. Later, Jefferson Bank connected the structure to a large new addition. It was destroyed to make way for the Twin Towers.

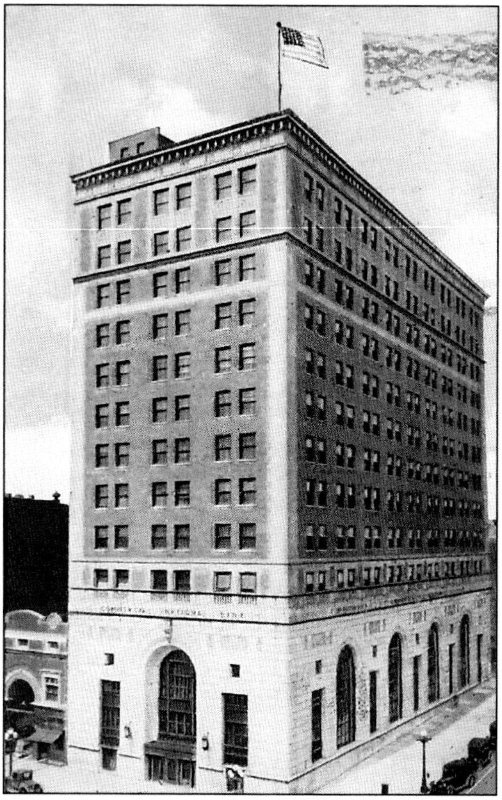

The private bank of Callender, Ayers, and Company was organized in 1881. By 1885, the partners reorganized as the Commercial National Bank. No less than six banks merged when Commercial National Bank was constructed at 301 South Adams—the building pictured here—in 1926. Also pictured, to the far left, is a portion of the Duchess Theater. When Commercial National Bank added this annex in 1930, the theater was razed.

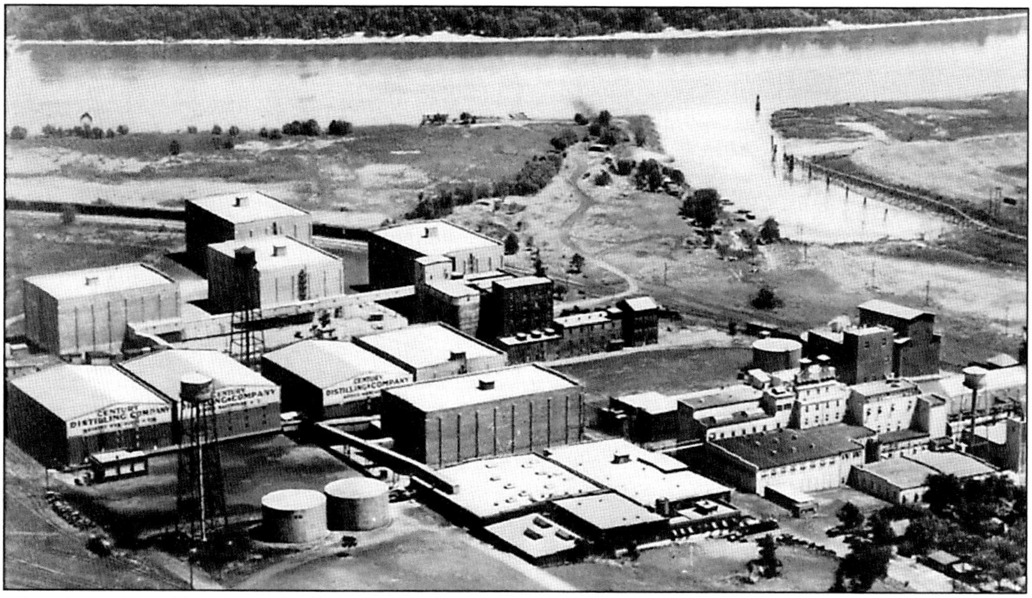

The Atlas Distillery was built in 1894 by the Woolner family, as shown above, and was the largest in the city at that time. The name was eventually changed to the Century Distilling Company. From 1945 to 1953, this plant was a part of the National Distillers. The 1960s brought about a change at this plant from distillery to warehouse use. In 1975, the complex became the headquarters for the N.E. Finch Company.

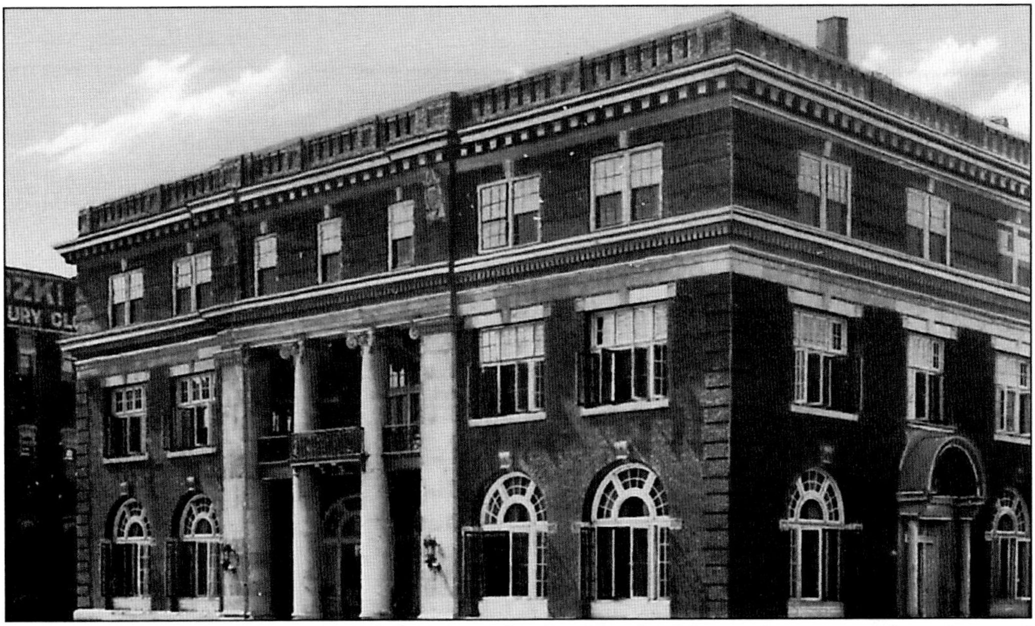

The Creve Coeur Club was founded on March 13, 1894, by 13 area business and professional men, to promote both business and social artistries. It was named the Creve Coeur Club to honor the first European settlement in the Peoria area. The original building (pictured above) was built between 1903 and 1904 at Liberty and South Jefferson. It was razed in the late 1960s, and a new facility was built.

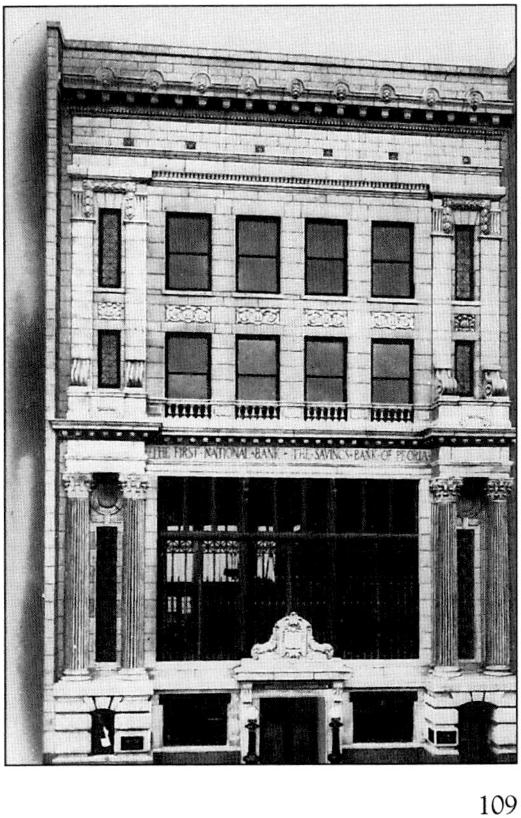

The First National Bank of Peoria, founded in 1863 (its national charter number was 176), was Peoria's oldest bank prior to the merger with Commerce Bank in the mid-1990s. It was originally housed at Main and Washington and moved to the building pictured here in 1911. This institution purchased the Alliance Life Insurance Company building in 1946 for a reported $935,000. After much remodeling, the bank was moved to the new building at Jefferson and Main in 1949. The building shown here was remodeled into the men's department of the Bergner Department Store, and was razed in 1997 to make way for the new Technology Center, which is now under construction.

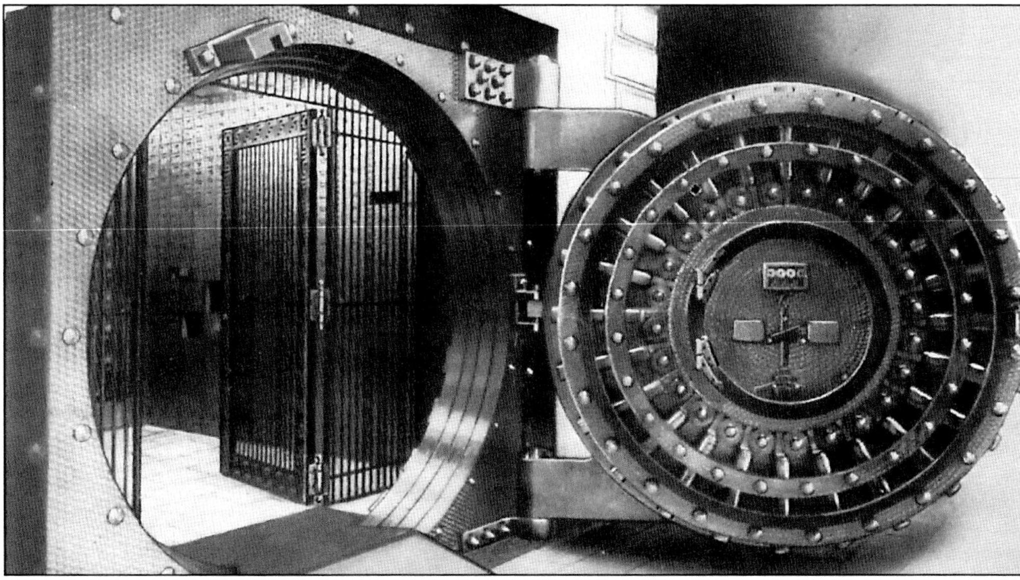

The Savings Bank of Peoria, founded in 1868, was located at Washington and Main Street. On July 17, 1906, the bank moved to 317 Main Street. In 1917, the Savings Bank and First Trust consolidated to form the First Trust and Savings Bank. The First National Bank and First Trust Bank consolidated in 1930.

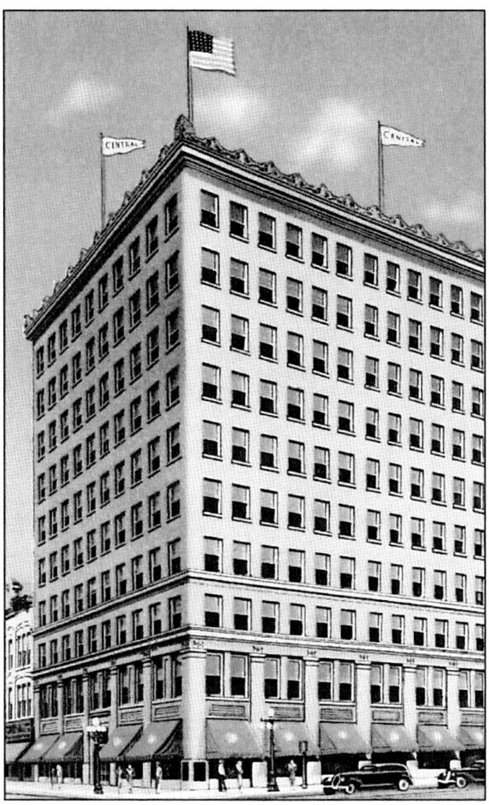

The Central National and Trust Company was organized in 1879 and incorporated in 1884 at 211 Main Street. By 1893, the bank leased and occupied a building at the northwest corner of Main and Adams. In 1909, a lease was signed for 99 years that triggered the erection of the ten-story building pictured here. In the 1960s, the Central Bank and Trust merged with Commercial National Bank and relocated to their building. The building was restored in the 1990s, and now houses a branch of the South Side Bank on the first floor.

Ten

CHURCHES

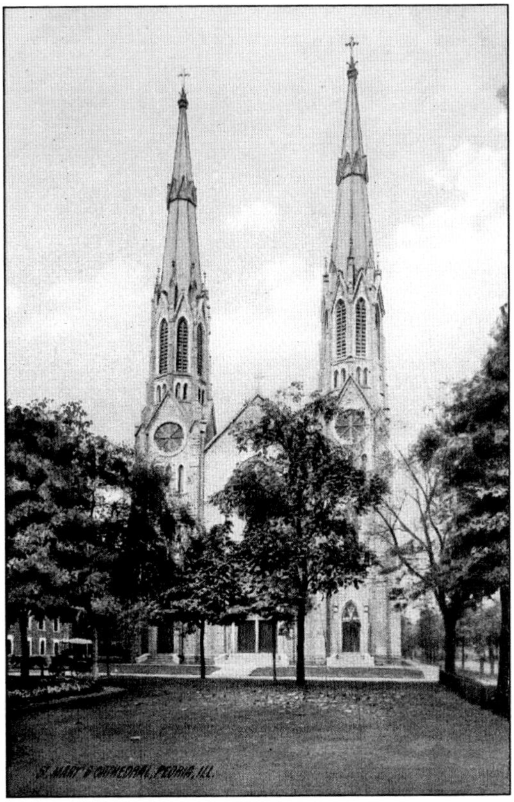

The most photographed Catholic Church in Peoria is St. Mary's Church, which is shown here. St. Mary's Church was succeeded by St. Mary's Cathedral, which stands at Madison and Green Street and was dedicated on May 15, 1989. The church still stands today.

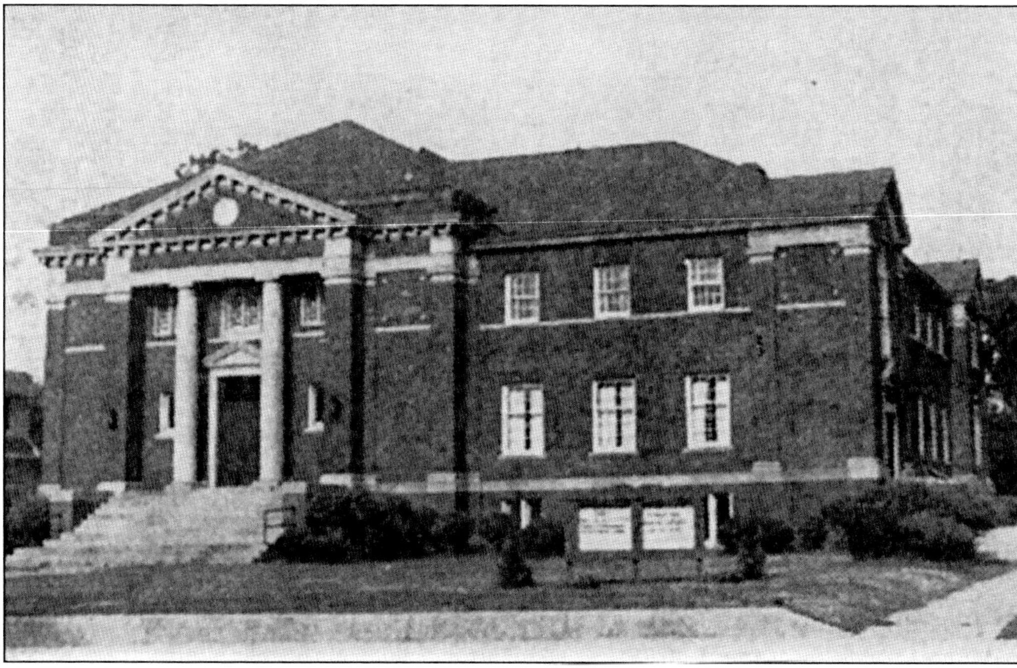

The Union Congregational Church was organized in 1890 as Union Church. In 1893, the name changed to the Union Congregational Church. By 1894, a building was erected at Illinois and Deckman. In 1917, the church constructed a building at Knoxville and Nebraska. The above building burned in 1970, and the church never rebuilt.

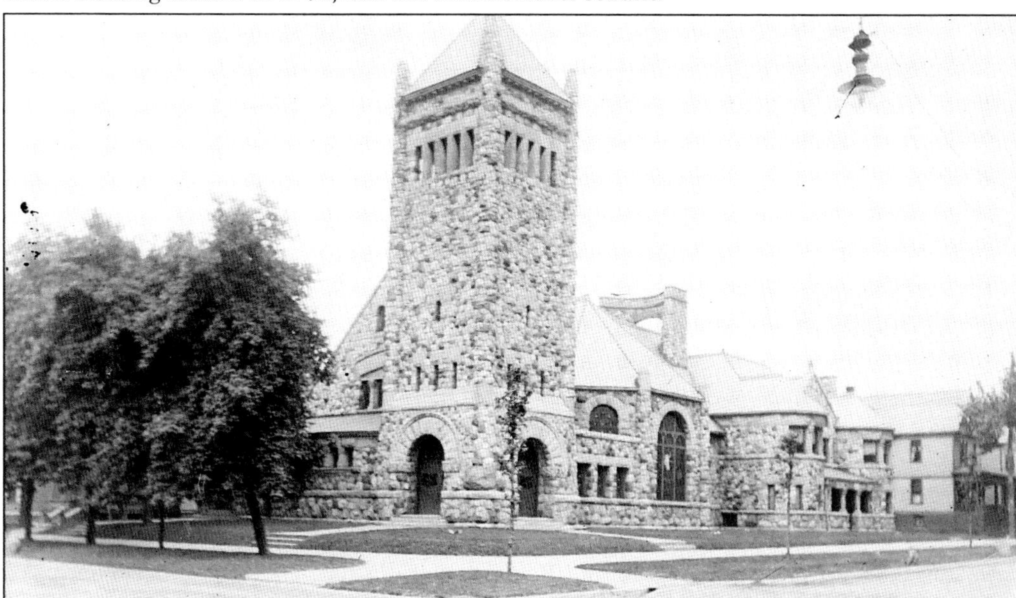

The Second Presbyterian Church formed from a division of the First Church before the Civil War. The First Church building was located at Madison Avenue and Jackson Streets in 1855. The building pictured above (built in 1889) was the second building, erected at the cost of $50,000. In 1937, a merger between the First Congregational Church and the Second Presbyterian Church created the First Federal Church. The above building still stands.

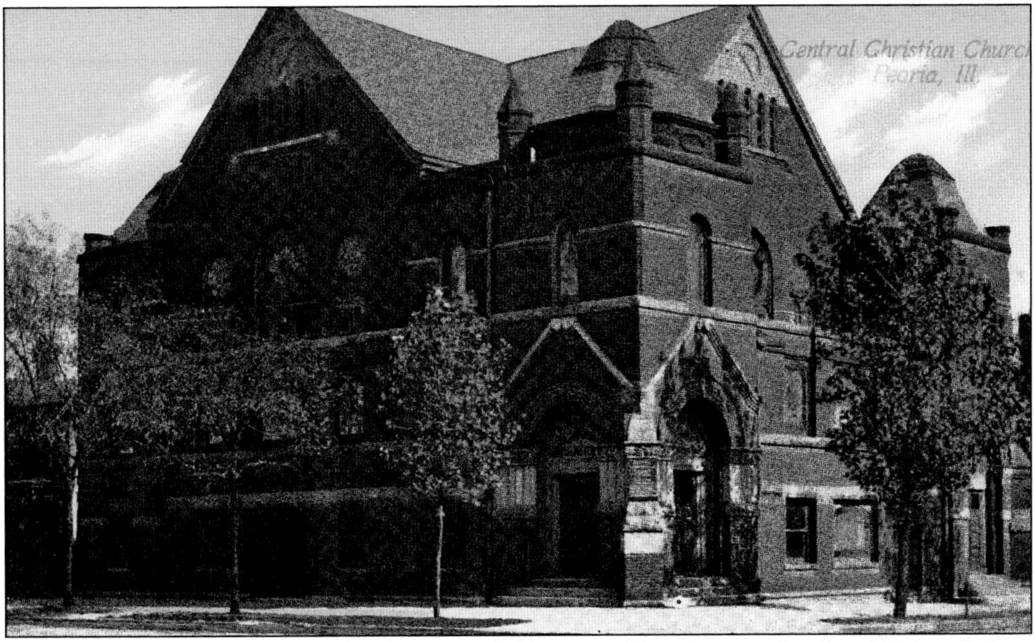

This was the house of worship for the Central Christian Church, completed in 1894 on Fulton Street at Monroe Street at the cost of $25,000. It was at this time that the name was changed to the Central Christian Church. The building was destroyed by fire on January 7, 1913.

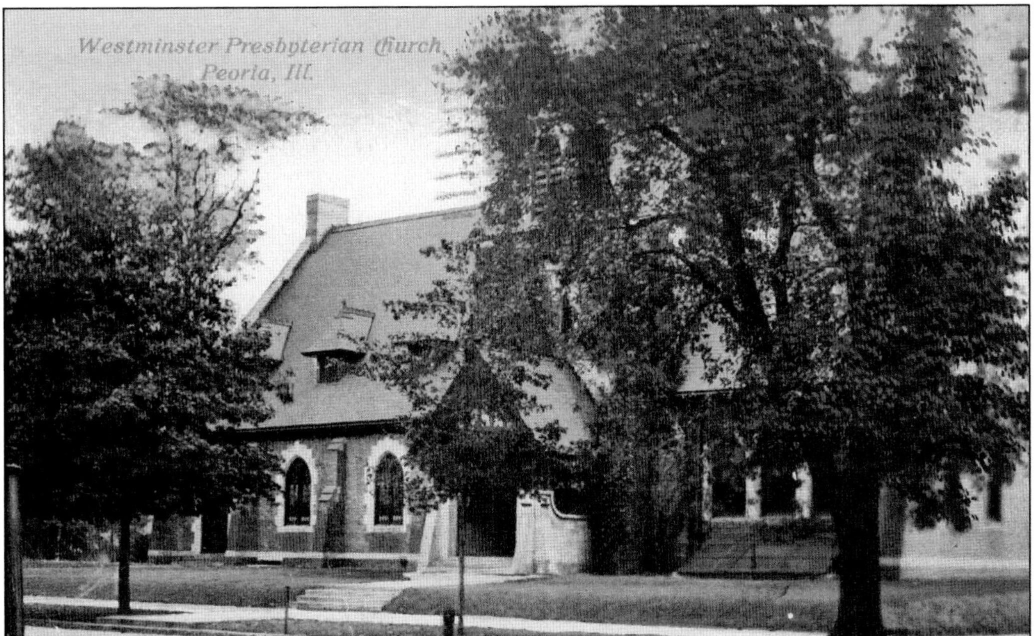

The Westminster Presbyterian Church was founded in 1897 at 1420 Moss Avenue. In 1898, the church pictured here was completed. Note that the use of large, ornamental boards on the new entrance was compatible with the original, Gothic architectural style. The building burned in 1985, and the church was rebuilt on the same site.

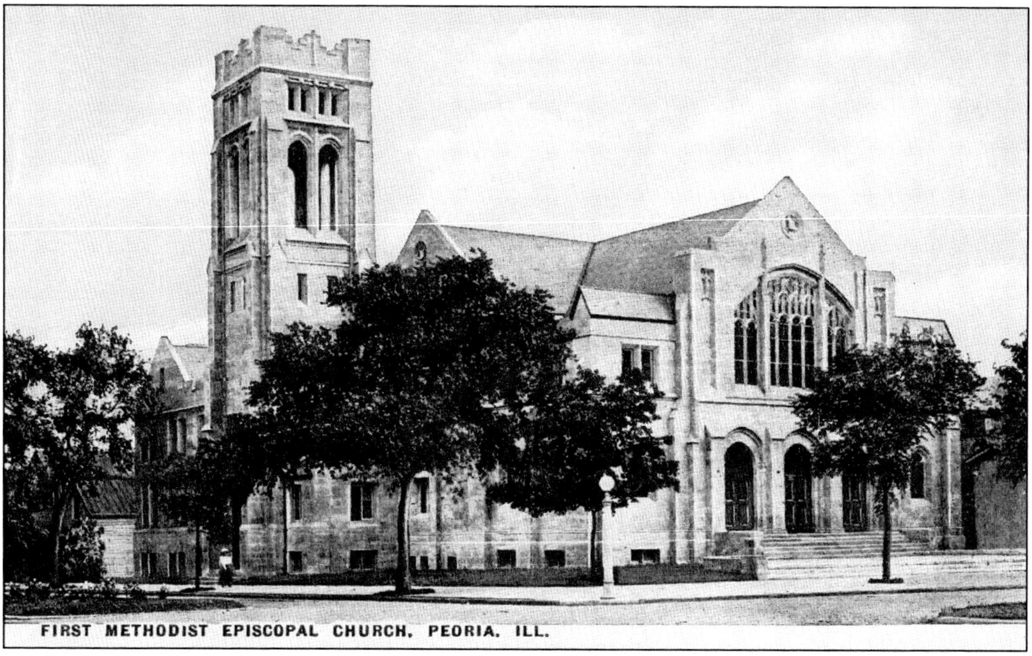

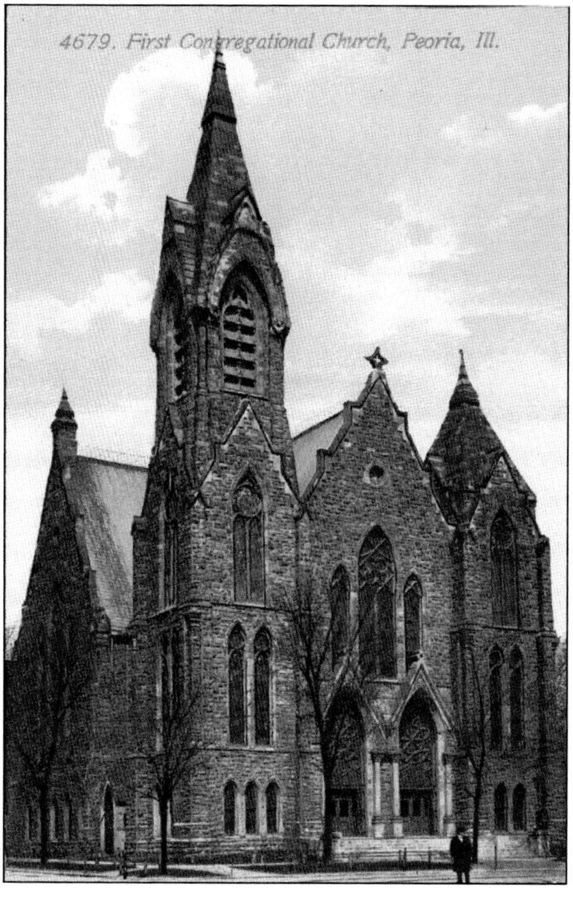

After three former church homes, the First Methodist Episcopal Church, located at the corner of Perry and Hamilton Boulevard, was completed. This stone building was dedicated in 1916. The church continues to expand into the downtown area. The name has changed, from the original name in 1830, to the First United Methodist Church today.

The First Congregational Church, which dates back to 1834, was a predecessor of the Main Street Congregational Church. A lot at Hamilton Boulevard and Monroe Avenue was secured, and the cornerstone was laid in 1876. The building shown here was completed and dedicated in September of 1883. It was destroyed by fire on March 21, 1936. In June of 1937, the First Congregational and the Second Presbyterian Churches were amalgamated, creating the First Federated Church.

The congregation of St. Paul's Episcopalian Church, founded in 1848, erected their second building (shown here) at Main and Monroe in 1890 at a cost of $33,000. Later, St. Paul's relocated to War Memorial Drive and opened their new building in 1956. The former building was removed, and is now a parking lot.

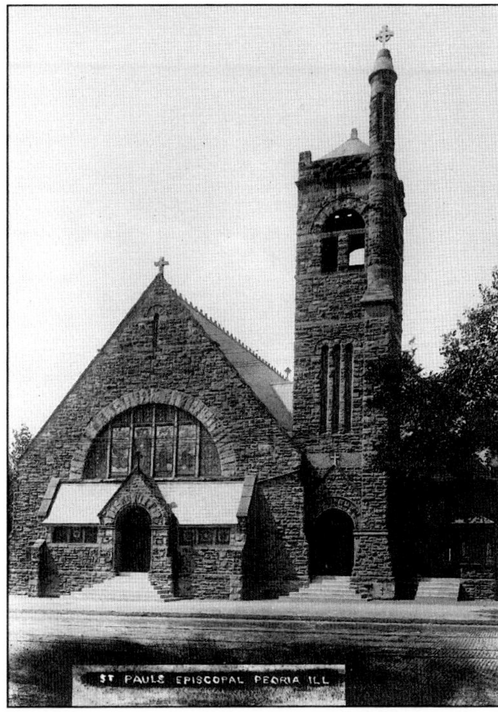

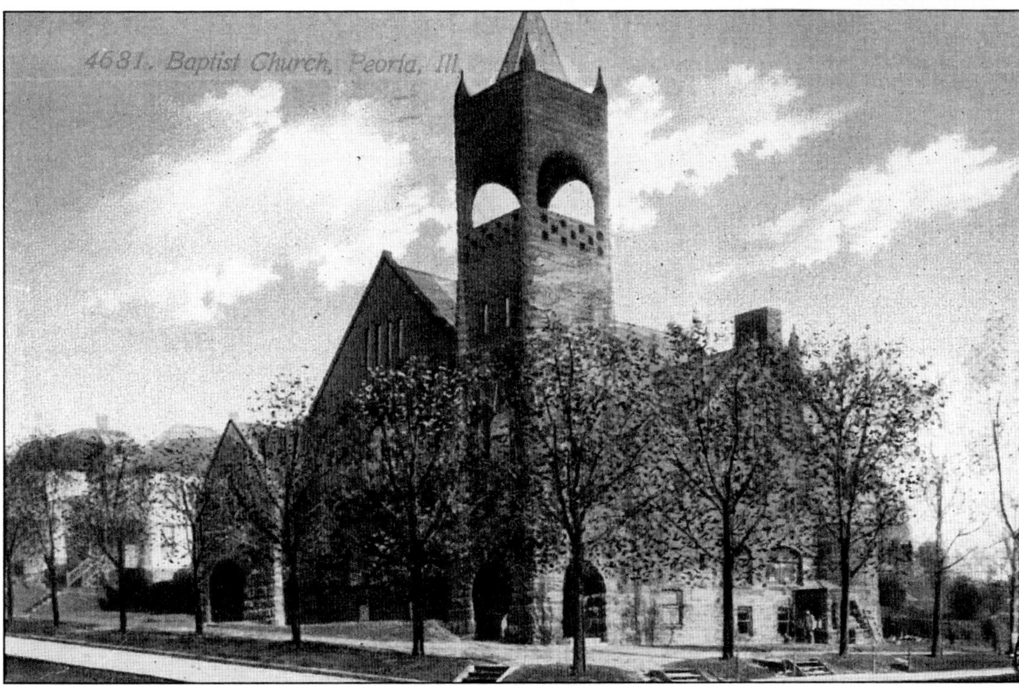

The First Baptist Church, after meeting in several different houses of worship, opened this new building in 1890 at the corner of Hamilton Boulevard and Glen Oak. It was constructed of large stones and included a tower. The congregation remained here until 1957, when their new location at 411 Lake Avenue was opened. The merging Methodist Hospital Complex acquired the building and had it removed in 1959.

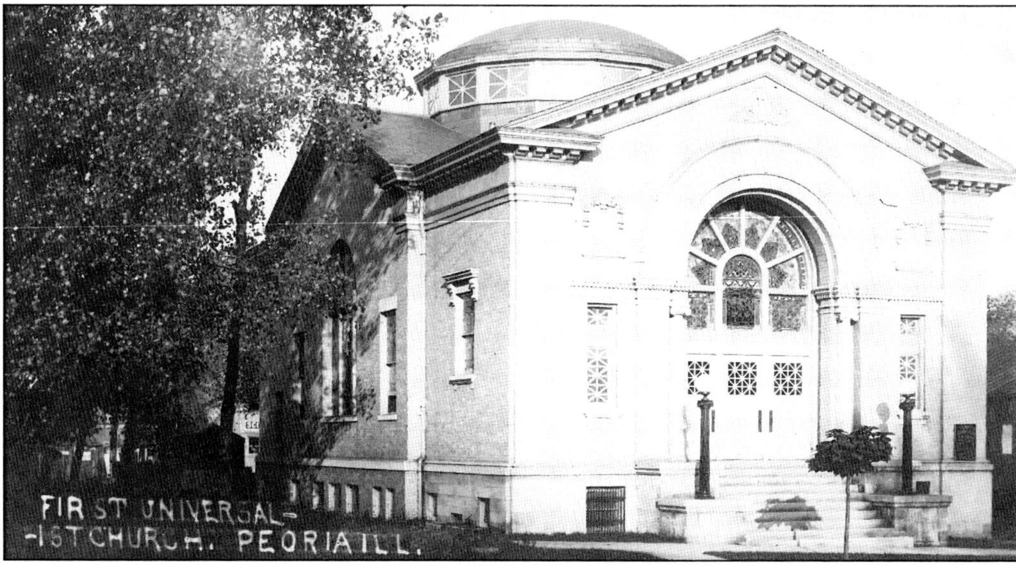

Organized in 1843, the Universalist Unitarian Church held their first meetings at the courthouse. The congregation would continue to hold services at several different locations until 1867, when a new church was erected and named Church of the Messiah. Around 1885, the name of the church was changed to Bradley Memorial First Universalist Church, in memory of longtime member Tobias S. Bradley. The building pictured here was erected in 1902, and is located at 908 Hamilton Boulevard.

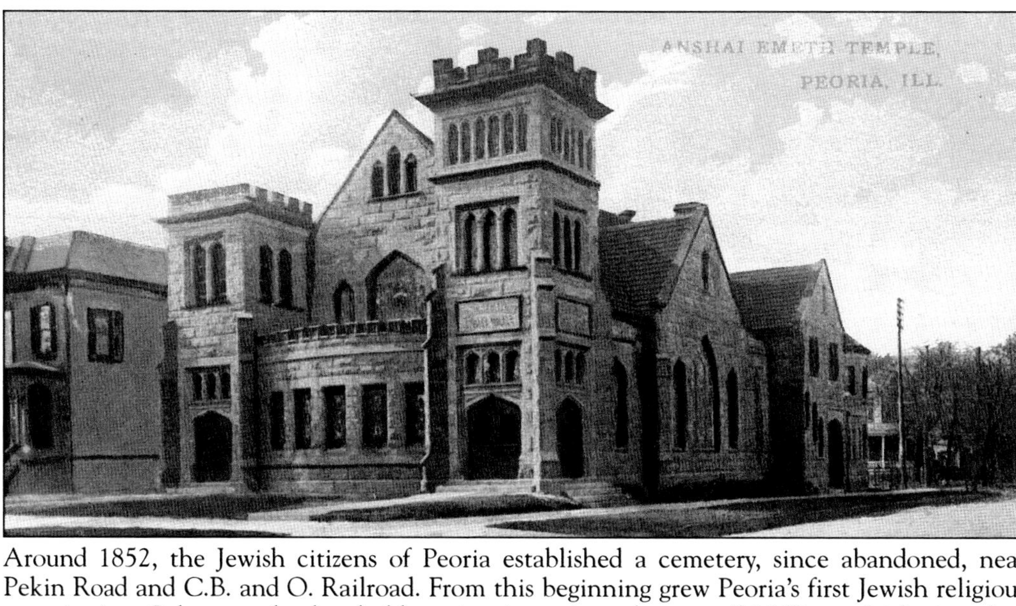

Around 1852, the Jewish citizens of Peoria established a cemetery, since abandoned, near Pekin Road and C.B. and O. Railroad. From this beginning grew Peoria's first Jewish religious organization. Subsequently, they held services in various places until 1863, at which time they purchased the Universalist's building on Fulton Street. From this beginning, the Congregation Anshi Emeth arose. After their temple, located at Jefferson and Liberty Street, was destroyed by fire in 1896, the congregation then erected the building pictured above at Monroe and Hancock. This temple is clad in Lake Superior sandstone, and it was dedicated in 1898. The Christian Assembly Church occupies the building today. Temple Anshi Emeth is today located at 5614 North University.

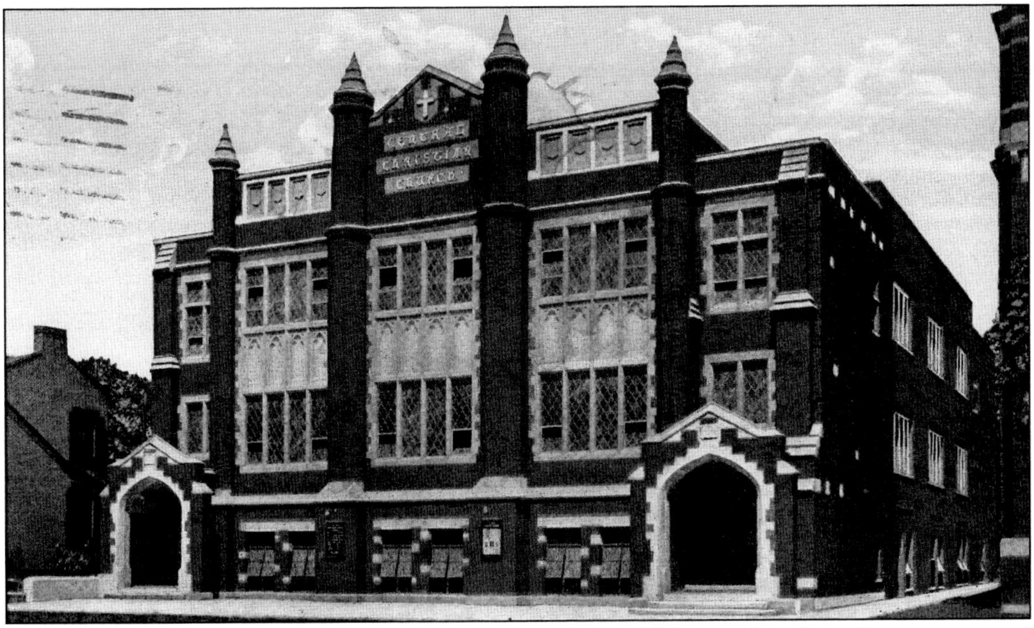

The Christian Church of Peoria was founded in 1845. As with many churches, the congregation moved to several different places. After their building on Fulton was destroyed in 1913, the membership purchased the former English Reformed Lutheran Church building at 209 North Madison Avenue. In 1916, that building was removed and a new brick building (shown here) was erected on the same site at a cost of $69,000. The name Central Christian Church was adopted in 1896. The above building was razed in 1973 to make way for the Voyager Inn. The First Christian Church is today located at 6400 University.

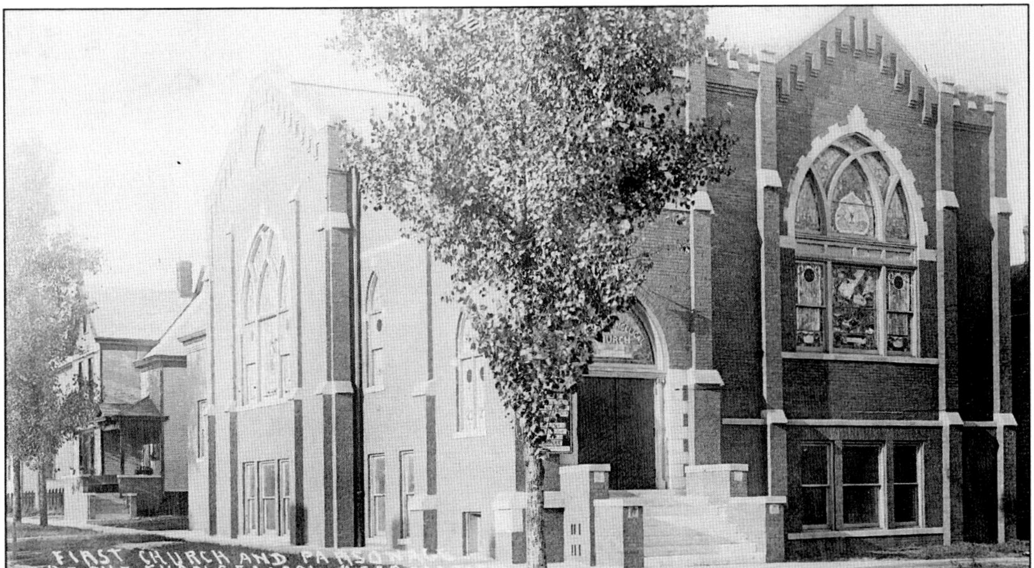

This postcard was never mailed, and the exact location is not known. However, the Evangelical Alliance was organized in 1847. In 1873, a frame building was built to house the Alliance at First and State Streets. The above church is believed to have been a later building, housing both the First Church and Alliance.

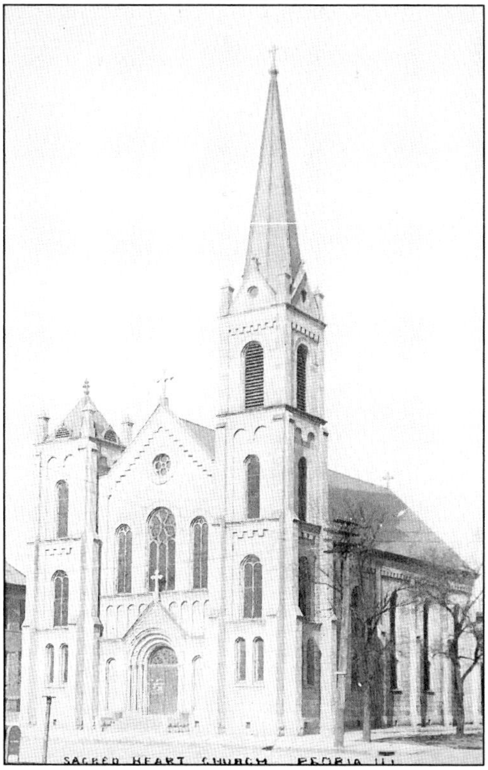

The Sacred Heart Church at Fulton and Madison was dedicated in 1906. This Gothic design was built with Indian limestone by a Catholic monk, Brother Adrian. This downtown landmark is no longer in a residential neighborhood, and the church now serves people from other areas.

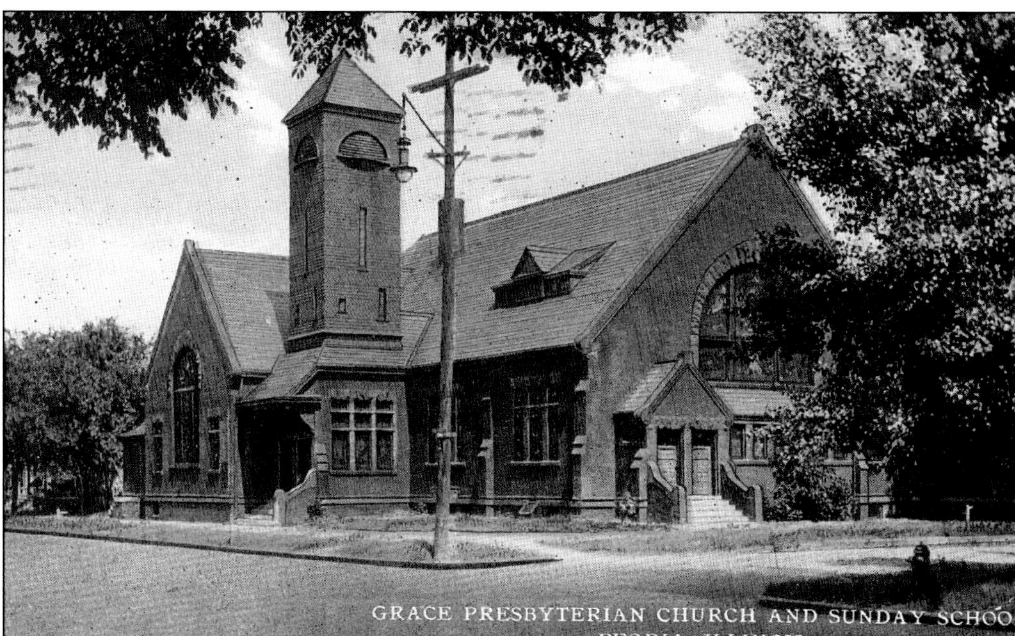

The Grace Presbyterian Church and Sunday School was organized in 1862. Several houses of worship were used in the beginning, including a railroad coach car. The building pictured above was located at Madison and Wayne and was constructed in the late 1890s. The church is presently located on West Forest Hill.

At his death, Asahal Hale bequeathed $12,000 and a parcel of land for the erection of a Methodist chapel, which was built at High and Main Streets. The first chapel was dedicated in 1869. On June 13, 1901, the building pictured, known as Hale Chapel, was dedicated. These rusticated limestone walls and Gothic-style windows, along with the central tower, are still intact. Another faith still uses this facility.

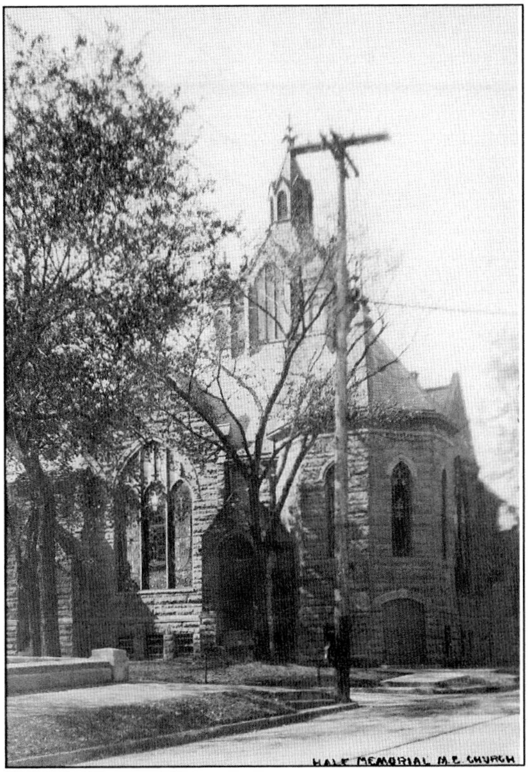

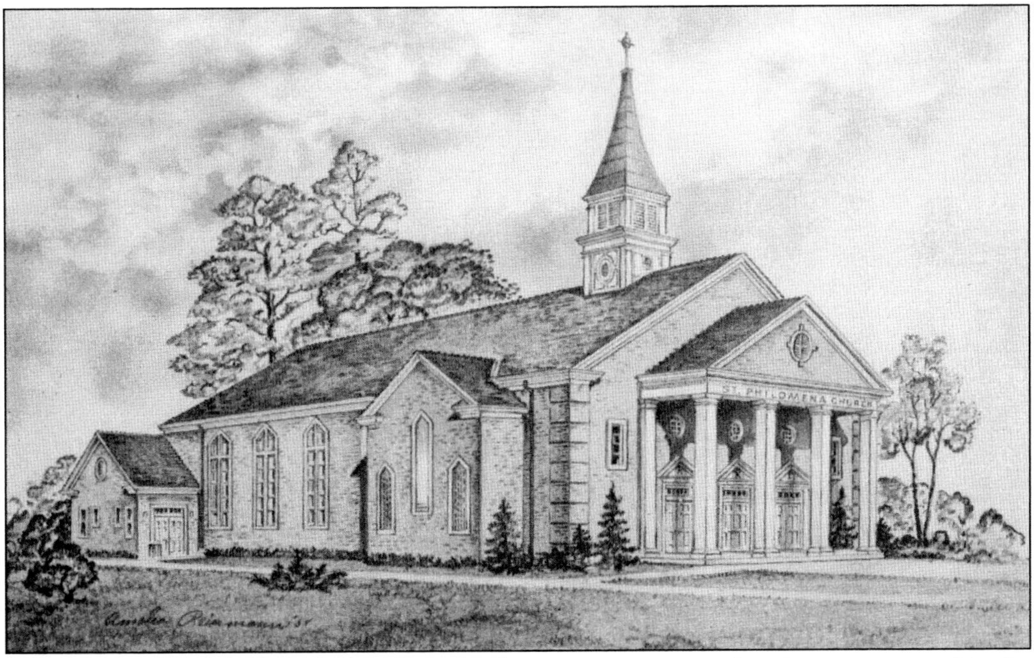

As the population of Peoria shifted from the downtown area, new churches were opened in the suburbs. St. Philomena Catholic Church was founded in 1946 and is an example of moving churches to the suburbs. The new building was completed in 1954 at 1000 Albany. This church was a modified Colonial style.

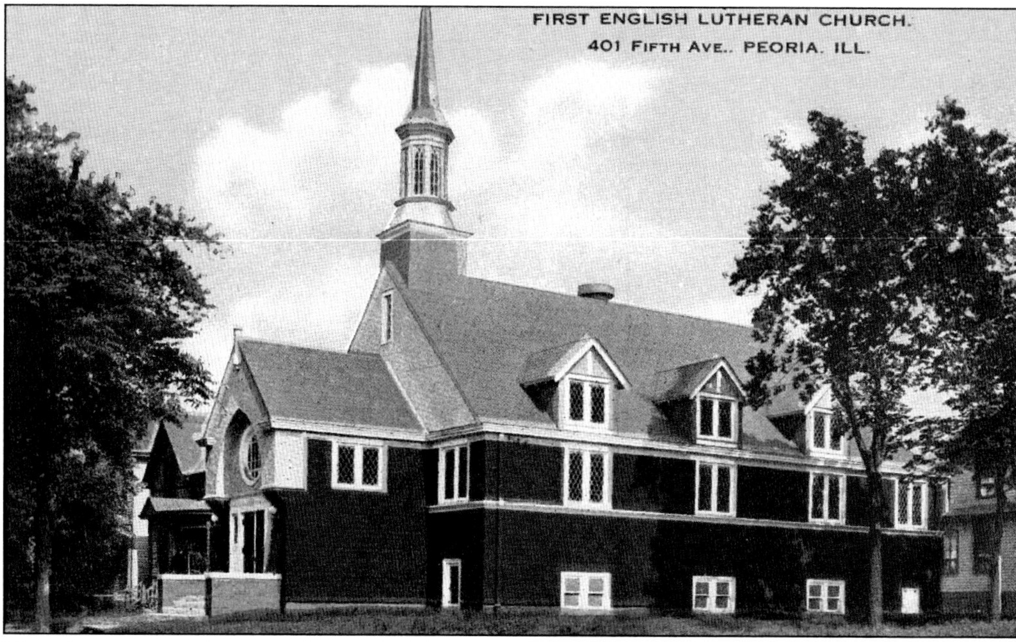

The above postcard was mailed in 1917, just one year after the First English Lutheran Church was dedicated in March of 1916. The design was Colonial and Gothic. The church relocated, in the early 1950s, to 715 East Forest Hill. The new church was dedicated in 1953. The 5th Street building has been razed.

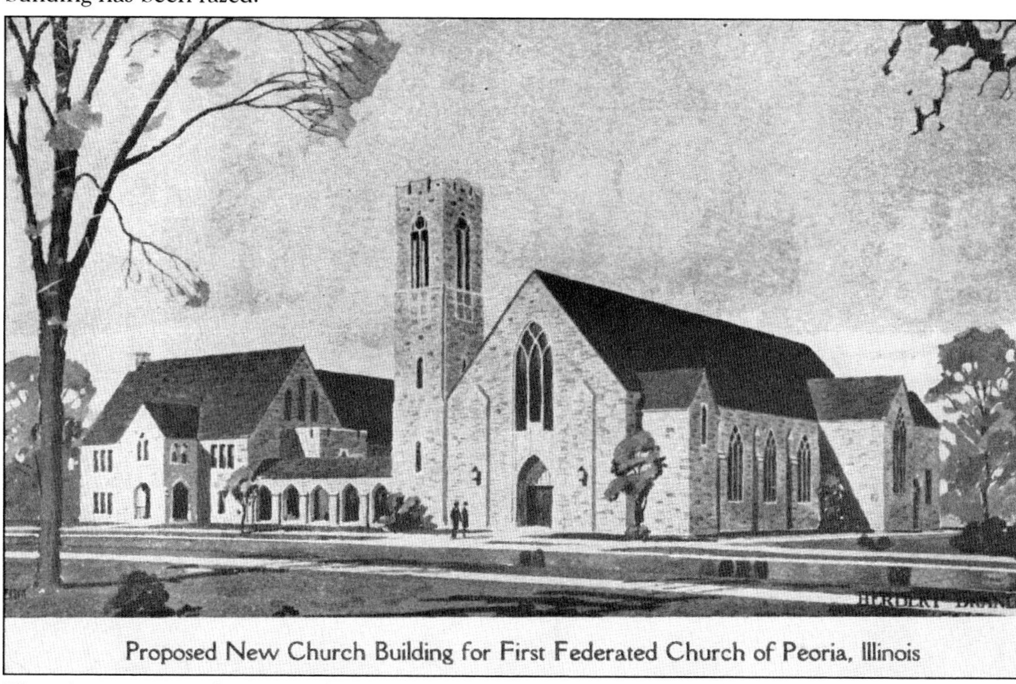

Proposed New Church Building for First Federated Church of Peoria, Illinois

The above postcard projected the new church building that was constructed beginning on July 1, 1948, at Florence and North Sheridan Road. The new building was dedicated in 1949. This merger between the First Congregational Church and the Second Presbyterian Church took place in January of 1937.

Eleven

PEORIA HEIGHTS

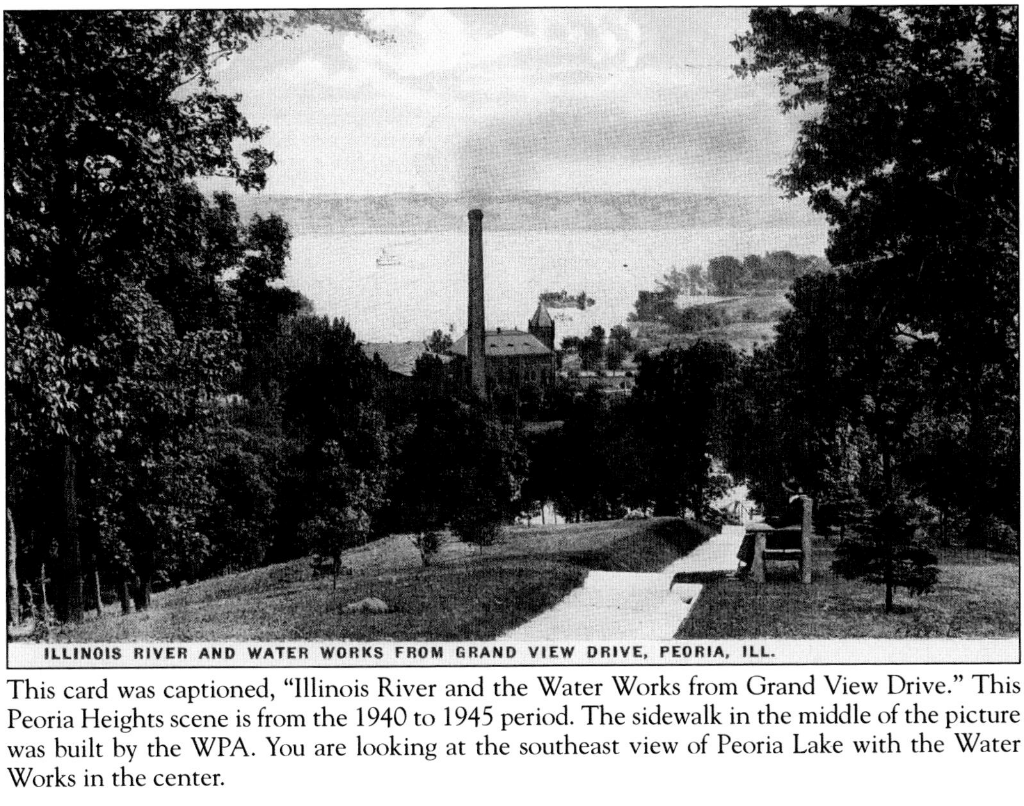

This card was captioned, "Illinois River and the Water Works from Grand View Drive." This Peoria Heights scene is from the 1940 to 1945 period. The sidewalk in the middle of the picture was built by the WPA. You are looking at the southeast view of Peoria Lake with the Water Works in the center.

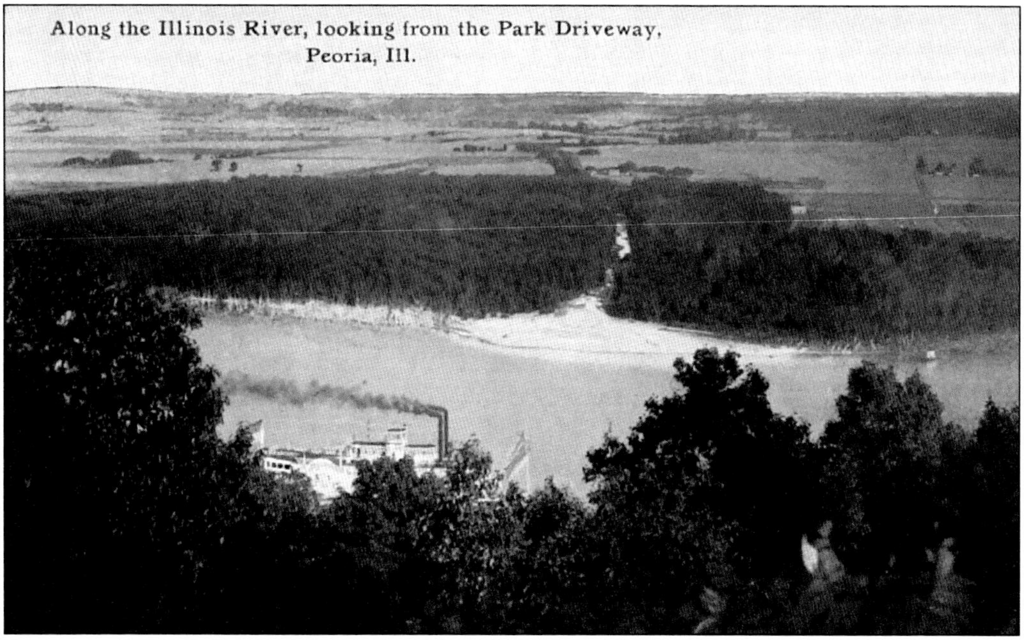

Dramatic daytime postcards were reproduced from the time Grand View Drive was begun in 1903. With horse teams, picks, and shovels, the Park Driveway became Grand View Drive and was constructed as such. The graveled roadway was 30 feet in width and 8 inches deep, and was finished on December 7, 1904. The name Grand View Drive was selected by the park board.

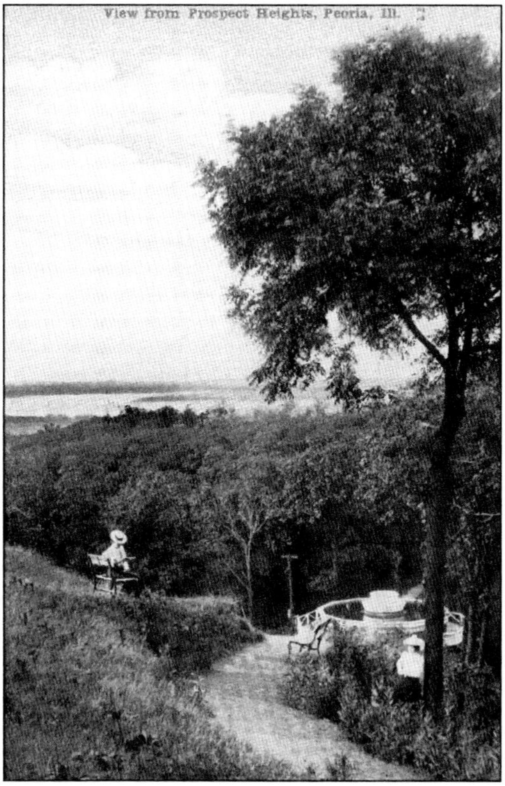

Visitors to the hillside are enjoying the scenery from the park, overlooking the Illinois River. It is believed that this path could be Gibson Path, which was acquired in 1911. A drinking fountain and lighting were installed to allow for a safer visit. This path was also led by a sulphur spring. The path led to Al Fresco Park and Wilwin Dane Hall, both located on Galena Road.

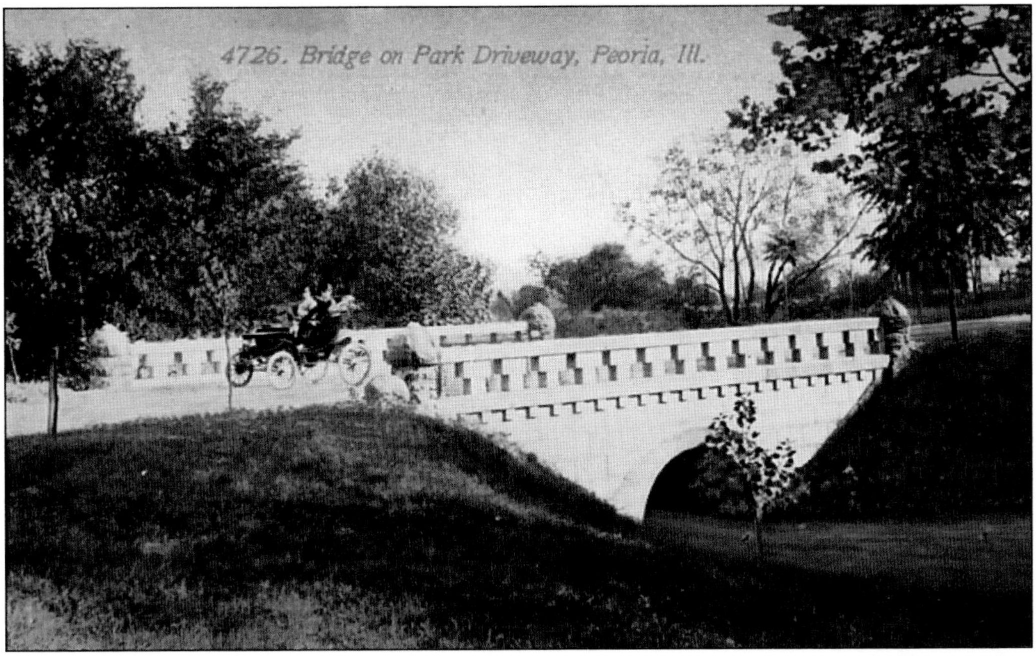

The grand entrance from Galena Road was made possible by the elaborate bridge, pictured in this early card. Note the early auto that is beginning its approach to the slope, ascending the hill. This bridge is still in use today.

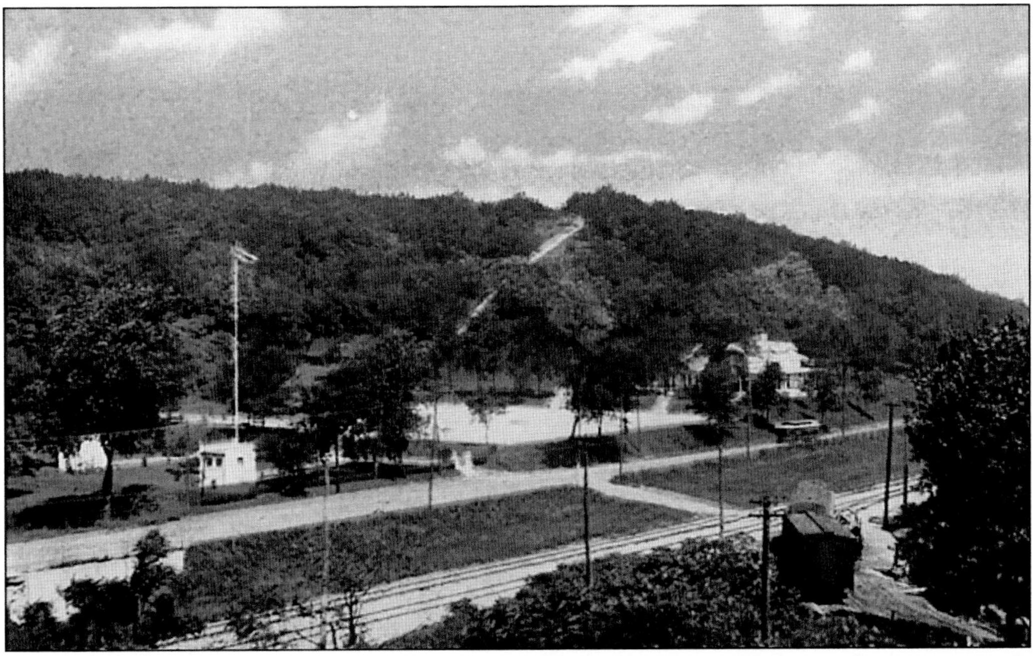

This view of Grand View playground was taken from the Water Works on the opposite side of Galena Road. By 1934, thanks to the National Recovery Act (WPA), Roosevelt Road was constructed. Its zigzag effect greatly improved the former right-of-way. It became the connecting road between the top and bottom of the hill. The construction of the road provided much needed employment in the area.

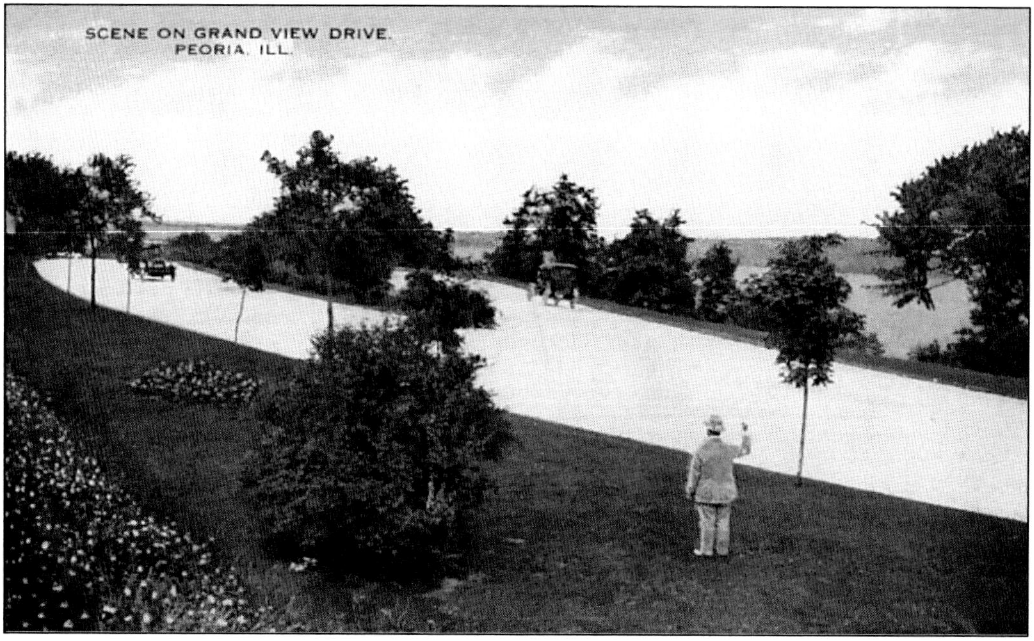

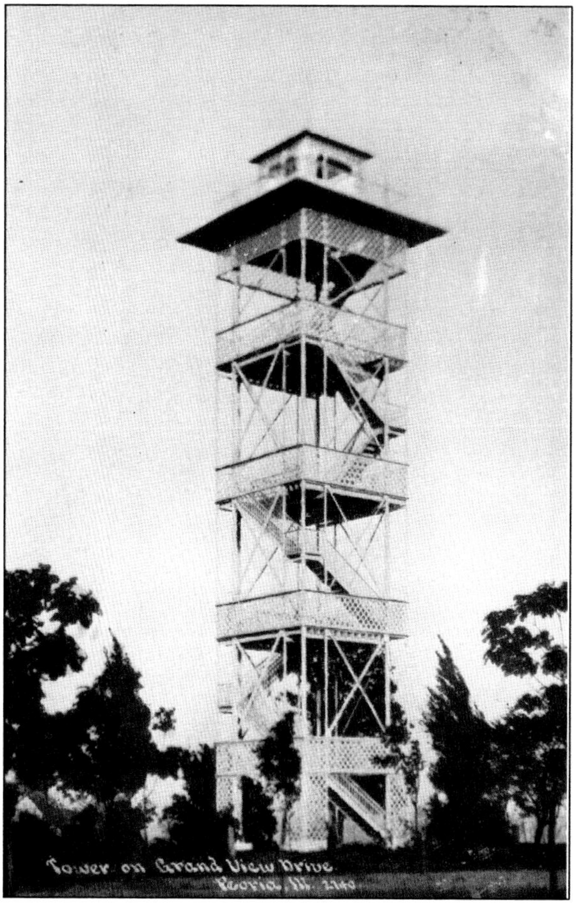

The postcard view above is believed to have been taken around 1936. Grand View Drive was paved that year, and many trees were planted as well. The visitor in the card is unknown. Also added that year were picnic grounds, two tennis courts, and two softball diamonds.

The 75-foot observatory tower was begun in 1905 and completed in 1906. It was 89 feet from the ground to the roof, and 450 feet from the river level to the top floor. The tower was five stories and could be ascended by a series of steps numbering 126. A view of up to 30 miles was possible. However, World War II brought a need for scrap metal and the tower was destroyed.

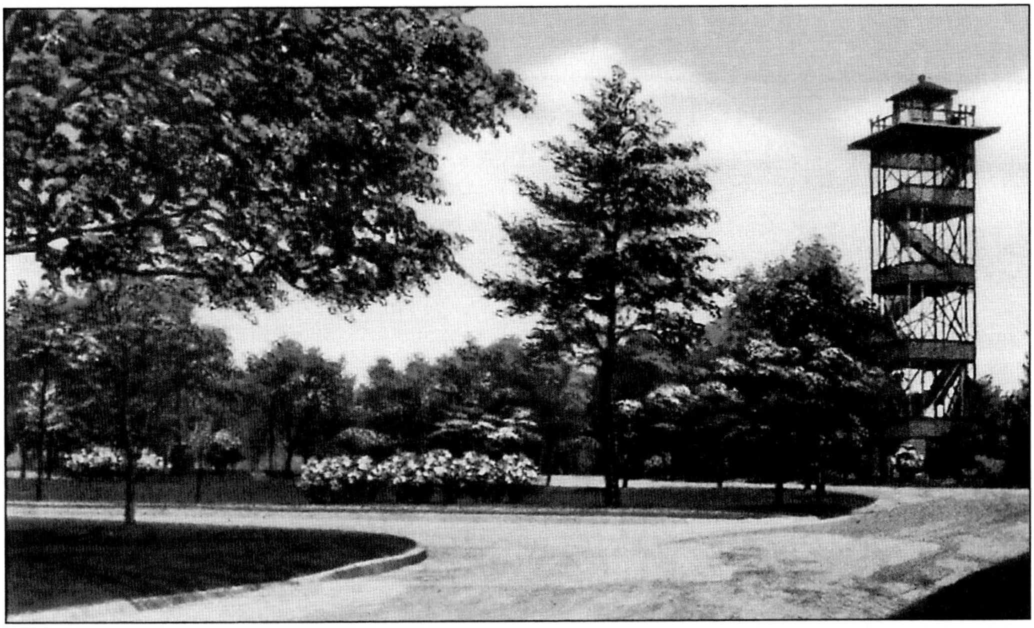

This picturesque, broad valley of the Illinois River is from a picture taken in the late 1930s. The Grandview observation tower stood at Kingman and Grandview Streets. The metal, estimated at over 100 tons, was removed as a patriotic gesture for the war effort. In its place is now a picnic area.

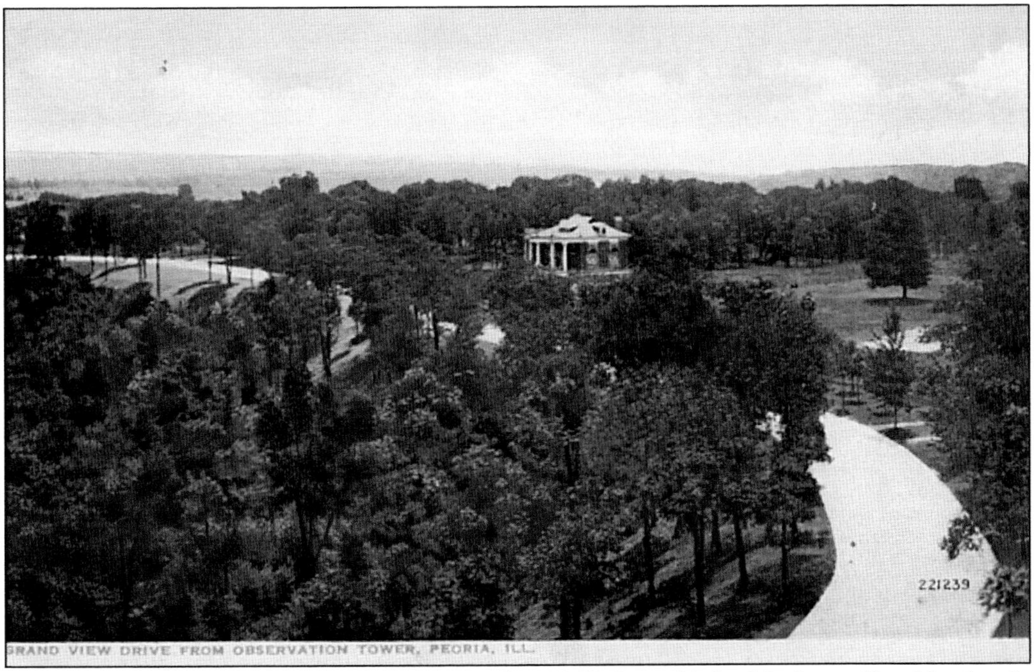

A view of nature was the dominant reason Walter H. Kirk established for himself and his family this handsome residence known as Valley View. The house was one of the first built on the new Grand View Drive. Walter died in 1924; his widow, Mrs. Kirk, remained in the house until her death. This house still stands and has been restored with great care.

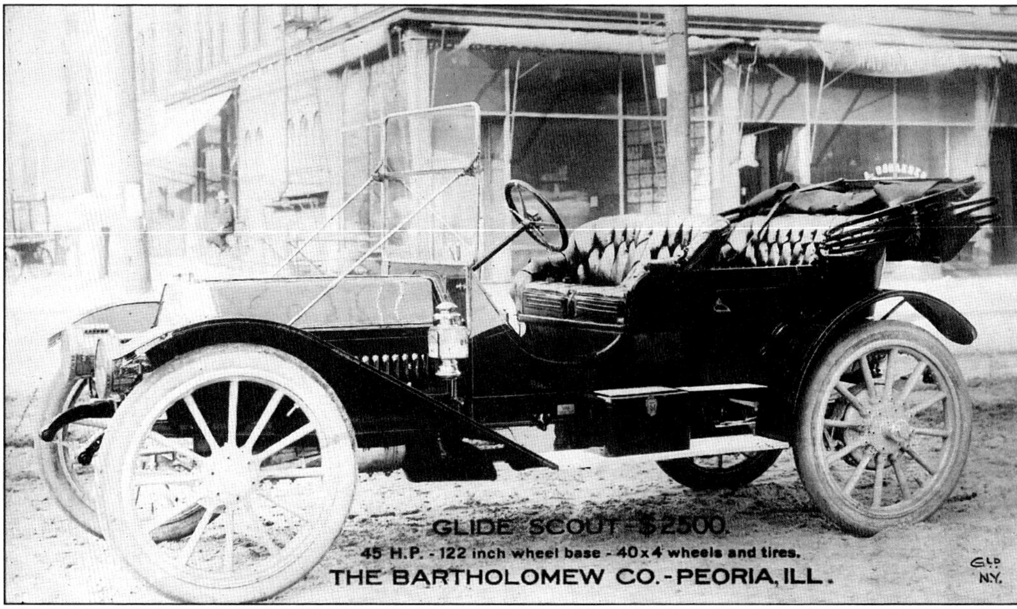

Pictured on this postcard is a fine image of a 1910 Peoria Heights Glide-Scout. It was manufactured by the Bartholomew Company, which also offered other models, including touring cars, roadsters, and semi-racers. These models ranged in cost from $2,250 to $2,500 and they weighed almost 2 tons. Their top speed was 25 miles per hour, and they were driven by a 40-horsepower, 4-cylinder engine.

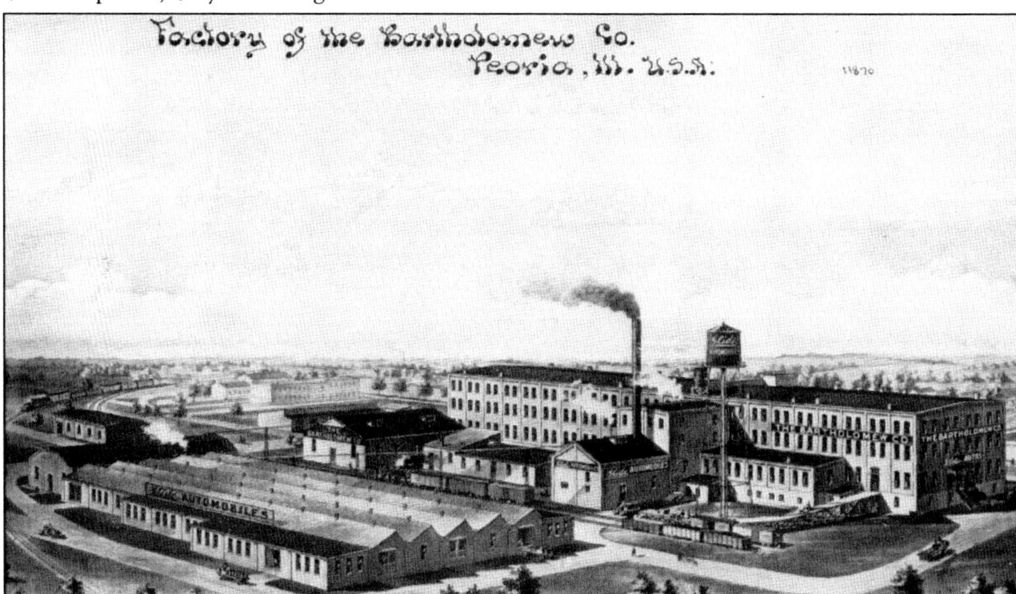

John B. Bartholomew began manufacturing the Glide Automobile in 1902, at the plant pictured above. Production would continue until 1917. In 1920, the last Glide truck was produced. Prior to Glide, this plant housed the Peoria Rubber and Manufacturing Company, the Pete Bicycle Company, the Duryea Automobile Company, the Peoria Buggy Company, and the St. Louis Motor Car Company. Later, this complex would become part of Premier Company. In 1933, the Premier Malt Products Company would merge with Pabst Brewing.

The central courtyard was the hub around which the production of Pabst Blue Ribbon Beer was created. Carloads of grain to be made into beer, which was made famous in Milwaukee, arrived daily. From 1933 until the late 1980s, the plant was the largest in Illinois. The buildings, except for the main offices, have all been removed.

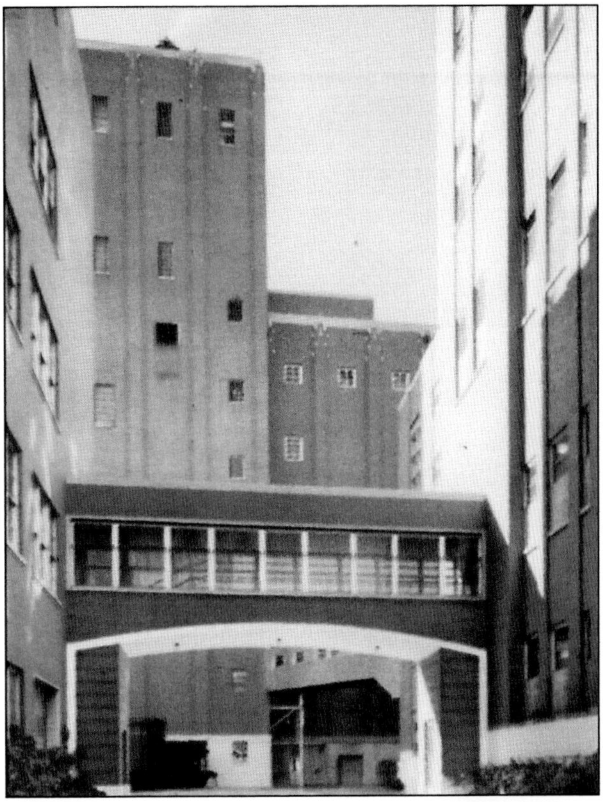

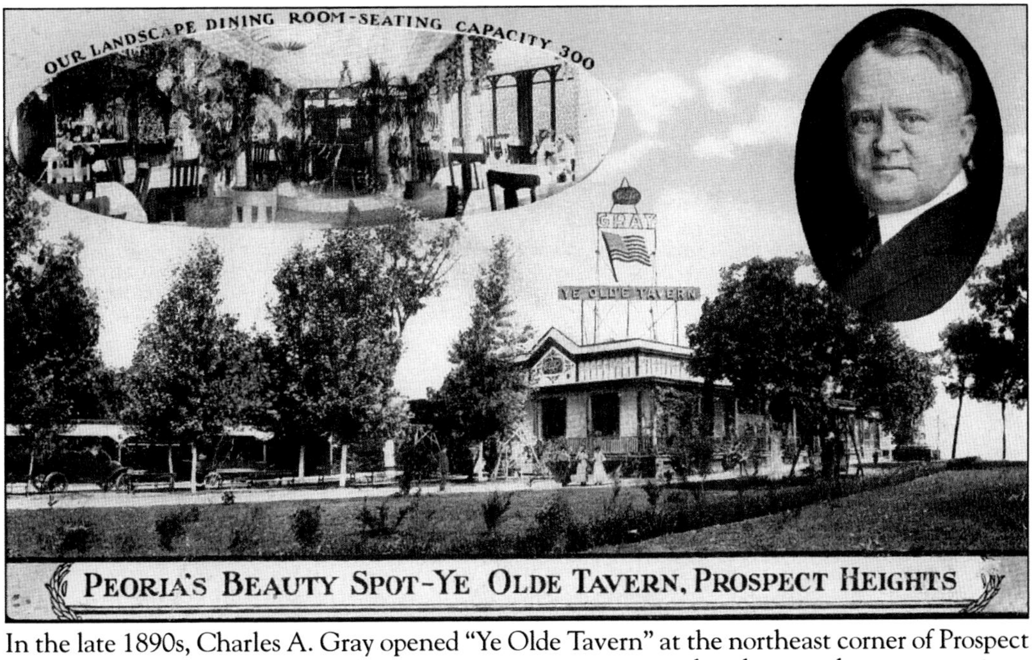

In the late 1890s, Charles A. Gray opened "Ye Olde Tavern" at the northeast corner of Prospect Road and Grand View Drive. This tavern was open year-round and enjoyed prosperous times until 1919, when Prohibition was enforced. On November 20, 1923, a fire destroyed the entire building at a cost of $15,000 in damages.

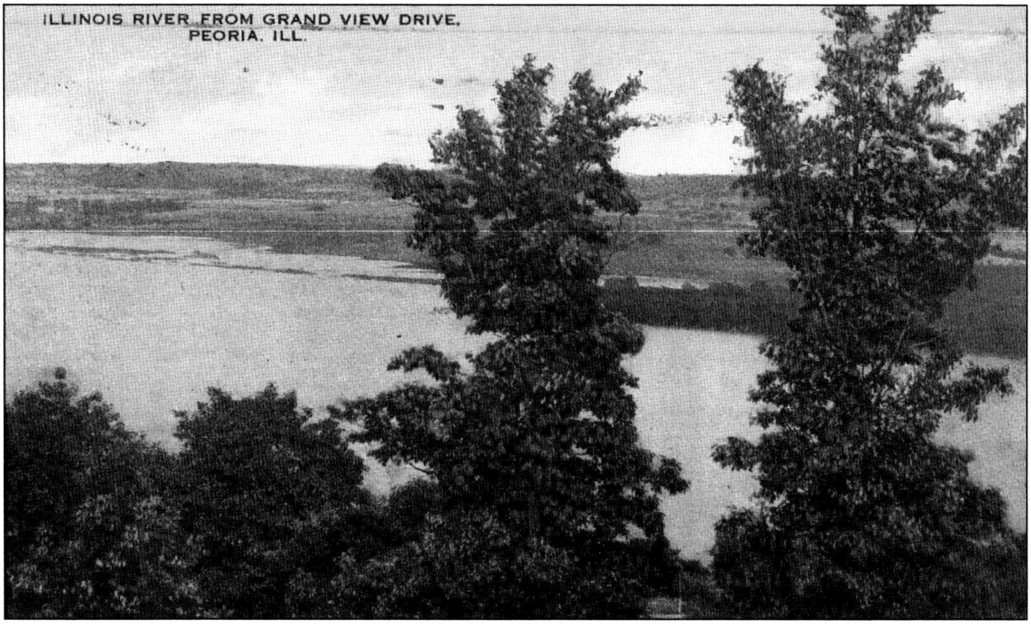

Captioned "Illinois River from Grand View Drive, Peoria, ILL.," this is yet another photo taken from the "World's Most Beautiful Drive"—so named by President Theodore Roosevelt on October 10, 1910. Roosevelt was en route to "Ye Olde Tavern" for dinner. The President was in town on a campaign tour for his re-election.

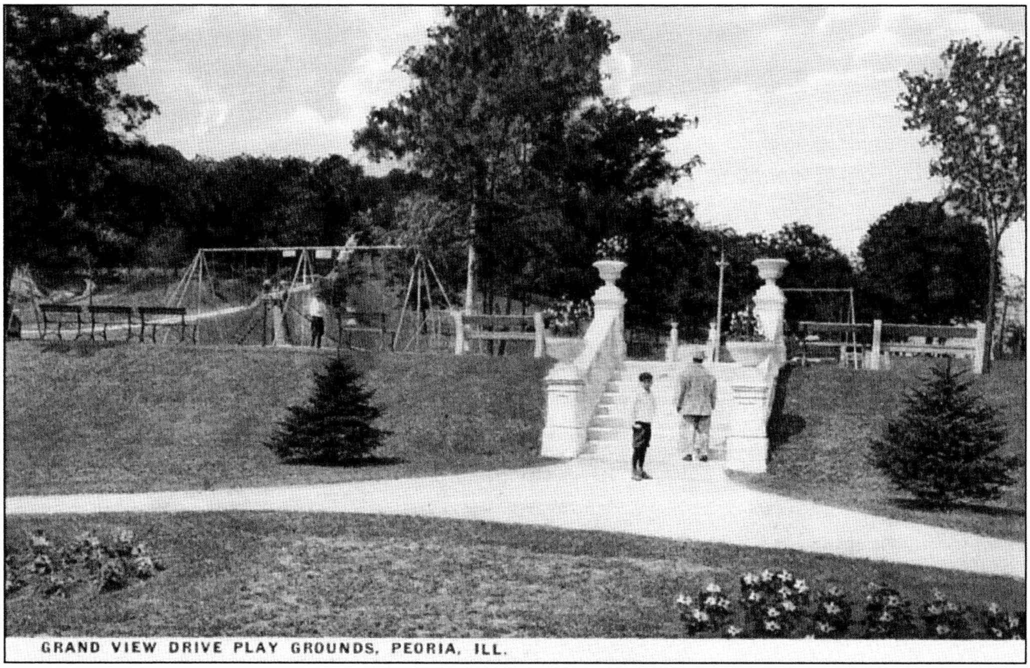

At the foot of Grand View Drive is the playground pictured above. A large new pavilion was completed in 1918 which offered a view of the Illinois River from Galena Road. This pavilion was carefully restored to its original look in the 1980s, through the use of private funds.